Reviewers of Selected Articles, This Issue
   Ethnic-racial Stigma and Physical Health Disparities in the United States of America: From Psychological Theory and Evidence to Public Policy Solutions
   Luis M. Rivera & Danielle Beatty

Issues in Progress
   Ethnic-Racial Stigma and Physical Health Disparities in the United States of America: From Psychological Theory and Evidence to Public Policy Solutions; Issue Editors: Luis M. Rivera and Danielle Beatty.
   Milgram's Obedience Studies 50 Years On: Extensions, Explanations, Applications; Issue Editors: Art Miller, Alex Haslam, and Steve Reicher.
   Confronting and Reducing Sexism: Interventions that Work; Issue Editors: Julia Becker, Matthew Zawadzki, and Stephanie Shields.
   Media Representations of Race and Ethnicity: Implications for Identity, Intergroup Relations, and Public Policy; Dana Mastro and Riva Tukachinsky.
   The Social Past in the Personal Present: Psychology, History and Social Issues; Andrea G. Hunter and Abigail J. Stewart.
   Resisting and Confronting Disadvantage: From Individual Coping to Societal Change; Katherine Stroebe and Soledad de Lemus.
   Understanding Activism; Craig McGarty, Anna Kende, and Nicola Curtin.
   Behavior across Group Boundaries: Seeking and Maintaining Positive Interactions with Outgroup Members; Birte Siem, Stefan Stürmer, and Todd Pittinsky.

Editorial Advisory Board
   Dominic Abrams, University of Kent at Canterbury, United Kingdom
   Manuela Barreto, University of Exeter, United Kingdom
   Allan B.I. Bernardo, University of Macau, Macau
   Chi-yue Chiu, Nanyang Technological University, Singapore
   Jacquelynne Eccles, University of Michigan, United States
   Carolin Hagelskamp, New York University, United States
   Nick Haslam, University of Melbourne, Australia
   Ying-yi Hong, Nanyang Technological University, Singapore
   Melanie Killen, University of Maryland, College Park, United States
   Jason Plaks, University of Toronto, Canada
   Luisa Ramirez, Universidad del Rosario, Colombia
   Jennifer Richeson, Northwestern University, United States
   Lisa Rosenthal, Yale University, United States
   Adam Rutland, University of Kent at Canterbury, United Kingdom

Isis Settles, Michigan State University, United States
Beth Shinn, Vanderbilt University, United States
Maykel Verkuyten, Utrecht University, The Netherlands
Johanna Vollhardt, Clark University, United States

Past JSI Editors
Rick H. Hoyle (2006–2009)
Irene Hanson Frieze (2001–2005)
Phyllis Katz (1997–2000)
Daniel Perlman (1993–1996)
Stuart Oskamp (1988–1992)
George Levinger (1984–1987)
Joseph E. McGrath (1979–1983)
Jacqueline D. Goodchilds (1974–1978)
Bertram H. Raven (1970–1973)
Joshua A. Fishman (1966–1969)
Leonard Solomon (1963)
Robert Chin (1960–1965)
John Harding (1956–1959)
M. Brewster Smith (1951–1955)
Harold H. Kelley (1949)
Ronald Lippitt (1944–1950)

2014 Vol. 70, No. 1

Social Exclusion of Children: Developmental Origins of Prejudice

Issue Editors: Dominic Abrams and Melanie Killen

INTRODUCTION

Social Exclusion of Children: Developmental Origins of Prejudice 1
Dominic Abrams and Melanie Killen

SECTION I: PSYCHOLOGICAL FOUNDATIONS OF INCLUSION AND EXCLUSION

Peer Group Rejection in Childhood: Effects of Rejection Ambiguity, Rejection Sensitivity, and Social Acumen 12
Drew Nesdale, Melanie J. Zimmer-Gembeck, and Natalie Roxburgh

When Do Children Dislike Ingroup Members? Resource Allocation from Individual and Group Perspectives 29
Kelly Lynn Mulvey, Aline Hitti, Adam Rutland, Dominic Abrams, and Melanie Killen

Does Moral and Social Conventional Reasoning Predict British Young People's Judgments About the Rights of Asylum-Seeker Youth? 47
Martin D. Ruck and Harriet R. Tenenbaum

Do Adolescents' Evaluations of Exclusion Differ Based on Gender Expression and Sexual Orientation? 63
Justin E. Heinze and Stacey S. Horn

SECTION II: REVEALING AND CHALLENGING EXCLUSION NORMS

Of Affect and Ambiguity: The Emergence of Preference for Arbitrary Ingroups 81
Yarrow Dunham and Jason Emory

How Young Children Evaluate People With and Without Disabilities 99
Lauren K. Huckstadt and Kristin Shutts

Can Fostering Children's Ability to Challenge Sexism Improve Critical Analysis, Internalization, and Enactment of Inclusive, Egalitarian Peer Relationships? 115
Erin Pahlke, Rebecca S. Bigler, and Carol Lynn Martin

Ethnic Classroom Composition and Peer Victimization: The Moderating Role of Classroom Attitudes 134
Jochem Thijs, Maykel Verkuyten, and Malin Grundel

How Peer Norms of Inclusion and Exclusion Predict Children's Interest in
      Cross-Ethnic Friendships 151
  Linda R. Tropp, Thomas C. O'Brien, and Katya Migacheva
What Makes a Young Assertive Bystander? The Effect of Intergroup
      Contact, Empathy, Cultural Openness, and In-Group Bias
      on Assertive Bystander Intervention Intentions 167
  Nicola Abbott and Lindsey Cameron

SECTION III: COMMENTARY
Intergroup Social Exclusion in Childhood: Forms, Norms, Context, and
      Social Identity 183
  Mark Bennett

Social Exclusion of Children: Developmental Origins of Prejudice

Dominic Abrams[*]
University of Kent

Melanie Killen
University of Maryland

Over the past decade, developmental and social psychological research has explicitly adopted a developmental intergroup framework, integrating social and developmental psychology fields to understand the origins of social exclusion and prejudice. This article argues that a social developmental analysis of how groups and individuals experience, evaluate, and understand exclusion is essential for a complete picture of the human experience, interpretation, and consequences of exclusion. What has been missing in much of the social psychological research on exclusion is an incorporation of developmental perspectives; likewise, what has been missing in development psychological research is a focus on group identity and group dynamics for understanding the basis for exclusionary behavior in childhood. Yet, the roots of adult forms of exclusion can be documented in childhood, and children who experience exclusion are particularly at risk for negative outcomes, and especially when exclusion is based on group membership. Moreover, interventions designed to ameliorate social problems associated with exclusion need to be based on an understanding of how, why, and under what conditions, children and groups make decisions to exclude others, how they experience this exclusion, and how exclusion originates and changes over the course

---

[*]Correspondence concerning this article should be addressed to Dominic Abrams, School of Psychology, Keynes College, University of Kent, Canterbury CT2 7NP, United Kingdom. Tel: 44 (0)1227-827475 [e-mail: D.Abrams@kent.ac.uk].

We would like to thank Sheri Levy for her encouragement and enthusiasm for ideas about a volume that integrates social and developmental psychology approaches to prejudice, Ann Bettencourt for her wonderful assistance with moving the volume forward, and to Johnny Siever for his careful attention to details. In addition, we thank our contributors for their timeliness throughout the editorial process, and for submitting important and forward-looking research papers on social exclusion in childhood. As always, we thank the children, adolescents, parents, and school staff who participated in the research studies reported in this volume.

of the lifespan. Thus, a growing body of psychological work, exemplified in this issue of the Journal of Social Issues *(2014), highlights implications for theory in psychology and related social sciences, and for interventions and policies to tackle social exclusion.*

Social science accounts of social exclusion in childhood have largely focused on the structural exclusion of particular sectors of society (see Abrams & Christian, 2007). Children living in optimal environments with high-quality parenting, access to early childhood education, and economic stability are more likely to thrive than children without these opportunities, who suffer in many ways from a perpetual cycle of stress, disengagement, and negative healthy outcomes. The United Nations Convention on the Rights of the Child (UNICEF, 1989) was created to address the problems stemming from children excluded from basic fundamental human rights (see Killen, Rutland, & Ruck, 2011). In this *Journal of Social Issues* volume on *Social Exclusion in Childhood*, ten cutting-edge, novel, and substantive approaches to social exclusion in childhood reveal the complexities of how exclusion emerges, the factors that children become aware of very early in life, and the central role that group identity plays in how children both experience, and perpetuate exclusion.

A Social Developmental Perspective on Exclusion

Only recently has the psychological dynamics of exclusion in childhood been featured across the broad social science spectrum, including economics and social policy (for an exception see Ludwig et al., 2008). Yet developmental and social psychology has much to say about children and social exclusion, particularly focusing on children's relationships with groups, and how group dynamics contribute to the exclusion cycle that begins in early development. For children, among the negative personal consequences of being socially excluded are lack of motivation to succeed in school, problematic peer relationships, and psychological maladjustment, such as depression and anxiety (Juvonen & Graham, 2001). These distressing consequences reflect the power of exclusion to threaten people's fundamental psychological needs to belong to and be part of social relationships (Baumeister & Leary, 1995; Kerr & Levine, 2008; Williams, 2007).

In fact, over the past decade, developmental and social psychological research has explicitly adopted a developmental intergroup framework, integrating social and developmental psychology fields (e.g., Abrams & Rutland, 2011; Bennett & Sani, 2004 Dunham & Degner, 2010; Enesco & Guerrero, 2011; Levy & Killen, 2008). We argue that a social developmental analysis of how groups and individuals experience, evaluate, and understand exclusion is essential for a complete picture of the human meaning and consequences of exclusion. What has been missing in much of the social psychological research on exclusion is an incorporation of developmental perspectives; likewise, what has been missing in development psychological research is a focus on group identity and group dynamics for understanding the basis for exclusionary behavior in childhood. Yet, the roots of adult forms of exclusion can be documented in childhood, and children who experience exclusion are particularly at risk for negative outcomes, and especially when exclusion is based on group membership.

Interventions designed to ameliorate social problems associated with exclusion need to be based on an understanding of how, why, and under what conditions, individuals and groups make decisions to exclude others, how they experience this exclusion, and how exclusion originates and changes over the course of the lifespan. Therefore, this growing body of psychological work is important for policy as well as for other social sciences perspectives.

As an example, academic achievement gaps overall, and particularly in Science, Technology, Engineering, and Math (STEM) subjects are of concern to policy makers, economists, and sociologists. Exclusion is a part of this process because, for example, ethnic minority students who feel excluded from their peers in the social context of school become less motivated to be in school (Brown & Bigler, 2005; Juvonen & Graham, 2001). More directly, ability stereotypes associated with gender create stereotype threat effects on performance in young children (Hartley & Sutton, 2013).

We believe that examining the psychological connection between children and wider social structures, defined by group and social category memberships, can shed much light on children's experiences of social exclusion. The collection of papers in this issue draws on both social and developmental psychology and highlights the question of how children's relationships with peers and with different social groups and categories may either create or prevent various forms of social exclusion.

Why is it so important to focus specifically on social exclusion and childhood? Economic exclusion that affects children is known to create cycles of disadvantage, and many believe that investment in children can help to break such cycles (European Commission, 2013; cf. Micklewright, 2002). Beyond material and economic forces, there are four key reasons for a psychological perspective on children's social exclusion. First, social exclusion is every bit as detrimental for children as it is for adults (Abrams, Weick, Colbe, Thomas, & Franklin, 2011; Eisenberger, Lieberman, & Williams, 2003). Therefore, it is imperative to find ways to minimize the short- and long-term negative outcomes of social exclusion so that the problems associated with exclusion are not exacerbated. Second, social attitudes and experiences developed through childhood have implications for subsequent adult cognition and behavior. Children who exclude others on the basis of implicit or explicit stereotypes may, as adults, perpetuate negative patterns of social interactions in the workplace, furthering social inequities and social hierarchies, based on unfair criteria. Children who are persistently excluded by others may find it difficult to establish trusting relationships. Hence, tackling processes of social exclusion during childhood should help to reduce levels of social exclusion perpetrated and experienced by adults. Third, by adulthood the biases and stereotypes that contribute to exclusionary behavior are deeply entrenched. This suggests that interventions early in childhood are uniquely powerful for creating changes in attitudes, given that these attitudes are not yet fully formed (Killen et al., 2011).

Finally, social exclusion is a multifaceted phenomenon. There are contexts in which social exclusion is legitimate to make groups work well. Groups create inclusion and exclusion criteria, which are often viewed as necessary to make the group function smoothly, such as the criteria associated with entrance exams, auditions, and tryouts. For example, it may be defensible and appropriate to exclude someone from a group because he or she fails objective entry criteria, or transgresses laws. Thus, attempting to prohibit all exclusion would neither be practical or effective. However, enabling children to differentiate between exclusion that is legitimate from exclusion that is based solely on group membership preference or prejudicial criteria is essential for reducing unjust or cruel social group exclusion.

In fact, part of studying social exclusion involves taking into consideration issues of hierarchy, power, and status, on the one hand, and intentionality, social goals, and motivations, on the other hand. There is little question that those children at the bottom of social hierarchies status are psychologically "at risk" (Killen & Rutland, 2011; Ruck & Horn, 2008; Turiel, 2002). Drawing from Tajfel and Turner's (1979) insight that groups and social identity are largely defined in comparative terms, what we think is notable here is that exclusion of others often arises through a process of ingroup preference—it is the world view, the social relationships, and the shared identity that binds such people together and provides the boundaries for the social capital they provide. Less powerful groups and individuals become excluded psychologically by ingroup preferences among members of higher status groups (Aboud, 2003; Brewer, 1999) and exclusion is likely amplified through other social processes. Therefore, who is included has implications for who is excluded, and the two processes are generally related in meaningful ways.

Unfortunately, children, and especially children who are, for whatever reason, socially excluded, have almost no formally recognized voice in most societies—no vote, no money, and no power. This means that their needs are often obscured or misunderstood. Thus, it is easy to view children themselves as the problem, and their social exclusion to result from dysfunctional social development. We contend that funding for research and interventions must address the wider underlying social and developmental processes that are involved in exclusion, as reported in this volume.

Because children lack political voice it is important that psychologists discover children's experiences, perceptions, and evaluations of about exclusion, and then explain and share what we discover to be relevant to policy and practitioner audiences. Consequently, contributors to this issue were asked to address the nature of children's and adolescents' experiences of exclusion, how they detect, evaluate, and perhaps engage in exclusion in typical school and family contexts. The broader aim of pursuing these different lines of research and drawing them together is to inform interventions to reduce the negative aspects of exclusion. This will help to promote healthy social development and a civil and just society.

Importantly, then, we consider that children are key actors in processes of social exclusion and inclusion; they are making sense of their social context and establishing an identity within that context, one that is meaningful to themselves and their peers but one that changes with age and experience. Therefore, we can conceptualize children as being at a focal point of exclusion—as targets, sources and observers of exclusion, making sense of it, and relating it to their social context and identity.

Finally, a reason for focusing on the intersection of social and developmental psychology is that we consider social exclusion to be a fundamentally relational process (Doise, 1986), and these relationships are nowhere more focal than in the social and psychological worlds of children. Elsewhere, we have developed this idea through a fairly comprehensive relational taxonomy, or matrix, that tries to capture some of the multifaceted aspects of social exclusion by distinguishing between four components that are involved: different "actors"; "levels" of relationship (e.g., interpersonal, group, societal); different "modes" of exclusion; and different "dynamics" of exclusion (e.g., Abrams & Christian, 2007; Abrams, Hogg, & Marques, 2005). We have focused particularly on explicating the connections and differences between interpersonal and intergroup exclusion (e.g., Killen, Mulvey, & Hitti, 2013; Killen & Rutland, 2011).

Current Research Featured in this Issue

The empirical articles in this collection reflect a fascinating cross-section of research areas within our relational framework and show how a social developmental perspective rather naturally draws on different elements of it. The collection addresses at least four general themes central to the study of social exclusion in childhood: (1) evaluations of inclusion and exclusion (how do children evaluate it?); (2) resistance and vulnerability to exclusion (why do children resist exclusion and how are their own experiences with it implicated in their ability to cope with it?); (3) intergroup contact (how does contact affect exclusive and inclusive social orientations?); and (4) theories of change (how can exclusive attitudes be changed?).

The different contributions span a wide age range and multiple contexts. Four papers consider exclusion among elementary age and preschool children, whereas six papers focus on similar processes in the more socially experienced and adept, as well as cognitively mature adolescent age range. One set of papers focus on ethnicity and race, another set is concerned with gender and sexuality, and others explore more transitory groups, such as teams, minimal groups, or classrooms. The research is drawn from several different continents and cultural contexts, including Australia, Europe, and the United States. Across these samples and contexts there are strong theoretical and conceptual themes that interlock across contributions. For example, social reasoning about exclusion is explored in detail in several papers, and the potential efficacy of intergroup contact for reducing exclusion is a common theme across several others. Across all of these issues and contexts, the authors have also provided clear directions for future research and considered the practical or policy implications of their findings.

Specific Papers

Nesdale, Zimmer-Gembeck, and Roxburgh (2014) focus on the relationship context to show how inter- and intragroup sources of exclusion matter. Their findings reveal how the group dynamics may depend on the target's own social motivational orientation in the form of their application of social acumen and their rejection sensitivity, resulting in intrapersonal exclusion. Mulvey, Hitti, Rutland, Abrams, and Killen (2014) focus on exclusion dynamics in the moral domain, involving resource inequality in inter- and intragroup relationship contexts. Surprisingly, pressures to be fair dominate over group loyalty, perhaps highlighting that exclusion is less likely to arise when digressions from equality norms are easy to perceive. Yet, Mulvey et al. also find that, with age, children expect that groups will consider group functioning goals along with equality goals, reflecting an age-related increase in the understanding of group dynamics.

Ruck and Tenenbaum (2014) consider the transnational/societal and intergroup levels of relationship to investigate how young people view the human rights of asylum seekers. Here, the modes of exclusion are partly ideological and partly categorical, and the dynamics need to be understood in the context of a longer time frame—a continuous process of decisions whether to accept or reject asylum seekers into one's country. What is interesting is how the justification for a source's (the ingroup country's) treatment of a target (asylum seeker) may switch from moral to social conventional reasoning depending on whether the target is to be included or excluded, respectively.

Also examining moral and social conventional expectations, Heinze and Horn (2014) explore a key issue for adolescents—the complex connection between inclusion and exclusion based on gender conformity and that based on heterosexuality. Here, the relationship context is particularly salient as there are pressures to form close interpersonal relationships at the same time as strong intergroup distinctions between genders, reinforcing strong intragroup relationships. Thus, the modes of exclusion are liable to be complex and to include representational, categorical, physical, and communicative forms, and the dynamics are likely to center on different motivations, and different perceptions of interdependence.

Dunham and Emory (2014) consider how it is that children are prepared to affiliate with ingroup members rather than outgroup members—how children become sources of exclusion. Here, the relationship context is intergroup and the mode of exclusion is purely categorical. What is revealed is how the dynamics of intergroup exclusion may proceed with relatively little help from outside. Between the ages of 3 and 6 years children become much more predisposed to prefer members of minimal ingroups than outgroups. Extrapolating to the emerging dynamics in this relationship, if followed through in behavior, children's propensity to relate more positively to ingroup members could result in intergroup resource inequality and a competitively interdependent intergroup relationship, which would likely to generate still more intergroup exclusion.

Huckstadt and Shutts (2014) document 3- to 5-year-olds' preferences for unfamiliar individuals with and without disabilities. They also consider the role of the institutional context to investigate whether being part of an inclusion program would affect these preferences. Although this variable turned out not to be influential, the study raises the question of how schools, teachers, and carers can relate institutional policies or strategies to children in a way that enables children to apply the relevant concepts to their interpersonal relationships with peers. A similar challenge is considered by Pahlke, Bigler, and Martin (2014). They considered how children's interpretation of exclusion might be honed, and in particular whether children aged 4–10 years might be helped to recognize gender bias. This requires children to recognize the relationship context (e.g., as interpersonal) and modes of exclusion (e.g., representational, categorical, or communicative), and to respond critically to it (influencing their motivational orientation). Evidence from the study showed that it was possible to equip children to identify sexism in the media by specifically addressing that particular categorization and relevant types of communication.

The paper by Thijs, Verkuyten, and Grundel (2014) explores exclusion in a relationship context that links intergroup to the societal levels (Dutch and Turkish–Dutch adolescents in school classes), and they consider the two groups both as being sources and targets of exclusion. Thijs et al. focus on dynamics that arise from interdependence and resource inequality, operationalized in terms of relative group sizes, and social power. Their study reflects issues of status and hierarchies in the immigrant context in the Netherlands, which has only recently become a focus for educational curricula and positive interventions.

Tropp, O'Brien, and Migacheva (2014) report two survey studies to examine the relationship between perceptions of peer norms of interethnic exclusion and children's interest in forming cross-ethnic friendships. The sources and targets differed across two studies (European American and either African American or Latino American). This research highlights that a potentially powerful psychological route for tackling exclusion is to address how children link their personal preferences with their group's norms. This highlights that wider societal pressures or institutional norms may be less compelling routes than working from within peer groups to tackle exclusion. Moreover, this study reflects a much needed in-depth examination of how intergroup contact and cross-group friendships is related to a reduction of prejudice in childhood.

Abbott and Cameron (2014) focus on the role of cross-group contact as a basis for children to intervene between sources and targets in episodes of intergroup exclusion. The concern is very much with the physical and communicative modes of exclusion, and in influencing children's motivational orientation on witnessing exclusion. Interestingly, this study exposes potentially important mediating roles of cultural openness and greater empathy. Thus, it raises the possibility of countering the intergroup level of exclusion using either the institutional/societal or interpersonal levels of relationship.

Bennett (2014), as the commentator, draws from these contributions to formulate a set of questions for future work. He argues for deeper investigation of the role of social identity in all of these exclusion contexts. He identifies a key research challenge, namely, to find ways to capture the way that the self-concept becomes implicated in exclusion and inclusion processes. There is scope for new, more dynamic, and sensitive measures of identification, and new methods for assessing how different aspects of identity are involved in social exclusion. Finally, he reinforces the value of developing a richer and fuller taxonomy of social exclusion processes relevant to children's social development.

Conclusion

As a whole, this set of papers reflects the positive outcomes of social and developmental researchers working closely together, sharing ideas and methods to move the field forward. This integrative approach enables social and psychological research to examine the emergence of the inevitable tensions that exist between affiliating with social groups (group identity) and valuing the goals of inclusion, fairness, and prosociality. This conflict exists in childhood through adulthood. Studying the onset, change, and emergence of inclusion and exclusion is the key to facilitating social justice, and particularly in the next generation. This is important territory for psychologists, and provides a basis for informing strategies and policies to create healthy social development.

References

Abbott, N., & Cameron, L. (2014). What makes a young assertive bystander? The effect of intergroup contact, empathy, cultural openness and in-group bias on assertive bystander intervention intentions. *Journal of Social Issues, 70*(1), 167–182.

Aboud, F. E. (2003). The formation of ingroup favoritism and outgroup prejudice in young children. *Developmental Psychology, 39*, 48–60. doi: 10.1037/0012-1649.39.1.48.

Abrams, D., & Christian, J. N. (2007). A relational analysis of social exclusion. In D. Abrams, J. N. Christian, & D. Gordon (Eds.), *Multidisciplinary handbook of social exclusion research* (pp. 211–232). Chichester: Wiley-Blackwell.

Abrams, D., Hogg, M. A., & Marques, J. M. (Eds.). (2005). *The social psychology of inclusion and exclusion*. New York: Psychology Press.

Abrams, D., & Rutland, A. (2011). Children's understanding of deviance and group dynamics: The development of subjective group dynamics. In J. Jetten and M. Hornsey (Eds.), *Rebels in groups: Dissent, deviance, difference and defiance* (pp. 135–157). Oxford: Blackwell.

Abrams, D., Weick, M., Colbe, H., Thomas, D., & Franklin, K. M. (2011). On-line ostracism affects children differently from adolescents and adults. *British Journal of Developmental Psychology, 29*, 110–123. doi: 10.1348/026151010×494089.

Baumeister, R. F., & Leary, M. R. (1995). The need to belong: Desire for interpersonal attachments as a fundamental human motivation. *Psychological Bulletin, 117*, 497–529. doi: 10.1037/0033-2909.117.3.497.

Bennett, M. (2014). Intergroup social exclusion in childhood: Forms, norms, context and social identity. *Journal of Social Issues, 70*(1), 183–195.

Bennett, M., & Sani, F. (2004). *The development of the social self*. New York: Psychology Press.

Brewer, M. B. (1999). The psychology of prejudice: Ingroup love or outgroup hate? *Journal of Social Issues, 55*, 429–444. doi:10.1.1.197.4614.

Brown, C. B., & Bigler, R. S. (2005). Children's perceptions of discrimination: A developmental model. *Child Development, 76*, 533–553.

Doise, W. (1986). *Levels of explanation in social psychology*. Cambridge: Cambridge University Press.

Dunham, Y., & Degner, J. (2010). Origins of intergroup bias: Developmental and social cognitive research on intergroup attitudes. *European Journal of Social Psychology, 40*, 563–568.

Dunham, Y., & Emory, J. (2014). Of affect and ambiguity: The emergence of preference for arbitrary ingroups. *Journal of Social Issues, 70*(1), 81–98.

Eisenberger, N. I., Lieberman, M. D., & Williams, K. D. (2003). Does rejection hurt? An fMRI study of social exclusion. *Science, 302*, 290–292. doi:10.1126/science.1089134.

Enesco, I., & Guerrero, S. (Eds.) (2011). Introduction. *Anales de Psicologia (Special Issue on Social and Developmental Aspects of Prejudice during Childhood and Adolescence), 27*, 575–581. Retrieved October 10, 2013, from http://www.redalyc.org/pdf/167/16720048001.pdf

European Commission. (2013). *Commission recommendation: Investing in children: Breaking the cycle of disadvantage*. Brussels, 20.2.13 778 final. Retrieved from http://ec.europa.eu/justice/fundamental-rights/files/c_2013_778_en.pdf

Hartley, B. L., & Sutton, R. M. (2013). A stereotype threat account of boys' academic underachievement. *Child Development, 84*, 1716–1733.

Heinze, J. E., & Horne, S. S. (2014). Do adolescents' evaluations of exclusion differ based on gender expression and sexual orientation? *Journal of Social Issues, 70*(1), 63–80.

Huckstadt, L. K., & Shutts, K. (2014). How young children evaluate people with and without disabilities. *Journal of Social Issues, 70*(1), 99–114.

Juvonen, J., & Graham, S. (Eds.) (2001). *Peer harassment in school: The plight of the vulnerable and victimized*. New York: The Guilford Press.

Kerr, N. L., & Levine, J. L. (2008). The detection of social exclusion: Evolution and beyond. *Group Dynamics, 12*, 39–52.

Killen, M., Mulvey, K. L., & Hitti, A. (2013). Social exclusion in childhood: A developmental intergroup perspective. *Child Development, 84*, 772–790. doi:10.1111/cdev.12012.

Killen, M., & Rutland, A. (2011). *Children and social exclusion: Morality, prejudice, and group identity*. NY: Wiley/Blackwell Publishers.

Killen, M., Rutland, A., & Ruck, M. D. (2011). Promoting equity, tolerance, and justice in childhood. *Society for Research in Child Development (SRCD) Social Policy Report, 25*, 1–25.

Levy, S. R., & Killen, M. (Eds.). (2008). *Intergroup attitudes and relations in childhood through adulthood*. Oxford: Oxford University Press.

Ludwig, J., Liebman, J., Kling, K., Duncan, G. J., Katz, L. F., Kessler, R. C., & Sanbonmatsu, L. (2008). What can we learn about neighborhood effects from the Moving to Opportunity experiment? A comment on Clampet-Lundquist & Massey. *American Journal of Sociology, 114*, 144–188.

Mickelwright, J. (2002). Social exclusion and children: A European view for a US debate. *Centre for the Analysis of Social Exclusion*, CASEpaper 51, London, UK: London School of Economics.
Mulvey, K. L., Hitti, A., Rutland, A., Abrams, D., & Killen, M. (2014). When do children dislike ingroup members? Resource allocation from individual and group perspectives. *Journal of Social Issues, 70*(1), 29–46.
Nesdale, D., Zimmer-Gembeck, M. J., & Roxburgh, N. (2014). Peer group rejection in childhood: Effects of rejection ambiguity, rejection sensitivity, and social acumen. *Journal of Social Issues, 70*(1), 12–28.
Pahlke, E., Bigler, R. S., & Martin, C. L. (2014). Can fostering children's ability to challenge sexism improve critical analysis, internalization, and enactment of inclusive, egalitarian peer relationships? *Journal of Social Issues, 70*(1), 115–133.
Ruck, M. D., & Horn, S. S. (2008). Charting the landscape of children's rights. *Journal of Social Issues, 64*, 685–699. doi: 10.1111/j.1540-4560.2008.00584.x
Ruck, M. D., & Tenenbaum, H. R. (2014). Does moral and social conventional reasoning predict British young people's judgments about the rights of asylum-seeker youth? *Journal of Social Issues, 70*(1), 47–62.
Tajfel, H., & Turner, J. C. (1979). An integrative theory of intergroup conflict. In W. G. Austin & S. Worchel (Eds.), *The social psychology of intergroup relations* (pp. 33–47). Monterey, CA: Brooks/Cole.
Thijs, J., Verkuyten, M., & Grundel, M. (2014). Ethnic classroom composition and peer victimization: The moderating role of classroom attitudes. *Journal of Social Issues, 70*(1), 134–150.
Tropp, L. R., O'Brien, T. C., & Migacheva, K. (2014) How peer norms of inclusion and exclusion predict children's interest in cross-ethnic friendships. *Journal of Social Issues, 70*(1), 151–166.
Turiel, E. (2002). *The culture of morality: Social development, context, and conflict*. NY: Cambridge University Press.
UNICEF (1989). The United Nations Convention on the Rights of the Child. London: UNICEF UK. Retrieved from http://www.unicef.org.uk/Documents/Publication-pdfs/UNCRC_PRESS200910web.pdf
Verkuyten, M. (2011). Cross ethnic friendships and parents. *Society for Research in Child Development SRCD Social Policy Report, 25*, 28–29.
Williams, K. D. (2007). Ostracism. *Annual Review of Psychology, 58*, 425–452.

DOMINIC ABRAMS is Professor of Social Psychology and Director of the Centre for the Study of Group Processes at the University of Kent. His research focuses on the psychological dynamics of social exclusion and inclusion within and between groups. He is co-Editor with Michael A. Hogg of the journal *Group Processes and Intergroup Relations*, and with Julie Christian of the *Wiley Multidisciplinary Handbook of Social Exclusion Research* (2007). His research is funded by the British Academy, the Economic and Social Research Council, and Age UK. He serves on the Council of the Academy of Social Sciences. He is a Fellow of the British Academy, and currently a council member of the Academy of Social Sciences, trustee of the Anne Frank Trust and President of the Society for the Psychological Study of Social Issues.

MELANIE KILLEN, PhD, is Professor of Human Development and Quantitative Methodology at the University of Maryland. She is the author of *Children and Social Exclusion: Morality, Prejudice and Group Identity* (2011) with Adam Rutland, co-editor of *Social Development in Childhood and Adolescence: A Contemporary Reader* (2011) with Robert Coplan, and serves as the Editor of the *Handbook on*

Moral Development (2006, 2014) with Judith Smetana. She is Associate Editor at *Child Development*, and has received funding from the *National Science Foundation* and the *National Institute of Child Health and Human Development* for her research on social exclusion, moral reasoning, and intergroup attitudes.

Peer Group Rejection in Childhood: Effects of Rejection Ambiguity, Rejection Sensitivity, and Social Acumen

Drew Nesdale*, Melanie J. Zimmer-Gembeck, and Natalie Roxburgh
Griffith University

This study examined the reactions of 6 to 12 year old children (N = 144) to in-group members who accepted or rejected them, and assessed whether their reactions were influenced by their rejection sensitivity (RS) and social acumen (SA). After completing measures of RS and SA, children participated in an intergroup simulation in which they were accepted or unambiguously versus ambiguously rejected by their group. Findings indicated that whereas ambiguously rejected children understood that they had been rejected, they nevertheless retained greater in-group identification and more positive attitudes than the rejected children, although less than the accepted children. However, as with rejected participants, ambiguously rejected children still opted to change groups whereas accepted children did not. SA children liked the in-group less, whereas those with SA liked the in-group more. Discussion focused on children's selection of peer groups, as well as the effects of their rejection from them.

Peer group membership is of critical importance to children during the middle childhood years. Consistent with social identity development theory (SIDT, Nesdale, 2007), children willingly become group members, identify with their group, display behaviors that favor the in-group over any out-group, seek to defend and strengthen the status of their group, conform to group norms, and are prepared to exclude members who do not conform (see Abrams, Rutland, Cameron, & Marques, 2003; Dunham & Emory, 2014; Nesdale, 2007; Rubin, Bukowski, & Parker, 2006).

---

*Correspondence concerning this article should be addressed to Professor Drew Nesdale, School of Applied Psychology, Griffith Health, Griffith University, Parklands Drive, Southport, 4222, Queensland, Australia [e-mail: d.nesdale@griffith.edu.au].

Funding for this Discovery Research Project was provided by the Australian Research Council, DP1096183, 2010–2012 to the first two authors.

Given the obvious importance of social groups to children, it might be expected that the experience of peer group rejection, or even the threat of such rejection, would have the potential to impact greatly on them and research has confirmed this (Rubin et al., 2006).

Of particular concern to this study, however, were children's responses toward those group members who actually rejected them, and whether these responses changed with age. The study also examined whether their reactions differed according to whether they experienced unambiguous compared with ambiguous peer group rejection, as well as whether their responses were influenced by their rejection sensitivity (RS) and/or social acumen (SA).

Peer Group Rejection and Its Effects

Given the significance of peer acceptance to children, it is unsurprising that peer rejection has long been associated with diverse indicators of internal distress, including anxiety, unhappiness, anger, loneliness, and depression (Sandstrom & Zakriski, 2004). In addition, rejected children perform less competently on a range of cognitive tasks, including attending to and interpreting peer cues, solving social problem tasks, and understanding appropriate display rules for behavior (Jones, Abbey, & Cumberland, 1998; Nelson & Crick, 1999). Rejected children are also frequently more aggressive and disruptive, spend less time on tasks, initiate less social contacts, become more socially withdrawn, experience less success in joining others and engaging in prosocial play, display less social competence, and have more negative interactions with teachers (Coie, Dodge, & Kupersmidt, 1990).

Although much has been learnt about peer rejection, the main focus to date has been on chronic or ongoing rejection (Nesdale, 2008). While this is not surprising, it is also important to know what sorts of negative effects are instigated by occasional or episodic rejection, how long they last, as well as what sorts of implications they have for the child's interpersonal and intergroup relations. This study focused on the last of these issues.

This Study

The first aim was to examine the responses of children toward the members of their peer group following an episode of rejection by that group, using a peer group simulation paradigm that has been used to examine children's peer group rejection (Nesdale, 2008). Whereas research using this paradigm has revealed the extent to which unambiguous rejection has immediate effects on children's affective responses and their self-esteem, as well as their risk-taking and negative interpersonal behaviors (see Nesdale, 2008), less attention has been given to the rejected individuals' responses toward the members of the rejecting group.

For example, do rejected children immediately lose all trust and liking for the group members such that they instantly stop wanting to be in that group and, instead, decide not to have anything further to do with the group members? Do they feel sufficiently negative such that they are instigated to seek hostile forms of retribution? Do they immediately seek membership in other groups or do they engage in a period of social withdrawal and solitude before attempting to reengage with other children? The first aim of this study was to assess children's affective reactions toward the rejecting group, as well as their wish to join another group.

The second aim was to assess children's reactions to unambiguous compared with ambiguous rejection from a peer group. Because peer group acceptance is important to children by school age, and they are already likely to have experienced at least some instances of rejection, one possibility was that children might interpret an ambiguous peer group rejection episode as an instance of unambiguous rejection such that they might react to both with the same (negative) response. Alternatively, in the interests of maintaining a sense of acceptance by the peer group, children might seek to block out, ignore, or misinterpret cues that might suggest that other members did not want them in the group. Finally, another possibility was that they might be less positive toward members of the rejecting group than were accepted children, but would be more positive than those unambiguously rejected. Because a rejected child's responses would likely impact on their present and future relationships with individuals and group members, examining the effects of ambiguous and unambiguous rejection, compared with acceptance, is an important issue to address.

The third aim of the study was to assess the extent to which two individual difference variables influence the impact of a peer group rejection experience on a child. One variable, rejection sensitivity (RS), refers to a pattern of social information processing that includes a heightened tendency to anxiously expect, readily perceive, and overreact to implied or overt interpersonal rejection (Levy, Ayduk, & Downey, 2001). According to the RS model, RS develops when people's desires to belong are repeatedly unrealized resulting in ongoing expectations of rejection. These expectations are activated in situations where rejection is possible leading individuals to readily perceive innocuous cues as evidence of rejection. Rejection expectations may be accompanied by defensively oriented emotions of anxiety (i.e., anxious expectations) or anger (i.e., angry expectations) that prepare the individual to defend the self against subsequent rejection. Furthermore, the model proposes that the specific type of anticipatory affect (i.e., anxious or angry expectations) predicts the type of behavioral reaction enacted (i.e., social withdrawal or hostility and aggression, respectively), the particular behavioral response being dependent on the relative levels of anxious or angry expectations that are instigated.

While research with adults has yielded broad support for the RS model (see Levy et al., 2001; Zimmer-Gembeck & Nesdale, 2013), recent studies have also revealed that children may acquire RS during middle childhood and that both parental and peer rejection are associated with its emergence (i.e., anxious, angry, and rejection expectations). Moreover, as with adults, anxious RS was associated with more social withdrawal responses to rejection, whereas angry RS was associated with more hostility and retribution responses (Downey, Lebolt, Rincon, & Freitas, 1998; Nesdale & Zimmer-Gembeck, 2014).

On this basis, we anticipated that children's higher levels of RS (anxious, angry, and rejection expectations) would be associated with more negative reactions toward their in-group. In addition, we assessed whether higher RS might amplify the negativity of unambiguous and ambiguous rejection on children's in-group reactions.

The fourth aim of the study was to evaluate the extent to which peer group rejection might be influenced by a second individual difference variable, children's social acumen (SA). According to Nesdale and colleagues (Nesdale, 2013; Nesdale & Lawson, 2011), SA refers to children's knowledge of how the social system works, their social perceptiveness, and their skill in engaging positively and effectively in social interactions with others. Given that an array of evidence supports the SA construct (see Nesdale, 2013), we anticipated that children's higher compared with lower SA might be associated with more positive in-group reactions. In addition, we assessed whether higher compared with lower SA might minimize the effect of unambiguous and ambiguous rejection on children's negative in-group reactions because children with higher SA would be less concerned by an instance of rejection than would those with little SA. Finally, the study included boys and girls ranging from 6 to 12 years of age to test for possible age and gender effects during the middle childhood years, especially in relation to RS and social acumen.

Method

Participants

The sample included 144 Anglo-Australian children with equal numbers of boys and girls from grades two through five at two elementary schools serving the same lower middle class community. The sample included younger and older participants to allow for age comparisons, with the former ($n = 72$) ranging from 6 to 9 years ($M = 7.85$ years, $SD = 0.70$ years), whereas the latter ($n = 72$) ranged from 9 to 12 years of age ($M = 10.11$ years, $SD = 0.76$ years). The study had a 2 (age: 7, 10) × 2 (gender: boys, girls) × 3 (peer status: accepted, ambiguous rejected, rejected) factorial between subjects design with approximately equal numbers of boys and girls at each age level randomly allocated to one of the three peer status conditions. All children participated with parental permission.

Materials

Photographs. The photos used were drawn from a set of photos that has been developed and pretested by the authors. Within age and gender, the head-and-shoulder color photos selected were of Anglo-Australian children who were matched for expression (not smiling) and attractiveness (moderate). Each photo was 150 × 110 mm and was attached to a display board.

Response booklet. A response booklet was prepared for each participant containing a series of questions, each with an accompanying unipolar or bipolar scale, with each point on each scale labeled appropriately.

The Child Rejection Sensitivity Questionnaire (CRSQ; Downey, Freitas, Michaelis, & Khouri, 1998) was used to measure participants' anxious, angry, and rejection expectations. Because of the young age of the children, a reduced set of six vignettes from the CRSQ involving peers and teachers was used (e.g., Imagine you're back in your classroom and everyone is splitting up into groups to work on a special project together. You sit there and watch lots of other kids getting chosen. As you wait, you wonder if the kids will want you for their group). Following each vignette, the participant responded to three questions, with the first measuring anxious expectations (i.e., How nervous would you feel right then about whether or not they would choose you), and had response options ranging from 1 (*Not nervous at all*) to 3 (*Yes, a lot nervous*). The second question measured angry expectations (i.e., How mad would you feel right then about whether or not they would choose you) with response options from 1 (*No, not mad at all*) to 3 (*Yes, a lot mad*). The third question measured the participants' perception of the likelihood of an accepting or rejection outcome (i.e., Do you think the kids in your class will choose you for their group) with response options from 1 (*No*) to 3 (*Yes*). Three RS (i.e., rejection expectations) scores were computed for each participant (i.e., anxious, angry, rejection) by averaging their responses on each measure across the six vignettes. In each case, higher scores indicated higher RS. Validation of the RS constructs has been revealed in studies showing that RS angry expectations were correlated with attributions of hostile intent by others, angry reactions to ambiguously intentioned rejection, and retribution intentions (Downey et al., 1998; Nesdale & Zimmer-Gembeck, 2014) whereas RS anxious expectations were correlated with social withdrawal intentions (Nesdale & Zimmer-Gembeck, 2014). Cronbach's α for each measure were anxious expectations = .69, angry expectations = .66, and rejection expectations = .58. (Findings involving the last measure need to be interpreted with caution.)

Social Acumen Scale (SAS, Nesdale, 2013) consisted of 16 questions, each of which was responded to on a five-point scale ranging from 1 (*Not at all*) to 5

(*A lot*). Items tapped participants' social knowledge (e.g., When I am not sure how to act in a group I watch others to see what to do), perceptiveness (e.g., I can tell how someone is feeling), and social skill (e.g., I can get others to do what I want). Items were averaged to compute a total SAS score, with higher scores indicating higher SA. SAS scores are positively correlated with social intelligence and emotional empathy, and negatively correlated with RS and aggression (Nesdale, 2013). The SAS had a Cronbach's $\alpha = 76$.

Manipulation check items. Perceived acceptance by the team was checked using a single question (How much did the other children want you in the team?) with responses from 1 (*Not at all*) to 5 (*A lot*).

In-group identification was checked using a single question (How much do you like being in your team?) with the responses options from 1 (*Not at all*) to 5 (*A lot*).

Main dependent measures. In-group attitudes: Participants' attitudes toward members of the in-group were measured by summing their responses on three questions, each having an associated five-point unipolar scale. Participants indicated how much they liked the members of their team (How much do you like the children in your team?), ranging from 1 (*I don't like them at all*) to 5 (*I like them a lot*), how much they trusted the members of their/ team (How much do you trust the children in your team?), on a scale ranging from 1 (*I wouldn't trust them at all*) to 5 *(I would trust them a lot)*, and how much they would like to play with the members of their team (How much would you like to play with the children in your team?), on a scale ranging from 1 (*I wouldn't like to play with them at all*) to 5 (*I would like to play with them a lot*). The Cronbach's α for the in-group attitude or liking scale $= .84$.

Change groups: Participants were asked how much they would want to change groups (i.e., How much would you want to change into the other team?), as well as how much they thought children in the other team would want to change teams (i.e., How much do you think the children in the other team would want to be in your team?). Both questions were answered using a five-point unipolar scale, ranging from 1 (*Not at all*) to 5 (*A lot*).

Procedure

Participants were asked by their teachers to draw themselves on a 145 × 210 mm piece of paper and, 1 week later, each was told individually by the experimenter that s/he would be asked some questions about themselves and would play a pretend game. The participant then practiced the unipolar and bipolar scales, and completed the SAS, and CRSQ.

The participant was then asked to pretend that s/he was going to participate in an intergroup drawing competition, that all the children's drawings had been judged by an artist, and that s/he had been put into a team of drawers just like him/herself. An instant head-and-shoulders photo was then taken of the participant and s/he was shown (randomly selected) photos of the other two same-aged, -gender, and -ethnicity members of their team (i.e., the in-group), and they attached their own photo between those of the other team members. These instructions were designed to encourage the child's self-categorization into his/her team.

To manipulate peer group status, participants in the peer group acceptance condition were asked to pretend that the other members of their team really wanted the participant in the team because s/he had made a great drawing. S/he was also told that another child had wanted to be in the team but that the team members had chosen the participant instead and wanted the participant to choose the team color and name.

In contrast, participants in the peer group rejection condition were asked to pretend that the experimenter had just remembered that the children in the team had actually wanted another child in the team more than the participant because the other child drew a better picture. The participant's photo was then removed from the team photos and placed to one side while the experimenter worked out what to do. The participant was told that the team members had already chosen the team color and name.

Participants in the ambiguous peer group rejection condition were also told that the children in the team had actually wanted another child in the team but they were then told that the other child decided to go to another team. The experimenter then indicated that the participant could fill the space left in the team and that the team members had already chosen the team color and name. Thus, the rejection was ambiguous in that the team preferred another child rather than the participant, but that the preferred child rejected the team in favor of another team. This enabled the participant to be assigned to the team (albeit by the researcher) but the team members did not raise any further objections.

Participants were then shown the photos of the competitor team (i.e., the out-group) who were of the same age, gender, and ethnicity, as their own team. The participant was then directed to her/his response booklet and completed the remaining questions in the booklet.

Participants who had experienced one of the rejection manipulations were then taken through the full acceptance manipulation to ensure that they understood that they had participated in a pretend game and that no one had really been rejected or accepted by another group. The children were then given their photos and thanked for their participation.

Results

Effects of Peer Group Status Manipulation

Perceived acceptance by the team. Analysis of participants' responses to this question (How much did the other children want you in the team?) in a 2 (age: 7, 10) × 2 (gender: boys, girls) × 3 (peer group status: accepted, ambiguous rejection, rejected) between groups ANOVA revealed two significant main effects, including a significant main effect for peer group status, $F(2,132) = 147.91$, $p < .001$, $\eta^2 = .69$. Comparison of the cell means using Duncan's Multiple Range Test ($p = .05$), indicated that the peer group accepted participants believed that they were wanted in the team ($M = 4.48$, $SD = .77$) significantly more than did the ambiguously rejected participants ($M = 1.77$, $SD = .99$) who did not differ from the rejected participants ($M = 1.56$, $SD = 1.05$).

The analysis also revealed a significant main effect for participant age, $F(1,132) = 8.80$, $p < .01$, $\eta^2 = .06$, which indicated that the younger children ($M = 2.83$, $SD = 1.64$) judged that the other children wanted them in the team significantly more than did the older children ($M = 2.37$, $SD = 1.59$).

In-group identification. Participants' responses on this item (How much do you like being in your team?) were analyzed in a 2 (age: 7, 10 years) × 2 (gender: boys, girls) × 3 (peer group status: accepted, ambiguous rejection, rejected) between groups ANOVA. The analysis revealed three significant main effects, including a significant main effect for peer group status, $F(2,132) = 11.44$, $p < .001$, $\eta^2 = .15$, that indicated that the peer group accepted participants identified with their team ($M = 4.29$, $SD = 1.00$) significantly more than did the ambiguously rejected participants ($M = 3.60$, $SD = 1.30$) who, in turn, identified with their team significantly more than did the rejected participants ($M = 3.12$, $SD = 1.33$).

The analysis also revealed a significant main effect for participant age, $F(1,132) = 5.24$, $p < .05$, $\eta^2 = .04$, which indicated that the younger children identified with their team ($M = 3.90$, $SD = 1.20$) significantly more than did the older children ($M = 3.44$, $SD = 1.37$). In addition, there was a significant main effect for participant gender $F(1,132) = 4.63$, $p < .05$, $\eta^2 = .03$, which indicated that the female participants identified with team ($M = 3.89$, $SD = 1.29$) significantly more than did the male participants ($M = 3.46$, $SD = 1.29$).

Main Dependent Measures

In-group attitudes. Participants' attitudes (i.e., like, trust, play with) toward the in-group members were analyzed in a 2 (age: 7, 10 years) × 2 (gender: boys, girls) × 3 (peer group status: accepted, ambiguous rejection, rejected) between groups ANOVA that revealed three significant main effects. There was a significant main effect for peer group status, $F(2,132) = 14.75, p < .001, \eta^2 = .18$, which indicated that the peer group accepted participants ($M = 12.12, SD = 2.79$) were significantly more positive toward their team than were the ambiguously rejected participants ($M = 10.23, SD = 3.19$) who, in turn, were significantly more positive than were the rejected participants ($M = 8.85, SD = 3.31$).

The analysis also revealed a significant main effect for participant age, $F(1,132) = 8.23, p < .01, \eta^2 = .06$, which indicated that the younger children were more positive toward their team ($M = 11.11, SD = 3.09$) than were the older children ($M = 9.69, SD = 3.49$). In addition, there was a significant main effect for participant gender, $F(1,132) = 9.23, p < .01, \eta^2 = .06$, which indicated that the female participants were more positive toward their team ($M = 11.15, SD = 3.23$) than were the male participants ($M = 9.65, SD = 3.35$).

Change teams. The participants' responses on whether they would wish to change to the other team were analyzed in a 2 (age: 7, 10 years) × 2 (gender: boys, girls) × 3 (peer group status: accepted, ambiguous rejection, rejected) between groups ANOVA. This analysis revealed only a significant main effect for peer group status, $F(2,132) = 5.33, p < .01, \eta^2 = .07$. Comparison of the cell means indicated that the peer group accepted participants ($M = 2.23, SD = 1.24$) wanted to change to the other team significantly less than did the peer group rejected participants ($M = 3.08, SD = 1.33$), and the ambiguous rejected participants ($M = 2.75, SD = 1.26$), who did not differ from each other.

The participants' responses on how much they thought the children in the other team would wish to change to their team were analyzed in a 2 (age: 7, 10 years) × 2 (gender: boys, girls) × 3 (peer group status: accepted, ambiguous rejection, rejected) between groups ANOVA. This revealed only a significant main effect for peer group status, $F(2,132) = 6.56, p < .01, \eta^2 = .09$; accepted participants ($M = 3.50, SD = 1.67$) considered that the children from the other team would want to change to the participant's team significantly more than did the ambiguous rejected participants ($M = 2.75, SD = 1.58$) who did not differ from the rejected participants ($M = 2.77, SD - 1.07$).

Effects of RS and SA on In-Group Attitudes

Simple correlations. Correlation coefficients were computed between the participants' scores on the RS variables, SA, and the participants' in-group attitudes (see Table 1). As indicated, anxious expectations were significantly correlated with angry expectations ($r = .38$), and rejection expectations ($r = .18$). In addition, there were significant negative correlations between SA and anxious expectations and rejection expectations ($rs = -.20, -.33$, respectively). As anticipated, this analysis also indicated that children who had more angry expectations,

Table 1. Correlations between All Variables ($N = 144$)

Variable	1	2	3	4	5
1. RS—Anxious	–				
2. RS—Anger	.38**	–			
3. RS—Rejection	.18*	.10	–		
4. In-group attitudes	−.11	−.19*	−.28**	–	
5. Social acumen	−.20*	−.06	−.33**	.26**	–
M (SD)	1.88 (0.45)	1.52 (0.36)	1.80 (0.31)	10.40 (3.37)	3.63 (0.51)

Note. RS = rejection sensitivity.
*$p < .05$. **$p < .01$.

and more rejection expectations, were less positive about the in-group members ($rs = -.19, -.28$, respectively). In contrast, children higher in SA had more positive attitudes toward the in-group ($r = .26$).

Multivariate analyses. Hierarchical multiple regression analyses were used to examine the unique associations of the participants' attitudes toward the in-group with their peer group status, RS, and SA. To examine peer group status, we designated peer group acceptance as the comparison group and created two dummy variables to compare unambiguous rejection with acceptance, and ambiguous rejection with acceptance. The dummy variables, together with RS anxiety, RS anger, RS rejection expectations, and SA, were entered at Step 1 of each hierarchical regression model. The interaction terms involving peer group status and other measures (RS and SA) were entered in Step 2. We tested one interaction term at a time, resulting in the estimation of four hierarchical regression models (Steps 2a, 2b, 2c, and 2d in Table 2).

The analysis revealed that peer group status, RS, and SA accounted for 29% of the variance in children's in-group attitudes, $F(6, 137) = 9.17, p < .01$. Consistent with the ANOVA above, children in the unambiguous rejection ($\beta = -.45$) and ambiguous rejection ($\beta = -.25$) conditions had less positive attitudes toward the in-group. Consistent with expectations, participants' RS and their SA were also significantly associated with their in-group attitudes. Specifically, children higher in RS anger ($\beta = -.16$), and expectations of rejection ($\beta = -.21$) had more negative in-group attitudes. In contrast, children higher in SA had more positive in-group attitudes ($\beta = .20$). None of the subsequent steps involving the interaction terms was shown to account for significant additional variance in children's in-group attitudes (see Table 2. After Step 2a, $F(8,135) = 7.11, p < .01$. After Step 2b, $F(8,135) = 7.70, p < .01$. After Step 2c, $F(8,135) = 7.02, p < .01$. After Step 2d, $F(8,135) = 6.90, p < .01$).

Table 2. Results of Regressing Attitudes toward the In-Group on Peer Group Status, Rejection Sensitivity, and Social Acumen ($N = 144$)

Independent variables	B (SE)	β
Step 1, $R^2 = .29, p < .01$		
Ambiguous condition	−1.78 (.59)	−.25**
Rejected condition	−3.22 (.60)	−.45**
RS—Anxiety	.62 (.60)	.08
RS—Anger	−1.43 (.72)	−.16*
RS—Expectation	−2.19 (.83)	−.21**
Social acumen	1.30 (.51)	.20*
Step 2a, $\Delta R^2 = .01, p = .39$		
RS anxious × ambiguous	1.00 (1.43)	.08
RS anxious × rejected	−.79 (1.37)	−.07
Step 2b, $\Delta R^2 = .03, p = .08$		
RS anger × ambiguous	3.24 (1.70)	.21*
RS anger × rejected	.12 (1.67)	.01
Step 2c, $\Delta R^2 = .01, p = .50$		
RS expect × ambiguous	−2.13 (1.99)	−.12
RS expect × rejected	−2.08 (2.02)	−.12
Step 2d, $\Delta R^2 = .00, p = .71$		
Social acumen × ambiguous	.87 (1.16)	.08
Social acumen × rejected	.85 (1.23)	.07

Discussion

This study revealed that children as young as 6 years display considerable perceptiveness when it concerns the state of their membership in a group (i.e., accepted, rejected, or ambiguously rejected) and that these perceptions influence their quite nuanced reactions to the group and its members. The findings also indicated that children's reactions to their group are independently influenced by two individual difference variables, including their acquired sensitivity to the possibility of rejection, and their level of SA.

Children's Perceptions of the Rejection Experience

The results indicated that accepted participants clearly understood that the group members wanted them in the team and preferred them to someone else whereas rejected participants had a clear view to the contrary. However, the views of the ambiguously rejected participants did not differ from those in the unambiguously rejected condition. Thus, whereas the ambiguously rejected participants might possibly have tried to "sugar-coat the pill," perhaps seeing themselves as more accepted (or, less rejected) than the unambiguously rejected group, such was not the case. Rather, having been told that the team members preferred another, and knowing that it was the experimenter who had actually placed them in the team, the ambiguously rejected participants apparently accepted the reality of their situation and saw themselves as no more accepted by the team members than did the unambiguously rejected participants.

Somewhat surprisingly, however, this pattern of perceptions did not coincide with the participants' attitudes toward the group members. Whereas the ambiguously rejected and rejected participants apparently saw themselves as being equally rejected, their attitudes toward the group members actually diverged significantly. The key to this divergence appears to have been the fact that the ambiguously rejected child actually did end up as a team member, whereas the rejected child did not. The effect of this was that the ambiguously rejected participant developed a sense of in-group identification whereas the unambiguously rejected participant did not.

Consistent with this, the participants' in-group identification responses revealed that accepted participants liked being in their team more than did the ambiguously rejected participants, but that the latter revealed significantly greater in-group identification than did the unambiguously rejected participants. Clearly, even though the ambiguously rejected participants only became team members through the experimenter's actions, it was sufficient for them to identify with their team more than did the rejected participants. It is possible that this feeling might also have been influenced by the knowledge that the preferred team member actually opted for another group thus leaving a legitimate place for the unambiguously rejected participant. That is, while the team members might initially have preferred another, when that person opted for another team, perhaps the team members might actually have welcomed the new member.

Children's Reactions to the Rejecting versus Accepting Group Members

Consistent with the in-group identification findings, the participants' in-group attitudes indicated that they were more positive toward the in-group when they had been accepted rather than ambiguously rejected and that, in turn, the latter were more positive toward the in-group than participants who had been unambiguously rejected.

However, contrary to these findings, the ambiguous and unambiguous rejected participants did not differ in wishing to change groups, and significantly more so than did the accepted participants. Moreover, the rejected participants (both ambiguous and unambiguous) believed that the members of the competitor team would not wish to join their (the participants') team, and significantly more so than did the accepted participants.

Thus, whereas the change group responses by both the accepted and unambiguously rejected participants were as might be expected, those of the ambiguously rejected participants were not because the latter had revealed that they identified with their team and had positive attitudes toward it. Instead, when it came to the possibility of leaving to join a new group, the fact that the in-group members had actually rejected them apparently came to the fore—better to leave this group and join another more welcoming group.

The preceding pattern of findings is noteworthy for several reasons. First, it indicated that the children's responses were quite nuanced, varying according to their peer status and the particular issue put to them. On some issues, the ambiguously and unambiguously rejected children agreed, but on others they were significantly different.

Second, even though it was clear to the ambiguously rejected participants that they were not wanted by their team, they still tended to identify with it and to express positive attitudes toward the team members, once they had been made a member. These findings are consistent with the view that children want to be group members and will seek to be included in a group if at all possible (Nesdale, 2007).

Third, consistent with the previous point, when the possibility of changing teams was raised, it was the issue of in-group acceptance that again came to the fore. Despite being made part of the team (by the researcher), and expressing some in-group identification and positive attitudes toward the in-group, the ambiguously rejected participants still were as likely to want to leave the in-group as the unambiguously rejected participants.

Fourth, in accordance with other research on children's tendencies to overestimate agreement with their own preferences, judgments, or decisions (i.e., social projection) (Augoustinos & Rosewarne, 2001), all the participants displayed social projection in their responses to the question of whether they thought that the members of the other team would wish to join their (the participant's) team. Thus, the ambiguously rejected and unambiguously rejected participants in this study anticipated that members of the out-group would show little interest in joining the participant's group whereas the accepted participants held a contrary view. Moreover, there was no age effect, as in other studies (see Abrams, 2011).

Finally, the results also revealed several independent age and gender effects on the different measures. Compared with the younger children, the older participants thought that the team was less likely to want them as members, they displayed less identification with the in-group, and they expressed less positive attitudes toward the in-group members. The most likely explanation for these effects is that they reflected the older children's greater SA (Nesdale, 2013). That is, based on their greater experience in dealing with individuals and groups, the older participants were more realistic in interpreting the behavior of the team members and this influenced their reactions toward them. Moreover, it is plausible that the reduced identification, and less positive attitudes, expressed by the male compared with the female participants, might have reflected the same factor.

Effects of RS on In-Group Liking

RS was measured in this study because, just as with adults and adolescents, recent research has shown that children in middle childhood who are subjected to chronic parental and peer rejection acquire RS (anxious, angry, and rejection expectations) and that anxious RS is associated with social withdrawal responses whereas angry RS is associated with hostility and retribution (Nesdale & Zimmer-Gembeck, 2014).

This study sought to extend these findings by examining the impact of children's RS on their reactions to a group in a context where their individual status with the group varied between acceptance and rejection. The findings indicated that as the children's angry expectations, and their expectations of rejection, increased, they were less positive toward the in-group. However, there was no evidence that the impact of RS was enhanced in the rejection compared with acceptance conditions.

There are several points about these findings. First, whereas angry and rejection expectations were inversely associated with positive in-group attitudes, the children's anxious expectations were not, presumably because they are more internally focused and linked with social withdrawal and isolation (Nesdale & Zimmer-Gembeck, 2014).

Second, regardless of their acceptance or rejection experience with the in-group, children higher in RS had less positive attitudes toward that in-group. Presumably, these responses reflect their many unsuccessful and unhappy experiences with such groups that have probably resulted in a jaundiced attitude toward all groups, even those who might appear to be accepting toward them.

Third, according to the RS model (Levy et al., 2001) and related research (Nesdale & Zimmer-Gembeck, 2014), one implication of the instigation of angry expectations is that they tend to be associated with an increased likelihood of retribution and hostility. Although the issue has not been addressed in relation to children, research with adults has shown that these responses only serve to increase the likelihood of peer group rejection with the further effect that the individual's dispositions toward RS are strengthened (Downey et al., 1998).

Effects of SA on In-Group Liking

SA was assessed because of the possibility that it might be positively associated with in-group attitudes. In addition, we assessed whether SA might interactively influence the impact of ambiguous and unambiguous rejection on in-group attitudes. The findings did not support the latter possibility, but did reveal that

SA was a significant positive predictor of the participants' in-group attitudes, regardless of the participants' peer group status.

This outcome serves to emphasize the importance of the SA construct. It indicates that children higher in SA have social knowledge and skills that can assist them in achieving successful interpersonal and intergroup interactions, in this case, responding positively even when other children do not initially accept them. This suggests that greater SA serves to enhance the child's positive responsiveness to the sorts of social upsets (e.g., rejection, hostility, aggression) that most children experience at some time or another during middle childhood, and their likely success in handling them. Consistent with this is the finding indicating that SA was negatively correlated with RS, as well as other research showing that SA is positively correlated with emotional empathy and negatively correlated with intentions to engage in interpersonal aggression (Nesdale, 2013).

Limitations

One issue concerns the manipulation of the ambiguous rejection condition. This situation was certainly ambiguous in that the participants were initially excluded by the team, and then included by the researcher, and without any further objections from the team. Consistent with this, the participants' in-group attitudes indicated that they viewed the situation differently from the unambiguously rejected participants. Against this, however, the former were rejected by the team in the same manner as were the latter participants. Clearly, more research is needed focusing on the manipulation of ambiguity to enable a more refined assessment of its impact on children's in-group and out-group attitudes.

A second issue concerns the use of a simulation rather than a more naturalistic paradigm. While the former has been used extensively in research and the findings parallel those obtained in real-world situations (Nesdale, 2007, 2008), there is still a need for naturalistic studies to confirm the present findings. Finally, whereas measures of in-group identification frequently err in terms of the redundancy of items (Nesdale, Rooney, & Smith, 1997), the reliability of the present single item measure would probably have been enhanced with additional items.

Conclusions

This research showed that even at 6 years of age, children are very perceptive concerning their experiences of acceptance and rejection, even ambiguous rejection, at the hands of the peer group and that their reactions to group members, including their desire for change, are quite nuanced. The results also indicated that both RS and SA are significant negative and positive predictors, respectively, of in-group attitudes, after accounting for the effect of peer group status. These findings, together with others, indicate that from as early as 6 years, children who suffer peer rejection experience negative emotional affect and that this impacts on their relationships with others (Nesdale, 2008). Moreover, if the rejection is ongoing or chronic, it can prompt the development of RS that recent research shows is linked to distorted cognition, anxiety, social withdrawal, and loneliness, or anger, retribution and aggression (Nesdale & Zimmer-Gembeck, 2014).

These findings have important social implications. First, they suggest that there should be an increased awareness of the possible need for early interventions designed to assist young children who are already experiencing problematic relationships with others. Second, the importance of drawing on the observations of multiple reporters, including other children, needs to be recognized and emphasized. Third, the basis of children's problems needs to be carefully assessed so that an appropriate intervention can be put in place for each child. For some, emphasis might be placed on moderating perceptual and processing distortions and biases, whereas others might need help in forming, holding, and improving friendships, while still others might need assistance in building coping strategies and emotional competence. Such activities would, of course, need to be experiential and very practical for such young children. Fourth, more research is needed to address the long-term effect of peer group rejection on later loneliness and depression, as well as relationship breakdown and violence. Given the devastating impact that peer group rejection can have on children, it is critical that these potential linkages are the focus of increased research.

References

Abrams, D. (2011). Wherein lies children's intergroup bias: Egocentrism. Social understanding, and social projection. *Child Development, 82*, 1579–1593. doi: 10.1111/j.1467-8624.2011.01617.x

Abrams, D., Rutland, A., Cameron L., & Marques, J. M. (2003). The development of subjective group dynamics: When in-group bias gets specific. *British Journal of Developmental Psychology, 21*, 155–176. doi:10.1348/026151003765264020

Augoustinos, M., & Rosewarne, D. L. (2001). Stereotype knowledge and prejudice in children. *British Journal of Developmental Psychology, 19*, 143–156. doi: 10.1348/026151001165912

Coie, J. D., Dodge, K. A., & Kupersmidt, J. B. (1990). In S. R. Asher & J. D. Coie (Eds.), *Peer rejection in childhood*. Cambridge Studies in Social and Emotional Development (pp. 17–59). New York: Cambridge University Press.

Downey, G., Freitas, A. L., Michaelis, B., & Khouri, H. (1998). The self-fulfilling prophecy in close relationships: Rejection sensitivity and rejection by romantic partners. *Journal of Personality and Social Psychology, 75*, 545–560. doi: 10.1037/0022–3514.75.2.545

Downey, G., Lebolt, A., Rincon, C., & Freitas, A. L. (1998). Rejection sensitivity and children's interpersonal difficulties. *Child Development, 69*, 1074–1091. doi: 10.2307/1132363

Dunham, Y., & Emory, J. (2014). Of affect and ambiguity: The emergence of preference for arbitrary ingroups. *Journal of Social Issues, 70*(1), 81–98.

Jones, D. C., Abbey, B. B., & Cumberland, A. (1998). The development of display rule knowledge: Linkages with family expressiveness and social competence. *Child Development, 69*(4), 1209–1222. doi: 10.2307/1132370

Levy, S. R., Ayduk, O., & Downey, G. (2001). The role of rejection sensitivity in people's relationships with significant others and valued social groups. In M. R. Leary (Ed.), *Interpersonal rejection* (pp. 251–289). New York: Oxford University Press.

Nelson D., & Crick, N. R. (1999). Rose-colored glasses: Examining the social information processing of prosocial young adolescents. *Journal of Early Adolescence, 19,* 17–38. doi: 10.1177/0272431699019001002

Nesdale, D. (2007). The development of ethnic prejudice in early childhood: Theories and research. In O. Saracho & B. Spodek (Eds.), *Contemporary perspectives on social learning in early childhood education* (pp. 213–240). Charlotte, NC: Information Age.

Nesdale, D., (2008). Peer group rejection and children's intergroup prejudice: Experimental studies. In S. Levy & M. Killen (Eds.), *Intergroup attitudes and relations in childhood through adulthood* (pp. 32–46).

Nesdale, D, (2013). Social acumen: The missing piece in the puzzle of children's prejudice. In M. R. Mahzarin & S. Gelman (Eds.), *Navigating the social world* (pp. 323–326). Oxford, UK: Oxford University Press.

Nesdale, D., & Lawson, M. J. (2011). Social groups and children's intergroup attitudes: Can school norms moderate the effects of social group norms? *Child Development, 82,* 1594–1606. 10.1111/j.1467-8624.2011.01637.x

Nesdale, D., Rooney, R., & Smith, L. (1997). Migrant ethnic identity and psychological distress. *Journal of Cross-Cultural Psychology, 28,* 569–588. doi: 10.1177/0022022197285004

Nesdale, D. & Zimmer-Gembeck, M. J. (2014). Peer rejection in childhood: Social groups, rejection sensitivity, and solitude. In R. J. Coplan & J. Bowker (Eds.), *A handbook of solitude: Psychological perspectives on social isolation, social withdrawal, and being alone* (pp. 129–149). New York: Wiley-Blackwell.

Rubin, K., Bukowski, W., & Parker, J. G. (2006). Peers, relationships and interactions. In W. Damon, R. Lerner, & N. Eisenberg (Eds.), *Handbook of child psychology: Vol. 3, Social emotional and personality development* (6th ed., pp. 571–645). Hoboken, NJ: Wiley. doi: 10.1002/9780470147658

Sandstrom, M. J., & Zakriski, A. L. (2004). Understanding the experience of peer rejection. In J. B. Kupersmidt & K. A. Dodge (Eds.), *Children's peer relations: From development to intervention* (pp. 101–118). *Decade of behavior.* Washington, DC: APA.

Zimmer-Gembeck, M. J., & Nesdale, D. (2013). Anxious and angry rejection sensitivity, social withdrawal and retribution in high and low ambiguous situations. *Journal of Personality, 81,* 29–38. doi: 10.1111/j.1467-6494.2012.00792.x

DREW NESDALE is a developmental social psychologist and carries out research on children's intergroup prejudice, peer rejection, bullying, and aggression.

MELANIE J. ZIMMER-GEMBECK is a life-span developmental psychologist and conducts research on social relationships and individual development during late childhood, adolescence and emerging adulthood.

NATALIE ROXBURGH is an Honors graduate in Developmental Psychology and a practicing psychologist.

When Do Children Dislike Ingroup Members? Resource Allocation from Individual and Group Perspectives

Kelly Lynn Mulvey[*]
University of South Carolina

Aline Hitti
Tulane University

Adam Rutland
Goldsmiths, University of Maryland

Dominic Abrams
Goldsmiths, University of London

Melanie Killen
University of Kent

Do children like ingroup members who challenge group norms about resource allocation? Further, do children evaluate from their own individual perspective? Participants ($N = 381$), aged 9.5 and 13.5 years, evaluated members of their own group who deviated from group norms about resource allocation by either: (1) advocating for equal allocation in contrast to the group norm of inequality; or

---

[*]Correspondence concerning this article should be addressed to Kelly Lynn Mulvey, Department of Educational Studies, University of South Carolina, 129 Wardlaw, Columbia, SC 29208 [e-mail: mulveykl@mailbox.sc.edu].

This project was supported, in part, by a grant from the National Science Foundation, BCS#-0840492, awarded to Melanie Killen. We acknowledge the undergraduate research assistance from Samantha Cibelli, Shawnee Cohn, Sara Edelberg, Shawnese Gilpin, Sonia Giron, Naomi Heilweil, Kimberly Hypolite, Aliya Mann, Madiha Moin, Kristina Shieh, Mehwish Quershi, Lisa Weinberg, Sarah Weindorf, and Rivka Weiss. We thank Fulbright Scholar Marcel Stefanik and the graduate students, Cameron Richardson, Shelby Cooley, Megan Clark Kelly, and Laura Elenbaas, for their research assistance. We thank the students, parents, and teachers who participated in this study.

(2) advocating for inequality when the group norm was to divide equally. With age, participants differentiated their own individual favorability from the group's favorability of deviant members of the ingroup. Further, when deciding between group loyalty and equal allocation, children and adolescents gave priority to equality, rejecting group decisions to dislike ingroup members who advocated for equality.

Do children like ingroup members who challenge group norms about resource allocation? Further, when do children expect that how favorable a group from their own individual perspective? Fairness in the context of resource allocation is a central moral concept, which emerges early in childhood and extends throughout the lifespan (Blake & McAuliffe, 2011; Turiel, 1983). Distributing resources fairly is a complex cognitive challenge, as decisions about resource distribution must take into account competing claims to a particular resource and must balance information about variables, including merit, need, and prior claims or history (Damon, 1977). Further, children begin to recognize that denying resources to others based solely on group membership is a form of social exclusion (Killen & Rutland, 2011). While merit and other factors, such as effort, often warrant unequal distributions of resources, group membership, such as gender, or ethnicity, is viewed as an unfair basis for unequal distribution. Thus, giving more resources to the ingroup than to members of an outgroup creates and reinforces social hierarchies, and can lead to exclusionary social decisions. When do children recognize the unfair, exclusionary nature of denying resources to others, especially in contexts when this behavior is condoned by children's peer groups?

Seminal research on resource allocation reaches back as far as Piaget (1932). Following Piaget (1932), Damon (1977) undertook a systematic examination of children's understanding of and reasoning about distribution of resources, identifying age-related differences in how children made allocation decisions. Fehr, Bernhard, and Rockenbach (2008) found that individuals display an ingroup bias when distributing resources. In addition, Blake and McAuliffe's (2011) findings indicate that, by age 8, children reject inequality, even when they are beneficiaries of the inequality.

Recently, moral judgment research on resource allocation has examined distribution decisions within intergroup contexts (Leman, Keller, Takezawa, & Gummerum, 2009), and in the context of group dynamics (Killen, Rutland, Abrams, Mulvey, & Hitti, 2013). Group contexts provide a particular challenge for individuals, as they must not only make decisions about fair resource allocation but recognize that to deny resources to an outgroup is a form of exclusion which requires balancing information about group dynamics, and group identity.

Research establishing the developmental subjective group dynamics model has revealed ways children resolve the tension between uncritically favoring other ingroup members: as children get older they are more likely to prefer outgroup members who adhere to ingroup norms than ingroup members who deviate from those norms (Abrams & Rutland, 2008). Recently, Killen et al. (2013) have examined these patterns using both moral and social conventional group norms, and found that group loyalty takes a different form depending on whether the norm is about morality (resource allocation) or social conventions (traditions about wearing club shirts). Deviance from the group was supported more strongly in the moral context than in the conventional context due to children's focus on equality.

What has not been investigated, however, is *favorability* toward group deviants (how much do you like someone who challenges the group's allocation decision?) and expectations about group favorability with respect to one's own individual favorability of group members who challenge the norm (how much will the group like the deviant?). While individuals may view dividing resources unequally negatively (keeping more for the ingroup), this does not mean that individuals do not like members who advocate unequal allocation. In fact, children may like those who want their group to get more, even when they evaluate this decision as wrong.

The goals of this study were to address these questions by examining children's favorability toward ingroup members who do, and do not support norms of equality and to compare children's expectations about group favorability with their own individual favorability. Most allocation of resources decisions are made by individuals in groups in which there is an identification with the group, and there is something to be gained by distributing a disproportional part of the resources to the ingroup. Further, disagreeing with the group potentially leads to social exclusion from the group (Hitti, Mulvey, Rutland, Abrams, & Killen, 2013). Taking an impartial or fair viewpoint requires understanding the conditions under which group membership should not be part of the decision-making process. The question is when do children take into account group loyalty when evaluating resource allocation? Do they understand groups may make decisions that do not align with their own sense of what is fair?

Evaluations of Normative and Deviant Group Members

In this study, we investigated how children thought groups would react toward normative group members who adhere to morally relevant group norms versus members who deviate from such norms. Research, primarily in social conventional contexts, indicates that groups generally dislike ingroup members who deviate from group norms and are willing to exclude these members from their group (Abrams & Rutland, 2008). Less is known about how children expect groups will respond to normative and deviant members when the group norms involve morally relevant resource allocation decisions. Is it the case that groups will dislike (and thus, be willing to exclude) group members who deviate from the group by urging equal allocation of resources? Deviance in this context protects others from the denial of resources. Research on bystander interventions, however, has shown that speaking out against morally unacceptable behavior is a difficult, but important act (Abbott & Cameron, 2014). In order to understand what is driving children's evaluations, we measured both judgments about group norms regarding resource allocation, and assessed children's social reasoning. Assessing social reasoning is important as this can provide a clear picture of whether children are making social decisions regarding resource allocation by focusing on the moral aspects (i.e., "keeping more for our group is unfair because it excludes the others") or the societal aspects (i.e., "he wants to help our group out by having us keep more") of a particular situation.

Children (9–10 years) and adolescents (13–14 years) were sampled to capture age-related differences in distinguishing between one's own perspective and the group's perspective. This ability to distinguish between one's own perspective and a whole group's perspective reflects a form of theory of mind abilities (Abrams, Rutland, Pelletier, & Ferrell, 2009) related to an understanding of how groups function in varying social contexts. Adolescents have more experiences with groups and are striving to be autonomous, thus they may be more able to differentiate between their own opinion and their expectations about groups. Research shows that children with greater social acumen show more support for their ingroup (Nesdale, Zimmer-Gembeck, & Roxburgh, 2014). Understanding contexts in which individuals may align with deviant members rather than the ingroup as a whole will provide insight into those instances where exclusionary group decisions may be rejected.

Current Study

The current study examined children's social cognitive judgments about two types of group norms, equal and unequal allocation of resources, in an intergroup context. Gender, a salient authentic form of group identity, served as the "ingroup" and "outgroup" categories for this study. Distinctions between girls and boys are frequently reinforced by functional labeling of gender groups by adults, for instance, in school contexts, and have been identified as an early marker for children regarding intergroup attitudes (Patterson & Bigler, 2006). Participants evaluated group favorability toward (i) normative members who adhered to the group's resource allocation norm, (ii) deviant members who rejected the group's norm, and (iii) their own individual favorability toward deviant members who reject the group norm.

Based on the developmental subjective group dynamics model (Abrams, Rutland, Ferrell, & Pelletier, 2008), it was expected that, generally, both children and adolescents would assert that groups would like normative group members, and dislike deviant group members. It was also expected, however, that deviance that advocated equal allocation of resources would be judged more favorably than would deviance that supported unequal allocation of resources. Based on research from social domain theory (Turiel, 1983), which has demonstrated that children focus more on group functioning with age (Horn, 2006), it was expected that judgments and reasoning would reveal a greater focus on issues of equality, equity, and fairness in young children and a greater focus on the group norm and group functioning in adolescents.

It was expected that children would show greater favorability toward deviant members who espoused equal, rather than unequal, distribution, and that this would change with age. Older children would show greater sophistication in differentiating their own view from the group's view of deviant members, recognizing that the group would give priority to the group's goals in evaluating deviant members and perceive that unequal allocations may be beneficial.

Materials and Methods

Participants

Participants ($N = 381$) from the suburbs of a metropolitan Mid-Atlantic city in the United States included two age groups: 122 (73 female) and 9–10 year olds ($M = 9.76$ years, $SD = .35$); and 259 (141 female) and 13–14 year olds ($M = 13.56$ years, $SD = .39$). Participants were middle- to middle-low-income students. Ethnicity was reflective of the U.S. population, and included approximately 30% ethnic minority participants. Parental consent was obtained.

Design and Assessments

Children were individually interviewed and adolescents were surveyed using a protocol developed in previous research, which measured participants' evaluations of deviance from groups (for example of the pictures used in the protocol, see Killen et al., 2013). All participants assessed two stories, which referenced moral group norms (*equal:* voting to divide resources equally between one's own group ($50) and another group ($50), and *unequal:* voting to divide resources preferentially between one's own group ($80) and another group ($20)). Participants were asked to consider a group resource allocation norm, and one member of the group (deviant member) who disagrees with the group norm. Two versions of the protocol varied as to which group norm was described first (equal or unequal). Participants were shown a picture of eight same gender children and completed a group identity assignment task, which was drawn from the minimal group paradigm (Nesdale, 2008). This task involved measures to heighten their affiliation with the group and make the intergroup context salient. For instance, they chose a color and a symbol for their group.

Including both versions of the protocol, there were four deviance scenarios (e.g., deciding on how to distribute funds from the student council to two groups). For each context, participants were introduced to their ingroup norm and the outgroup (defined by gender) norm, which was the opposite of the ingroup norm. Then, participants were introduced to a normative and deviant member of each group. Deviant members go against the group norm and advocate for the same norm as the other group. Two forms of deviance were included: advocating for equal distribution of resources when the group wants to keep more money for the ingroup, and advocating for unequal distribution of resources by keeping more money for the ingroup when the group desires an equal allocation. An example from the protocol follows:

> "The Student Council ... [has] $100 to give out to the groups ... In the past, when your group has talked about it they have voted to give $50 to your own group and $50 to the other group. In the past, when the other group has talked about it they have voted to give $80 to their own group and $20 to your group. The group has to vote on what to do. Your group is saving up for a big trip to a music show... Veronica, who is also in your group, always votes to give $50 to your own group and $50 to the other group. Sally, who is also in your group, wants to be different from the other members of the club. She says that your group should get $80 and the other group should get $20."

Measures

For each scenario children responded to five dependent measures: (1) *group favorability toward the normative member:* evaluation of how favorable the group will be toward a normative member who agrees with the group norm (e.g., How do you think the group feels about having X (normative member) in the group? $1 = very\ bad$ to $6 = very\ good$), (2) *group favorability toward the deviant member:* evaluation of how favorable the group will be toward the deviant member who challenges the group norm (e.g., How do you think the group feels about having X (deviant member) in the group? $1 = very\ bad$ to $6 = very\ good$), (3) *justification for group favorability toward the deviant member:* a justification for their evaluation (e.g., Why?), (4) *individual favorability toward the deviant member:* evaluation of how favorable the participant will be toward the deviant member who challenges the group norm (e.g., How much do you think you would like X (deviant member)? $1 = not\ much$ to $6 = a\ lot$), (5) *justification for individual favorability toward the deviant member:* a justification for their evaluation (e.g., Why?).

Procedure

Individual interviews were conducted by trained research assistants for 4th grade participants. Interviews occurred in a quiet room at the school, with sessions lasting approximately 25–30 minutes. For 8th grade participants, trained research assistants administered surveys in a classroom environment, with sessions lasting approximately 25–30 minutes. Groups of 8th grade participants were 20–30 participants. The protocol was identical in survey and interview format. Participants randomly received either a version with a group norm of equal allocation presented first or a version with a group norm of unequal allocation presented first. Participants completed two moral (one equal and one unequal) deviance scenarios.

Coding and Reliability

Responses to the justification assessments were coded using coding categories drawn from social domain theory (Smetana, 2006). The coding system comprised three categories, including: (1) *Fairness* (moral domain: e.g., "It is fair to split the money equally"); (2) *Group Functioning* (societal domain: e.g., "He's going against what the group wants"); and (3) *Autonomy* (psychological domain: e.g., "It's okay for him to be different"). Because less than 5% of the participants used two codes, interrater reliability of the use of double codes was not analyzed. Coding was conducted by three coders blind to the hypotheses of the study. On the basis of 25% of the interviews ($N = 96$), Cohen's $\kappa = .87$ for interrater reliability.

Data Analytic Plan

One-sample t-tests, univariate analyses of variance (ANOVAs) and repeated measures ANOVAs were conducted to analyze favorability judgments and justifications. If sphericity was violated, the Huynh–Feldt adjustment was used. Pairwise comparisons (Bonferroni) were conducted for between-subjects and interaction effects. ANOVAs included age group (9-year-olds, 13-year-olds) and gender of participant (male, female). When repeated measures analyses were conducted, factors were the assessment or types of justifications used. To test for ingroup preferences, separate analyses were made in which ANOVA statements included group (ingroup, outgroup) as a factor. Though participants affiliated with their gender group as indicated by their responses to the group assignment task, these tests were not significant. Therefore, group membership was dropped as a factor. Thus, analyses presented include participants' evaluations of both ingroup and outgroup members. Condition refers to the norm of the group.

Results

Group Favorability Toward the Normative and Deviant Members

In order to confirm our expectation that participants would be favorable toward normative members and not favorable toward deviant members, one-sample t-tests were conducted (tested against a neutral score of 3.5) separately for each condition for both normative and deviant members. Ratings were based on a 6-point Likert

Table 1. Means and Standard Deviations for Favorability Evaluations by Condition and Age

	9-year-olds	13-year-olds	Mean
Group norm: Unequal allocation			
Group favorability: Unequal normative member	4.60 (1.50)	4.69 (1.74)	4.66 (1.67)
Group favorability: Equal deviant member	3.34 (1.63)	3.15 (1.75)	3.22 (1.71)
Individual favorability: Equal deviant member	5.30 (0.90)	4.33 (1.73)	4.64 (1.58)
Group norm: Equal allocation			
Group favorability: Equal normative member	5.46 (0.81)	5.16 (1.32)	5.26 (1.19)
Group favorability: Unequal deviant member	2.80 (1.40)	3.02 (1.79)	2.95 (1.68)
Individual favorability: Unequal deviant member	2.63 (1.29)	3.25 (1.70)	3.05 (1.61)

Note. Evaluations are based on Likert scale responses ranging from $1 = $ *Very Bad* to $6 = $ *Very Good* for group favorability and $1 = $ *Not Much* to $6 = $ *A Lot* for individual favorability.

scale ($1 = $ *very bad* to $6 = $ *very good*). Our expectations were confirmed, with participants expecting the groups to rate the normative members favorably in both the equal, $t(379) = 28.94, p < .001, d = 1.49$ and unequal conditions $t(380) = 13.65, p < .001, d = .69$. Participants also expected the groups to rate the deviant members negatively in both the equal condition, $t(380) = -3.25, p < .001, d = -.16$, and unequal conditions, $t(378) = -6.41, p < .001, d = -.33$ (see Table 1). Even when groups hold unequal norms, children expect groups will like normative members and dislike deviant members.

To compare group favorability for a normative member with group favorability toward a deviant member, repeated measures ANOVAs were conducted with ratings of favorability for normative and deviant members as the repeated measures factor. Two ANOVAs were conducted, one in which a normative member was adhering to an unequal distribution group norm, while the deviant member wanted to be equal; and another in which the normative member was adhering to an equal group norm while the deviant advocated for more money for their ingroup. Thus, 2 (Age group: 9-year-olds, 13-year-olds) × 2 (Gender: male, female) × 2 (Group favorability: normative, deviant) ANOVAs were conducted with repeated measures on the last factor. Findings indicated that participants expected that the group would be more favorable toward the unequal normative group member than the equal deviant group member, $F(1, 376) = 73.35, p < .001, \eta^2 = .16$ (see Table 1). There were no age or gender findings. Thus, participants indicated that they believed the group would give priority to maintaining the group norm over equal resource allocation, essentially condoning excluding the other group from access to resources. Children do not expect groups to always prefer equality. They recognize that group goals may lead to group preferences for unequal allocation.

As expected, participants were more favorable to the equal normative member than to the unequal deviant member, $F(1, 374) = 346.15, p < .001, \eta^2 = .48$ (see Table 1). In addition, there was an age by group favorability interaction found for the equal normative and unequal deviant condition, $F(1, 374) = 3.923, p < .05, \eta^2 = .01$. Pairwise comparisons revealed that 9-year-olds asserted that the group would evaluate the equal normative member more positively than 13-year-olds ($p < .05$; see Table 1). There was no difference between 9-year-olds and 13-year-olds on their evaluations of group favorability for the unequal deviant member. Thus, younger children focused more explicitly on equality principles, while adolescents considered the potential benefits to the group of keeping more money for the group.

Justifications for Group Favorability Toward the Deviant Member

In order to examine more precisely differences by age, gender, and condition in participants' reasoning about how the group would feel about the deviant, the justifications used by participants to reason about the group's favorability toward the deviant member were analyzed. Repeated measures ANOVAs were conducted separately for participants who evaluated that the group would feel bad about having the deviant in the group versus those who evaluated that the group would feel good about having the deviant in the group. Responses to the group favorability toward the deviant member ($1 = really\ bad$ to $6 = really\ good$) were divided using a median split of 3.5. Analyses were conducted on proportions of the three codes used.

When the deviant wanted to be equal, a 2 (Age group: 9-year-olds, 13-year-olds) × 2 (Gender: male, female) × 2 (Group favorability toward the deviant: Bad, Good) × 3 (Reasoning: fairness, group functioning, autonomy) ANOVA was conducted with repeated measures on the last factor. An interaction effect was found for group favorability toward the deviant by reasoning, $F(2,698) = 100.41, p < .001, \eta^2 = .22$. Participants who thought that the group would feel good about the equal deviant being in the group used primarily fairness reasoning (see Table 2). Participants who thought that the group would feel bad about the equal deviant being in the group relied on group functioning reasons (for instance, "he is going against what the group wants"), making less use of fairness and autonomy (see Table 2). For fairness and group functioning reasoning, participants who responded that the group would feel bad differed significantly from those who responded that the group would feel good, $p < .001$. Participants who thought the group would feel good about having the equal deviant in the group focused on moral reasoning,

Table 2. Proportion of Justifications Used for Group Favorability: Deviant Member

	Bad	Good	Mean
Equal deviant act			
Fairness	.19 (.37)	.63 (.47)	.37 (.46)
Group functioning	.67 (.44)	.18 (.37)	.48 (.48)
Autonomy	.06 (.21)	.08 (.26)	.07 (.23)
Unequal deviant act			
Fairness	.57 (.47)	.17 (.36)	.45 (.48)
Group functioning	.29 (.43)	.59 (.48)	.38 (.47)
Autonomy	.07 (.24)	.05 (.21)	.23 (.23)

Note. Evaluations are based on a median split of 3.5 for responses to a Likert scale ranging from 1 = *Really Bad* to 6 = *Really Good*.

such as fairness. In contrast, participants who thought the group would feel bad about having the equal deviant focused on the impact that being different would have on the group. This suggests they thought the deviant member should go along with the group. In addition, for the equal deviant, a three-way interaction effect was found for age group by reasoning by group favorability toward the deviant, $F(2,698) = 5.06$, $p < .01$, $\eta^2 = .01$. Participants who thought that the group would feel good about having an equal deviant in the group differed significantly in their use of fairness reasoning, $p < .001$, with 9-year-old participants using more fairness reasoning ($M = .84$, $SD = .32$) than did 13-year-old participants ($M = .54$, $SD = .50$).

Similarly, the 2 (Age group: 9-year-olds, 13-year-olds) × 2 (Gender: male, female) × 2 (Group favorability, deviant: Bad, Good) × 3 (Reasoning: fairness, group functioning, autonomy) ANOVA that was conducted with repeated measures on the last factor for the unequal deviant group member revealed an interaction effect for group favorability toward the deviant by reasoning, $F(2,688) = 39.13$, $p < .001$, $\eta^2 = .10$. Participants who thought that the group would feel bad about having the unequal deviant group member in the group used mostly fairness reasoning (see Table 2). Participants who responded that they thought the group would feel good used primarily group functioning reasoning (see Table 2). For fairness and group functioning, participants who thought the group would feel bad differed from those who thought the group would feel good, p's < .001.

Individual Versus Group Favorability Toward the Deviant Group Member

In order to test our hypothesis that participants would, individually, like an equal deviant member and not like an unequal deviant member, one-sample *t*-tests were conducted (against the neutral score of 3.5) for the individual favorability ratings for the equal and unequal deviant members. Confirming our hypothesis, participants were favorable toward the equal deviant, $t(376) = 14.06, p < .001, d = .72$, and not favorable toward the unequal deviant, $t(376) = -5.41, p < .001, d = -.27$.

In order to assess favorability toward deviants from individual and group perspectives, 2 (Age group: 9-year-olds, 13-year-olds) × 2 (Gender: male, female) × 2 (Deviant favorability: group, individual) ANOVAs were conducted with repeated measures on the last factor, one for each type of deviance (equal deviant, unequal deviant). As expected, participants liked equal deviant members more than they expected the group would like equal deviant members. A main effect was found for the equal deviance condition, $F(1, 373) = 171.78, p < .001, \eta^2 = .31$ (see Table 1). In addition, an age interaction by deviant favorability was found, $F(1, 373) = 8.94, p < .01, \eta^2 = .02$. All participants differentiated between their own perspective and the group's perspective when favoring an equal deviant (p's < .001). However, 9-year-olds were more positive toward the equal deviant from their own point of view than were 13-year-olds ($p < .001$). There was no difference between 9-year-olds and 13-year-olds in their evaluations of group favorability.

When evaluating the unequal deviant member participants suggested that they would not like the deviant member and that the group would not like the deviant member (see Table 1). For the condition when the deviant was unequal there was an age interaction, $F(1, 371) = 4.45, p < .05, \eta^2 = .01$, which revealed that 9-year-olds did not differ in their favorability toward the deviant and their interpretation of the group's favorability toward the deviant, but that 13-year-olds did differentiate (see Table 1). Specifically, 13-year-olds expected that they would like the unequal deviant more than would the group, $p < .05$. Further, 13-year-olds asserted that they would be more favorable to the unequal deviant member than did 9-year-olds, $p < .001$, though both children and adolescents rated their individual favorability of the unequal deviant negatively (below the midpoint of 3.5). Thus, generally, all participants, both 9- and 13-year-olds, were able to separate their own opinions from those of the group, but this may be more challenging for 9-year-olds, given their lack of differentiation when evaluating an unequal deviant member.

Justifications for Individual Favorability Toward the Deviant Group Member

Differences in justifications were analyzed, using a median split of 3.5 on responses to the individual favorability toward the deviant member. This was necessary to test the hypothesis that children used different forms of reasoning when they liked, than when they did not like the deviant group members. Reasoning was analyzed on the proportional use of three codes. These codes were fairness,

Table 3. Proportion of Justifications Used for Individual Favorability: Deviant Member

	Not like	Like	Mean
Equal deviant act			
Fairness	.21 (.39)	.66 (.46)	.57 (.48)
Group functioning	.36 (.47)	.07 (.25)	.13 (.33)
Autonomy	.11 (.32)	.15 (.34)	.14 (.33)
Unequal deviant act			
Fairness	.63 (.47)	.22 (.39)	.48 (.48)
Group functioning	.14 (.34)	.32 (.45)	.20 (.39)
Autonomy	.12 (.32)	.19 (.39)	.15 (.35)

Note. Evaluations of a deviant act are based on a median split of 3.5 for responses to a Likert scale ranging from $1 = $ *Not Much* to $6 = $ *A Lot*.

group functioning, and autonomy. A 2 (Age group: 9-year-olds, 13-year-olds) × 2 (Gender: male, female) × 2 (Individual favorability: deviant: like, not like) × 3 (Reasoning: fairness, group functioning, autonomy) ANOVA was conducted with repeated measures on the last factor for the equal deviance condition. Differences were found between participants who said that they would like the equal deviant member and those who said that they would not, $F(2,700) = 6.59$, $p < .001$, $\eta^2 = .01$. Participants who said that they did not like the equal deviant member used all three forms of reasoning (see Table 3). Participants who said that they would like the equal deviant member, however, used primarily fairness reasoning (see Table 3). Participants who liked the deviant member used significantly more fairness reasoning than those who said they did not like the deviant member, $p < .01$.

For the unequal deviant member, a 2 (Age group: 9-year-olds, 13-year-olds) × 2 (Gender: male, female) × 2 (Individual favorability: deviant: like, not like) × 3 (Reasoning: fairness, group functioning, autonomy) ANOVA was conducted with repeated measures on the last factor. As expected, participants who judged that they would not like the deviant member used different forms of reasoning than did those who said that they would like the deviant member, $F(2,692) = 25.90$, $p < .001$, $\eta^2 = .07$. Specifically, participants who said they would not like the unequal deviant member used fairness reasoning (see Table 3). Participants who said they would like the unequal deviant member used all three forms of reasoning (see Table 3). Participants who evaluated that they would like the deviant member differed from those who said they would not like the deviant member on their use of fairness and group functioning reasoning at $p < .001$. Thus, the unequal member elicited the reverse pattern of the equal deviant, with those who do like the unequal deviant member using many forms of reasoning, while those who do not like the unequal deviant member focus strongly on fairness.

Discussion

The novel findings from this study revealed that in the context of resource allocation, children like members of their own group who challenge group norms, especially when the group norms are to distribute resources unequally. Thus, when deciding between group loyalty and equal allocation, children and adolescents give priority to equality, rejecting group decisions to exclude others from access to resources. This was surprising as we expected that while children might view a deviant member's decision to give more to the ingroup as unfair they might express a positive liking bias to such a member given that they would gain from it. Further, the findings stand in contrast to much previous research on intergroup dynamics in gender contexts, which has shown that children show ingroup bias very early (Patterson & Bigler, 2006). At the same time, it supports findings that have shown how strongly children care about equal allocation of resources (Fehr et al., 2008). The current study used a novel paradigm to measure the strength of this consideration in children's moral orientation.

In this study, children gave priority to fairness and inclusion over group loyalty while continuing to affiliate with the group. This study used gender as the intergroup context, a group membership category which children readily affiliate with in early childhood (Leaper & Bigler, 2011). Moreover, previous research using a similar identification task as the one used in the current study has shown that children very quickly identify with the groups to which they are assigned (see Nesdale, 2008). In this study, the intergroup gender context involved decisions about morally relevant group norms. We found that support for equal allocation was more salient for children than was group membership. Our findings held regardless of whether the group was representative of one's ingroup or outgroup. Thus, group members (ingroup or outgroup) who deviated from the group by advocating for an equal allocation of resources were viewed favorably, even when the group norm was to keep more resources for the ingroup.

The novel findings showed that the strong preference for equality often documented in children (Almås, Cappelen, Sørensen, & Tungodden, 2010; Fehr et al., 2008; Smetana, 2006) was related to children's evaluation of deviant group members. In addition, this study documented age-related differences in these evaluations. 13-year-olds were less likely than 9-year-olds to support an ingroup member who challenges an inequality group norm. There are several possible interpretations. On the one hand, it could be that adolescents prefer groups to give more to themselves than to another group, identified as the outgroup. This would support the findings from Leman et al. (2009), which identified greater egotism among adolescents than children in resource allocation decisions. Alternatively, it could be that adolescents recognize that there are times when some groups are more deserving of resources than other groups (Almås et al., 2010). They may attribute positive intentions to a group's norm about dividing up resources unequally because they are thinking about the group identity and affiliation (wanting more resources to accomplish the group goals). We propose that both orientations coexist and we found support for both views in the current study. On the one hand, participants liked ingroup members who rejected the inequality norm held by the group (for being unfair). On the other hand, adolescents were also more positive than were children about a member of the group who deviated by espousing an unequal allocation.

In addition, the findings confirmed developmental subjective group dynamics' predictions (Abrams et al., 2008) that children aged 9 years and above recognize that deviant members would be disliked by the group, since the deviant members disagree with their group. Both the children and adolescents in this study recognized that groups would prefer normative to deviant members, even in the context of intergroup allocation of resources. Our findings indicate that perceptions of group favorability were influenced by the type of norm. Participants expected that the groups would be more favorable to deviant members who challenged a group's inequality norm than those who challenge a group's equality norm. However, even when a group member challenges their group to support moral principles they will be disliked by the group. Previous research has shown that negative group favorability is related to greater acceptance of exclusion (Abrams & Rutland, 2008), thus it may be that even those group members who challenge groups to be equal are at risk of being excluded from their group.

While many studies have examined children's attitudes regarding resource allocation, few of these studies have explicitly measured reasoning. The reasoning used differed when evaluating deviant members who espoused equality from those who espoused inequality. Participants who expected groups to dislike equal deviant members reasoned that they were disliked for going against the group norms. In contrast, participants who expected groups to dislike unequal deviant members believed groups would not like these unequal deviants because of their unfair actions. Children who asserted that the group would like a deviant member who wanted to divide resources equally explicitly used fairness reasoning. Adolescents, however, focused on fairness issues but also showed an awareness of the importance of the group's goals. Individual reasoning about the decision making reflected moral, societal, and even psychological justifications. Participants weighed multiple factors, at times considering the personal rights of a group member to hold an opinion (autonomy reasoning) and the potential benefit of unequal allocation to the group (group functioning reasoning). These findings confirmed hypotheses posed by the social reasoning development perspective, which suggest that children will balance information about group identity and goals with their sense of morality, at times focusing on the unfair nature of excluding others from resources and at times focusing on the benefits to the ingroup of receiving resources (Rutland, Killen, & Abrams, 2010). Further, findings indicate that while both children and adolescents can balance group goals with a sense of morality that this ability becomes more sophisticated with age.

Moreover, participants were able to distinguish between the group's perspective and their own, understanding that while they would prefer equal allocations, groups would give preference to the unequal group norm. Adolescents showed stronger abilities to distinguish between individual and group perspectives, and greater capacity to attend to both group goals and moral principles than did children. Balancing information about equality principles with information about a group's goals posed a challenge for children (Rutland et al., 2010). Children focused more narrowly on their own equality preference, even when considering group favorability, as shown by the finding that children used more fairness reasoning than did adolescents.

Overall, participants recognized that when the group norm is about unequal allocation, the group will focus on the potential benefit of the allocation decision for the group, and show less support for a group member who advocates for equality. This is in contrast to children's and adolescents' individual perspective, which suggests a strong adherence to equality principles, even in these complex intergroup contexts. Extending previous theory, these findings reveal children's preference for equality in resource distribution (Almås et al., 2010; Blake & McAuliffe, 2011), and their understanding that groups are often not driven by principles of equality when they allocate resources. Participants' ability to differentiate their own position from the group's view reflects findings on theory of social mind, which indicate that, by age 9, children take group goals into consideration when making evaluations (Abrams et al., 2009).

What makes the current findings novel is that the focus was on favorability (how much a group would like a deviant member, or how much the participant would like the deviant member) and not only on act evaluation. Evaluating one's own and a group's favorability toward a group member who deviates from a group is a more cognitively complex task, as it requires one to balance information not only about the act itself, but also about the actor (including information about their group membership and one's own loyalty to the group). Thus, in the current study children were able to differentiate the individual and group perspective in intergroup resource allocation scenarios regarding expectations about favorability and liking, which differs from judgments involving evaluations of the right action.

Though much research indicates that children show an ingroup preference, we did not find differences when children were evaluating the ingroup versus the outgroup. The salience of the norms regarding equal allocation of resources trumped ingroup and outgroup preferences regarding gender in the context of this study. Thus, children supported equal division of resources between an ingroup and an outgroup, even though previous research using both implicit and explicit measures indicates an ingroup preference when sharing resources (Dunham, Baron, & Carey, 2011; Fehr et al., 2008). Future research should examine if the same pattern is present across different intergroup and normative contexts. In addition, though research indicates that children respond to hypothetical scenarios in similar ways as they respond to actual conflicts (Turiel, 2008), it would be fruitful to examine how children and adolescents evaluate deviance from group norms which derive from norms held by actual groups that they affiliate with at school. This could be done using a method similar to Horn's (2006) in which she conducted focus groups with adolescents about actual groups prior to creating her protocol.

Thus, children and adolescents gave priority to equality principles in their evaluations, while they recognized that groups would give priority to group loyalty. This research adds to our understanding of exclusion based on resource allocation, revealing that children and adolescents show an increasing ability to recognize that groups bring different claims, desires, and perspectives to their evaluations. While children favor principles of equality in the context of resource allocation, with age, the group perspective (including goals, desires, and needs) is increasingly taken into account. This is critical for our understanding of social issues, as it suggests that children do support group members who challenge their peer group to stand up to unfair or unjust treatment of outgroup members.

The implications of this research are broad, suggesting that with age children become more sophisticated in understanding both the pull of group loyalty and the importance of acting in ways which ensure just and fair treatment of others. In situations where group norms conflict with moral principles, individuals have to evaluate the type of norm under consideration, determine when a member of a group is challenging or supporting an ingroup norm, give priority to either the group norm or moral principle, and distinguish their own perspective from the group's perspective. We have demonstrated one context in which children can do this. In social life, these types of situations are pervasive, and learning how to evaluate the different aspects of the context provides a means for determining the most fair and least exclusive course of action.

References

Abbott, N., & Cameron, L. (2014). What makes a young assertive bystander?: The effect of intergroup contact, empathy, cultural openness and in-group bias on assertive bystander intervention intentions. *Journal of Social Issues, 70*(1), 167–182.

Abrams, D., & Rutland, A. (2008). The development of subjective group dynamics. In S. R. Levy & M. Killen (Eds.), *Intergroup relations and attitudes in childhood through adulthood* (pp. 47–65). Oxford, UK: Oxford University Press.

Abrams, D., Rutland, A., Ferrell, J. M., & Pelletier, J. (2008). Children's judgments of disloyal and immoral peer behavior: Subjective group dynamics in minimal intergroup contexts. *Child Development, 79*, 444–461.

Abrams, D., Rutland, A., Pelletier, J., & Ferrell, J. M. (2009). Children's group nous: Understanding and applying peer exclusion within and between groups. *Child Development, 80*, 224–243.

Almås, I., Cappelen, A. W., Sørensen, E. Ø., & Tungodden, B. (2010). Fairness and the development of inequality acceptance. *Science, 328*, 1176–1178. doi:10.1126/science.1187300

Blake, P. R., & McAuliffe, K. (2011). "I had so much it didn't seem fair": Eight-year-olds reject two forms of inequity. *Cognition, 120*, 215–224. doi:10.1016/j.cognition.2011.04.006

Damon, W. (1977). *The social world of the child*. San Francisco: Jossey-Bass.

Dunham, Y., Baron, A. S., & Carey, S. (2011). Consequences of 'minimal' group affiliations in children. *Child Development, 82*, 793–811. doi:10.1111/j.1467-8624.2011.01577.x

Fehr, E., Bernhard, H., & Rockenbach, B. (2008). Egalitarianism in young children. *Nature, 454*, 1079–1083. doi:10.1038/nature07155

Hitti, A., Mulvey, K. L., Rutland, A., Abrams, D., & Killen, M. (2013). When is it okay to exclude a member of the ingroup? Children's and adolescents' social reasoning. *Social Development*. doi: 10.1111/sode.12047

Horn, S. (2006). Group status, group bias, and adolescents' reasoning about treatment of others in school contexts. *International Journal of Behavioral Development, 30*, 208–218.

Killen, M., Rutland, A., Abrams, D., Mulvey, K. L., & Hitti, A. (2013). Development of intra- and intergroup judgments in the context of moral and social-conventional norms. *Child Development, 84*, 1063–1080. doi:10.1111/cdev.12011

Leaper, C., & Bigler, R. S. (2011). Gender. In M. K. Underwood & L. H. Rosen (Eds.), *Social development: Relationships in infancy, childhood, and adolescence* (pp. 289–315). New York, NY: Guilford Press.

Leman, P. J., Keller, M., Takezawa, M., & Gummerum, M. (2009). Children's and adolescents' decisions about sharing money with others. *Social Development, 18*, 711–727. doi:10.1111/j.1467-9507.2008.00486.x

Nesdale, D. (2008). Peer group rejection and children's intergroup prejudice. In S. Levy & M. Killen (Eds.), *Intergroup attitudes and relations in childhood through adulthood* (pp. 32–46). Oxford, UK: Oxford University Press.

Nesdale, D., Zimmer-Gembeck, M., & Roxburgh, N. (2014). Peer group rejection in childhood: Effects of rejection ambiguity, rejection sensitivity, and social acumen. *Journal of Social Issues, 70*(1), 12–28.

Patterson, M. M., & Bigler, R. S. (2006). Preschool children's attention to environmental messages about groups: Social categorization and the origins of intergroup bias. *Child Development, 77*, 847–860.

Piaget, J. (1932). *The moral judgment of the child*. New York: Free Press.

Rutland, A., Killen, M., & Abrams, D. (2010). A new social-cognitive developmental perspective on prejudice: The interplay between morality and group identity. *Perspectives on Psychological Science, 5*, 279–291. doi:10.1177/1745691610369468

Smetana, J. G. (2006). Social-cognitive domain theory: Consistencies and variations in children's moral and social judgments. In M. Killen & J. G. Smetana (Eds.), *Handbook of moral development* (pp. 119–154). Mahwah, NJ: Lawrence Erlbaum Associates.

Turiel, E. (1983). *The development of social knowledge: Morality and convention*. Cambridge, UK: Cambridge University Press.

Turiel, E. (2008). Thought about actions in social domains: Morality, social conventions, and social interactions. *Cognitive Development, 23*, 136–154.

KELLY LYNN MULVEY is an assistant professor of Educational Studies at the University of South Carolina. She completed her PhD (2013) in Human Development and Quantitative Methodology at the University of Maryland. Her research focuses on children's social-cognition, in particular moral and social development in intergroup contexts.

ALINE HITTI is a Visiting Scholar and Adjunct Faculty at Tulane University. She completed her PhD (2013) in Human Development and Quantitative Methodology at the University of Maryland. Her research interests include children's and adolescents' social cognitive and moral development in intergroup contexts based on ethnic, cultural, national, and religious affiliations.

ADAM RUTLAND is a Professor of Developmental Psychology at Goldsmiths, University of London. His research focuses on development and reduction of prejudice and social exclusion in childhood, peer relationships, and cross-ethnic friendships and children's understanding of group processes and morality. He is co-author of a book on *Children and Social Exclusion: Morality, Prejudice and Group Identity* with Melanie Killen.

DOMINIC ABRAMS is Professor of Social Psychology and Director of the Centre for the Study of Group Processes at the University of Kent. His research focuses on the psychological dynamics of social exclusion and inclusion within and between groups. He is co-Editor with Michael A. Hogg of the journal *Group Processes and Intergroup Relations*, and with Julie Christian of the *Wiley Multidisciplinary Handbook of Social Exclusion Research* (2007).

MELANIE KILLEN is Professor of Human Development and Quantitative Methodology at the University of Maryland. She is the author of *Children and Social Exclusion: Morality, Prejudice and Group Identity* (2011) with Adam Rutland, co-editor of *Social Development in Childhood and Adolescence: A Contemporary Reader* (2011) with Robert Coplan, and the Editor of the *Handbook on Moral Development* (2006, 2014) with Judith Smetana.

Does Moral and Social Conventional Reasoning Predict British Young People's Judgments About the Rights of Asylum-Seeker Youth?

Martin D. Ruck*
City University of New York

Harriet R. Tenenbaum
University of Surrey

Since the nearly universal ratification of the U.N. Convention on the Rights of the Child (U.N. General Assembly, 1989), children's rights have received increasing empirical attention. While there is an established body of research on how youth view their own rights, few studies have examined their views about the rights of out-group members. Employing a social-cognitive domain approach, the current study investigated British young people's (N = 260) views regarding the rights of asylum seekers. The data come from a secondary analysis of interviews on British young people's views about the religious and nonreligious rights of asylum seeker youth. Rather than being influenced by broader variables such as age, participants' judgments, and reasoning took into account the features of the specific rights situation under consideration. Moreover, the use of moral justifications was related to endorsing the rights of asylum seekers while social conventional justifications pertained to rejecting asylum seeker's rights. The implications for theory, future research and social policy are discussed.

Increasing awareness of the importance of children's rights is evident in the United Nations Convention on the Rights of the Child (CRC, U. N. General Assembly, 1989), which recognizes the inherent dignity of the child. The CRC

---

*Correspondence concerning this article should be addressed to Martin D. Ruck, The Graduate Center, CUNY, 365 Fifth Avenue, New York, NY 10016 [e-mail: mruck@gc.cuny.edu].

The authors would like to thank the Nuffield Foundation for supporting this research. In addition, they would like to thank Amy Messenger, Ruth Frost, Tope Ademosu, Andreea Rudas, Betul Alkhedairy, and Guler Dunne for help with data collection, coding, and transcription. Finally, they would like to thank the young people who so generously gave of their time.

outlines children's political, social, economic, and cultural rights. In addition, it also includes rights concerning children's nurturance (care and protection) and self-determination (autonomy and self-expression), which have importance for establishing psychological health and well-being in children and youth (Cherney, 2010; Ruck & Horn, 2008).

Despite the near universal ratification of the Convention, immigrant and asylum-seeking young people are more vulnerable to intergroup exclusion than their mainstream or majority counterparts (Killen, Rutland, & Ruck, 2011). This study employed a secondary analysis of interview data to examine situational variability in how host country majority young people judge and reason about the religious and nonreligious nurturance and self-determination rights of refugee and asylum seeker youth. Extending past research, this study examined whether endorsement of others' rights is related to reasoning about these rights.

Social cognitive domain theory provides the theoretical perspective for this study (see Smetana, 2006). According to this approach, individuals apply three domains of knowledge across a range of social situations. These domains include the moral (pertaining to fairness and rights), the social conventional (pertaining to social norms), and the psychological (pertaining to personal choice). Moral and social conventional reasoning were related to decisions about the acceptability of excluding others in examinations of children's and adolescents' judgments about intergroup exclusion (Heinze & Horn, 2014).

A number of studies employing a domain approach have examined young people's thinking about their own nurturance and self-determination across a range of situations and find that participants show consistent support for nurturance rights. Support for self-determination rights is more salient for older than younger participants (Ruck, Abramovitch, & Keating, 1998; Ruck, Tenenbaum, & Willenberg, 2011). Findings suggest that for nurturance rights, children, adolescents, and adults were more likely to consider the importance of social or familial roles and well-being (social conventional-based reasoning). In contrast, social reasoning for self-determination rights, corresponded to understanding of justice and equality (moral-based reasoning) and personal choice (psychological-based reasoning; Peterson-Badali & Ruck, 2008). Finally, with increasing age participants exhibited a more context-sensitive understanding of rights (Neff & Helwig, 2002).

While the various studies considered provide useful insight concerning how young people think about their own rights, few studies have examined how young people view the rights of immigrant groups such as asylum seekers. What we do know, however, is that in-group bias (Abbott & Cameron, 2014) and negative attitudes toward immigrants have become common across Europe and North America (Thijs, Verkuyten, & Grundel, 2014). Indeed, recent studies conducted in the United Kingdom (e.g., Cameron & Rutland, 2008) and Netherlands (e.g., Verkuyten & Steenhuis, 2005) showed that young people hold negative attitudes and stereotypes concerning asylum seekers and refugees.

Less empirical attention has focused on how majority group youth in host countries reason about the rights of immigrant and asylum seeking children. Reasoning about rights may involve either negative attitudes such as rejecting the rights of out-group members or in other cases involve tolerance and equity as seen when supporting the rights of out-group members. In the latter case, negative attitudes are distinct or separate from reasoning about rights. The UK represents an interesting context for examining attitudes towards these groups given that they are often characterized as "posing a threat to British culture" (MORI, 2003). Thus it is hardly surprising that there is growing political and public concern with the asylum-seeking population in the United Kingdom (MORI, 2003).

In one of the few studies examining how majority British youth reason about the rights of asylum seeking youth, Ruck, Tenenbaum, and Sines (2007) employed hypothetical scenarios where an asylum-seeking child's potential nurturance and self-determination rights were in conflict with the practices of authority. British youth were more likely to support asylum seeking children's nurturance than self-determination rights. Moreover, British youth's social reasoning was multifaceted. For example, when considering asylum seeking children's nurturance and protection rights, British adolescents were more likely to focus on issues of empathy and fairness. In contrast, for asylum-seeking children's self-determination and decision-making rights, participants were more likely to focus on adherence to authority.

Across Europe many asylum seekers and immigrants engage in religious practices that are often foreign to the majority population (Lynch & Cunninghame, 2000). In addition, Islam has become symbolic of the problems and issues associated with multiculturalism and immigration (Verkuyten & Slooter, 2007). However, only recently have studies begun to examine how majority group youth view Muslim's religious rights and related practices.

Recent work conducted in the Netherlands examined ethnic Dutch 12- to 18-year-olds' attitudes concerning the political and religious rights of Muslim immigrants. Verkuyten and Slooter (2007, 2008) found that ethnic majority Dutch adolescents showed less tolerance for the political and religious rights of Muslims than those of nonMuslims. Additionally, adolescents showed less tolerance toward Muslim religious practices (e.g., wearing a hijab or head scarf) than practices that were not at odds with participants' values.

Despite the large numbers of asylum seekers and immigrants in the United Kingdom from Muslim countries (United Nations High Commissioner for Refugees, 2011), little empirical attention has focused on how British youth view the religious rights of asylum-seeking youth. Available studies exploring how individuals conceptualize about either their own (e.g., Helwig, 1997) or others' religious rights (e.g., Verkuyten & Slooter, 2007) have viewed these rights from the perspective of self-determination or civil liberties. However, religious rights may also entail nurturance considerations in that some other agent (e.g., government) is held responsible for the fulfillment of the right under consideration. For example, food prepared according to certain religious procedures may implicate both nurturance and religious rights.

Addressing these issues, Tenenbaum and Ruck (2012) examined British 11- to 24-year-olds' understanding of nurturance and self-determination involving religious and nonreligious rights of asylum seeker youth. Tenenbaum and Ruck (2012) reported that participants' reasoning employed was consistent with a domain approach in that social reasoning was multifaceted and varied based on the type of right (nurturance or self-determination) and whether religious or nonreligious issues were implicated. Participants frequently appealed to practical issues when considering asylum seekers' religious nurturance rights. For nonreligious nurturance situations participants were apt to focus on issues involving parental responsibility. When considering religious self-determination rights participants supported the importance of respecting the asylum seekers' beliefs and customs. However, for nonreligious self-determination rights (which participants were less likely to endorse), youth were more likely to suggest that asylum seekers should "just be grateful for being allowed in the country."

The present study extended past research by measuring moral and social conventional reasoning when discussing social exclusion (MØller & Tenenbaum, 2011). Although research on social exclusion has found relations between reasoning and endorsement (Killen et al., 2002), work has not yet uncovered whether reasoning about the rights of minority group members is related to endorsement. This study addressed additional research questions about young people's reasoning about asylum seeker youth's religious and secular self-determination and nurturance rights. First, based on past research (Ruck et al., 2011), we expected that adolescents' endorsements and reasoning would vary based on the particular situation invoked. More specifically, it was hypothesized that young people would endorse fewer secular self-determination than other types of rights.

Second, past work has found that with increasing age, young people are less likely to endorse religious rights (Verkuyten & Slooter, 2007) for Muslims. Thus, we expected the older groups to endorse fewer religious rights and to justify these decisions with social conventional reasoning more than would younger participants. Similarly, we expected older adolescent to endorse fewer nonreligious self-determination rights than would younger adolescents (Tenenbaum & Ruck, 2012).

Finally, children tend to condone exclusion when they judge it to be a social conventional decision and to condemn exclusion when they view the situation as belonging to the moral domain (Killen et al., 2002). However, whether young people are more likely to endorse or extend rights to others when they use moral or social conventional reasoning has not been examined. Given that children have been found to condemn intergroup exclusion when using moral reasoning, we expected that they would endorse more rights to asylum seekers when using such reasoning. In contrast, we expected that they would endorse fewer Muslim rights for asylum seekers when using social conventional reasoning.

Method

Participants

The sample consisted of 260 participants from the greater London, U.K. Urban Area ranging in age from 11 to 24 years. The sample was divided into five age groups: 11–12 years (27 males, 29 females), 13–14 years (17 males, 29 females), 15–16 years (24 males, 28 females), 17–18 years (29 males, 35 females), and 19–24 years (15 males, 27 females).

We split the age groups into naturally occurring groups based on school grades. The 11- to 14-year-olds were split based on whether they were in the first 2 years of secondary school (11–12) or the next 2 years (13–14) of secondary school. The 15- to 16-year-old were enrolled in GCSE qualifications. All 17- to 18-year-olds were in the final 2 years of secondary school. The 19- to 24-year-old group attended a London university.

State schools were contacted to recruit the school-aged participants. Seventy-five percent of parents gave consent for their children to participate. The schools' catchment areas were economically diverse. The sample was representative of the greater London Urban Area (92% of the United Kingdom and 69.4% of greater London is White; Home Office, 2007). All participants were born in the United Kingdom. The majority, 204 (78.5%) identified as White British, 5 (1.9%) as mixed race, 17 as (6.5%) Asian British (mostly of Indian and Pakistani descent), 31 (11.9%) as Black African or Black Caribbean British, and 3 (1.2%) as East Asian British.

Procedures and Materials

Letters were sent home through schools. Parents of participants under aged 16 provided written consent and children gave verbal assent before being interviewed. Participants aged over 15 provided written consent. Participants were interviewed individually in their school. Eight hypothetical vignettes were presented to each participant. Half of the vignettes depicted situations involving an asylum seeking child's nurturance rights while the remaining four concerned self-determination rights. Two of the nurturance vignettes described situations where the child asylum seeker desired to have a religious right fulfilled (e.g., food prepared according to religious beliefs, religious expressing involving gender differentiation) while the other two implicated secular rights (e.g, access to parental support, school providing school uniform). Similarly for self-determination rights, two involved religious (e.g., freedom of religious expression unspecified, freedom of religious expression to wear a head scarf) and other two involved secular or nonreligious

Table 1. Justification Categories

Category	Description (and examples)
Moral[a]	Includes reference to fairness, rights and equality; appeals to the importance of respecting the asylum seekers' customs or religious beliefs (e.g., "Everyone should have the right to live where they want.").
Social-conventional	Includes references to group norm or functioning such as parents being responsible for looking after children; adherence to authority and rules; references to references to the asylum seeker being grateful for being allowed in the host country; (e.g., "Those people should be grateful for being here.").
Outcomes	Includes reference to general positive or negative outcomes of the situation (e.g., "He will get in trouble with his religion if he does that").
Practicality	Includes reference to practical issues or alternatives to solve the situation (e.g., "The school should lend him the uniform and when he has money he can buy his own").
Other	Miscellaneous

Note. [a]Because the focus of respecting others' religious decisions was based on respecting others for fairness reasons rather than focusing on referring to customs and conventions, we coded this type of reference as moral.

rights (e.g., right to choose where to live, right to personal privacy). All vignettes depicted situations where a child asylum seeker wanted to have children's right fulfilled that was in conflict with authority or government practices. Half of the situations took place in a detention center while the others took place in a school context. See Tenenbaum & Ruck (2012) for a complete description of all the vignettes used.

For each vignette, the age and gender of the story character was matched to the participant. A researcher read each vignette to the participants. For each vignette, participants were presented with an single item endorsement rating scale to assess whether the story character should be allowed to exercise the right in question using a 5-point scale ranging from *not at all* (–2) to *very much* (2). In addition, participants were asked to provide a justification for their response. All interviews were audio-recorded and transcribed. The order of presentation of the vignettes was counterbalanced.

Coding and Reliability

Based on past research (Tenebaum & Ruck, 2012) and a reading of the interviews, a justification coding system was developed. Multiple justifications were permitted. Only those justifications comprising 10% or more of responses for each vignette were analyzed. The coding system was based on four categories, including *moral, social-conventional, outcomes,* and *practicality*. Table 1 presents definitions of the coding categories.

Interrater agreement between the first author and a trained research assistant who was blind to the hypotheses was calculated on a randomly selected 21% of the protocols. Uncertainties or discrepancies in the coding were resolved through discussion. Cohen's kappa (κ) was calculated as a measure of interrater agreement. Interrater agreement was achieved with the following kappa coefficients: moral, $\kappa = 0.74$; social-conventional, $\kappa = 0.68$; outcomes, $\kappa = 0.88$; and practicality, $\kappa = 0.75$.

Results

Results are presented separately for endorsements and justifications. Preliminary analyses indicated no gender effects and therefore gender was excluded from all subsequent analyses. Where significant effects are indicated, Bonferroni post hoc tests were carried out by dividing the alpha by the number of tests conducted for each analysis. Only significant main effects and interactions are reported. For each vignette, endorsement scores could range from –2 (*not endorse at all*) to 2 (*endorse strongly*). Analysis of variance (ANOVA) models were used to examine the dichotomous justification data. These procedures are preferable to log-linear analytical procedures when analyzing dichotomous and repeated measures designs) and can be used when the degrees of freedom for the error terms are greater than 40 (Lunney, 1970).

Endorsements

A 5 (Age) × 8 (Individual vignettes) mixed-design ANOVA was conducted. Vignette served as repeated-measures factors while age served as a between-participants factor. All significant main effects and interactions related to the hypotheses are discussed below.

As predicted, there was a main effect of Vignette, $F(1, 1785) = 71.91$, $p = .0001$, $\eta_p^2 = 0.22$. Several interesting patterns of endorsement emerged from the results of Bonferroni follow-up tests. First, participants showed the greatest level of support for the asylum seeker child's nurturance right to parental emotional support ($M = 1.82$, $SD = 0.73$) and the asylum seeking child's religious self-determination right of being able to practice his or her own religion (unspecified), ($M = 1.69$, $SD = 0.79$) than the other vignettes. Second, participants were most likely to support the religious self-determination right of wearing a headscarf ($M = 1.34$, $SD = 1.31$), which differed from all other vignettes. Third, participants were less likely to support the nurturance right of the school paying for asylum-seeking children's school uniforms ($M = 0.94$, $SD = 1.44$), the religious nurturance right dealing with involving gender differentiation ($M = 0.84$, $SD = 1.57$), the religious nurturance right of food prepared according to religious beliefs ($M = 0.57$, $SD = 1.55$), and the asylum seeker child's self-determination right to privacy ($M = 0.57$, $SD = 1.73$) than the right to parental emotional support, freedom of religious expression (unspecified), and the religious practice of wearing a headscarf; these four former vignettes did not differ from each other. Finally, participants did not support the child asylum seekers' self-determination right to choose where to live ($M = -0.31$, $SD = 1.69$), which differed from all other vignettes.

There was a main effect of Age, $F(4, 255) = 4.22$, $p = .003$, $\eta_p^2 = 0.06$. Bonferroni post hoc tests indicated that 11- to 12-year-olds ($M = 9.39, SD = 4.32$) endorsed all vignettes more than did 15- to 16-year-olds ($M = 6.38$, $SD = 5.42$) or 17- to 18-year-olds ($M = 6.41$, $SD = 4.91$). 13- to 14-year-olds ($M = 8.70$, $SD = 5.96$) and 19- to 24-year-olds ($M = 6.48$, $SD = 5.30$) did not differ from other groups.

These effects were qualified by a significant Age × Vignette interaction, $F(23, 1491) = 2.87$, $p = .0001$, $\eta_p^2 = 0.04$. Bonferroni tests indicated significant age effects for three of the vignettes. First, there was a significant age effect regarding the religious nurturance right involving gender differentiation, $F(4, 255) = 4.16$, $p = .003$, $\eta_p^2 = .06$. Follow-up Bonferroni tests indicated that 11- to 12-year-olds ($M = 1.32$, $SD = 1.22$) were more likely to support this religious nurturance right than were 17- to 18-year-olds ($M = 0.27$, $SD = 1.74$). 13- to 14-year-olds ($M = 1.00$, $SD = 1.41$), 15- to 16-year-olds ($M = 1.04$, $SD = 1.43$), and 19- to 24-year-olds ($M = 0.84$, $SD = 1.57$) did not differ from other age groups.

Second, as predicted, there was an age effect for the religious nurturance right about having food prepared according to religious beliefs, $F(4, 255) = 3.80$, $p = .005$, $\eta_p^2 = 0.06$. Follow-up Bonferroni tests indicated that 11- to 12-year-olds ($M = 0.93$, $SD = 1.39$) were more likely to support this right than were 15- to 16-year-olds ($M = 0.00$, $SD = 1.76$). 13- to 14-year-olds ($M = 0.78$, $SD = 1.41$), 17- to 18-year-olds ($M = 0.34$, $SD = 1.55$), and 19- to 24-year-olds ($M = 0.93$, $SD = 1.40$) did not differ from other age groups.

Finally, there was a significant age effect regarding the nonreligious self-determination vignette of whether the child should be able to choose where to live, $F(4, 255) = 5.19$, $p = .0001$, $\eta_p^2 = 0.08$. Follow-up Bonferroni tests indicated that 11- to 12-year-olds ($M = 0.29$, $SD = 1.76$) were more likely to endorse this vignette than were 15- to 16-year-olds ($M = -0.62$, $SD = 1.55$) or 19- to 24-year-olds ($M = -0.62$, $SD = 1.60$). 13- to 14-year-olds ($M = 0.20$, $SD = 1.55$) endorsed this vignette more than did 19- to 24-year-olds. 17 to 18-year-olds ($M = -0.53$, $SD = 1.70$) did not differ from the other age groups.

Justifications

A 5 (Age groups) × 4 (Individual justification category) × 8 (Individual vignettes) mixed-design ANOVA was conducted. Justification category and vignette served as repeated-measures factors while age served as a between-participants factor. All significant main effects and interactions related to the hypotheses are discussed below.

There was a main effect of Justification, $F(3, 656) = 93.84$, $p = .0001$, $\eta_p^2 = 0.27$. Bonferroni pair-wise comparisons indicated that moral reasoning ($M = 3.07$, $SD = 1.63$) was used the most followed by references to outcomes ($M = 2.22$, $SD = 1.80$), which was followed by social-conventional reasoning ($M = 1.77$, $SD = 1.25$). Finally, participants made references to practicality ($M = 0.85$, $SD = 0.06$) the least. Each category differed significantly in usage from all other categories.

The main effect of Justification was qualified by a significant Justification × Age interaction as predicted by the second set of hypotheses, $F(10, 657) = 4.03$, $p = .0001$, $\eta_p^2 = 0.06$. Bonferroni follow-up comparisons indicated a significant effect of concerns about outcomes, $F(4, 255) = 6.33$, $p = .0001$, $\eta_p^2 = 0.09$. 11- to 12-year-olds ($M = 3.23$, $SD = 2.11$) were more likely to appeal to outcomes than 13- to 14-year-olds ($M = 2.04$, $SD = 1.66$), 15- to 16-year-olds ($M = 2.06$, $SD = 1.54$), 17- to 18-year-olds ($M = 1.86$, $SD = 1.57$), or 19- to 24-year-olds ($M = 1.86$, $SD = 1.57$).

There was also a significant Vignette × Justification interaction, $F(15, 657) = 35.64$, $p = .0001$, $\eta_p^2 = 0.12$. Follow-up comparisons with a protected alpha of 0.006 were employed. Table 2 displays the mean use of the different justifications across vignettes. Below findings are presented for religious and nonreligious nurturance and self-determination vignettes.

Justifications in religious nurturance and self-determination scenarios. For the freedom of religious expression involving food preparation, there was a significant difference in the frequency of justifications mentioned by participants, $F(3, 730) = 28.12$, $p = .0001$, $\eta_p^2 = 0.10$. Participants' justifications focused on moral considerations the most. Second, participants made references to outcomes. Third, social-conventional reasoning was used less than moral reasoning, and social-conventional reasoning did not differ significantly from the use of outcomes or practical considerations, which was used the least.

Second, the types of justifications participants employed varied when discussing religious expression involving gender differentiation, $F(3, 696) = 11.67$, $p = .0001$, $\eta_p^2 = 0.04$. Participants were most likely to mention outcomes and practicality, which did not differ from one another. Next, they were most likely to employ moral reasoning, which did not differ from practicality. Participants rarely invoked social-conventional justifications.

Third, for the freedom of religious expression (unspecified) scenario, there were significant differences in the types of reasoning participants used, $F(2, 464) = 275.45$, $p = .0001$, $\eta_p^2 = 0.52$. Follow-up Bonferroni pairwise comparisons indicated that participants were more likely to make appeals to moral reasoning than all other justifications. Second, participants were most likely to

Table 2. Means use of Justifications by Vignette

Justification category	Freedom of religious expression involving food preparation	Freedom of religious expression involving gender differentiation	Freedom of expression (unspecified)	Freedom of religious expression involving wearing a headscarf	Access to parental support	School provision of school uniform	Right to choose where to live	Right to personal privacy
Moral	0.49$_a$	0.22$_b$	0.79$_a$	0.25$_a$	0.29$_a$	0.25$_a$	0.25$_b$	0.55$_a$
	(0.48)	(0.41)	(0.41)	(0.43)	(0.46)	(0.43)	(0.43)	(0.50)
Outcomes	0.27$_a$	0.36$_a$	0.24$_b$	0.19$_{a,b}$	0.37$_a$	0.31$_a$	0.17$_b$	0.31$_b$
	(0.49)	(0.53)	(0.45)	(0.40)	(0.53)	(0.51)	(0.38)	(0.51)
Social-conventional	0.17$_{b,c}$	0.12$_{b,c}$	0.02$_c$	0.11$_b$	0.38$_b$	0.23$_a$	0.51$_a$	0.23$_b$
	(0.32)	(0.32)	(0.14)	(0.32)	(0.22)	(0.42)	(0.42)	(0.42)
Practicality	0.16$_{b,c}$	0.25$_{a,b}$	0.04$_c$	0.03$_d$	0.03$_b$	0.22$_a$	0.08$_c$	0.03$_c$
	(0.37)	(0.44)	(0.19)	(0.16)	(0.17)	(0.41)	(0.28)	(0.17)

Note. Standard deviations are in parentheses. Values in columns with different subscripts letters are significantly different from one another using protected Bonferroni comparisons in SPSS.

refer to outcomes. Finally, participants were least likely to make references to practicality or social-conventional justifications.

Fourth, for the freedom of religious expression scenario involving the wearing of a headscarf vignette, there was a significant difference in participants' reasoning, $F(3, 660) = 149.64$, $p = .0001$, $\eta_p^2 = 0.07$. Participants were most likely to consider moral justifications. This was followed by appeals to outcomes; participants made references to both types of justifications with equal frequency. Next, participants referenced social-conventional justifications, which was made with as equal frequency as references to outcomes. Finally, participants rarely made appeals to practicality.

Justifications in nonreligious nurturance and self-determination scenarios. Participants' reasoning revealed interesting patterns when discussing the access to parental emotional support vignette, $F(2, 624) = 31.84$, $p = .0001$, $\eta_p^2 = 0.11$. Participants made references to outcomes, social-conventional, and moral justifications the most and with equal frequency to each other. In contrast, participants rarely raised concerns about practicality.

There was not a significant difference in participants' reasoning about the school provision of school uniform scenario, $F(3, 759) = 1.71$, $p = .16$.

For the scenario dealing with the right of the asylum seeker to choose where to live, participants' reasoning also showed considerable variation, $F(2, 604) = 45.97$, $p = .0001$, $\eta_p^2 = 0.15$. Participants were most likely to employ social-conventional justifications. Second, they were most likely to reference moral reasoning, which did not differ from the use of outcomes. Finally, participants rarely made references to practical issues.

For the asylum seekers' rights to personal privacy analyses indicated significant differences in the types of reasoning participants' employed, $F(2, 601) = 53.99$, $p = .0001$, $\eta_p^2 = 0.17$. Participants were most likely to use moral reasoning. Next, participants were most likely to use outcomes and social-conventional reasoning with similar frequency. Respondents were least likely to consider practicality.

Finally, findings revealed a significant Vignette × Justification × Age interaction effect, $F(60, 3809) = 1.59$, $p = .003$, $\eta_p^2 = 0.02$. With a protected p-value of .002, there was a significant age effect in reference to outcomes for the freedom of religious expression involving the wearing of a headscarf scenario, $F(4, 255) = 4.69$, $p = .001$, $\eta_p^2 = 0.07$. 11- to 12-year-olds ($M = 0.38$, $SD = 0.52$) were more likely to refer to outcomes when discussing this vignette than were 13- to 14-year-olds ($M = 0.09$, $SD = 0.28$), 15- to 16-year-olds ($M = 0.13$, $SD = 0.34$), or 17- to 18-year-olds ($M = 0.13$, $SD = 0.33$). 19- to 24-year-olds ($M = 0.21$, $SD = 0.40$) did not differ from the other age groups.

Finally, we considered the relation between the type of reasoning employed and endorsement. We limited our focus to moral and social conventional reasoning

Table 3. Correlations between Young People's Endorsement and Reasoning

Type of vignette	Moral reasoning	Social conventional reasoning
Freedom of religious expression involving food preparation	0.54***	−0.07
Freedom of religious expression involving gender differentiation	0.23***	−0.02
Freedom of religious expression (unspecified)	0.47***	−0.09
Freedom of religious expression involving wearing a headscarf	0.02	−0.64***
Access to parental support	0.15**	−0.26***
School provision of school uniform	0.26***	−0.21***
Right to choose where to live	0.67***	−0.57***
Right to personal privacy	0.64***	−0.53***

Note. $*p < .05$; $**p < .01$; and $***p < .001$.

as preliminary analyses revealed that references to outcomes or the practicality were employed regardless of whether the right was endorsed or not endorsed. There were no significant main effects or interaction effects with age.

We expected that participants would be more likely to use moral reasoning when they endorsed an asylum-seeking youth's right than when the right was not endorsed. Furthermore, we expected that participants would be more likely to employ social-conventional reasoning when they did not support an asylum-seeking youth's rights than when they did. We conducted correlations between endorsement scores and these two types of reasons for each vignette in 16 separate correlation coefficients. To protect the alpha, we divided 0.05 by 16. Table 3 displays the correlations. Endorsement was positively related to the use of moral reasoning in six out of eight of the vignettes. Conversely, endorsement of rights was negatively related to the use of social conventional reasoning.

Discussion

This study investigated situational specificity in British young people's judgments and reasoning about the religious and nonreligious rights of asylum seeker youth. We examined relations between young people's endorsement of rights and their reasoning. We discuss the major findings pertinent and consider the limitations, policy implications, and conclusions. Overall participants took into account the features of the various rights situations to which they were asked to respond. In general, participants showed the greatest level of support for asylum-seeking children's right to parental emotional support and the right of freedom of religious expression (unspecified). In contrast, participants showed the lowest level of support for the asylum seeker child choosing where to live.

A number of interesting age-related findings with regard to endorsement also emerged. For the scenario involving freedom of religious expression involving gender differentiation the youngest participants were more likely than older participants to endorse this form of religious freedom. Similarly, the youngest participants were also more likely than older participants to support the scenario pertaining to freedom of religious expression involving food preparation. Thus, it seems that younger British youth were more likely to support religious self-determination for asylum seekers than were older British youth. This finding is in contrast with the fact that attitudinal surveys suggest that 72% of adults in the United Kingdom reported a favorable opinion of Muslims (Pew Global Attitudes, 2006). This is somewhat surprising given that such tolerance decreases with age.

Age-related findings were also found for the scenario involving asylum seeker children having the nonreligious self-determination right of choosing where to live. The two youngest groups of participants were more likely than older participants to favor the asylum-seeking child having this right. This right may not have been endorsed by older participants because of increasing housing costs. Simultaneously, there is concern that the cost of living in London is unaffordable (Osborn, 2008). As one 16-year-old female explained, "not everyone can afford to live in London." Older participants may be more concerned with living in London, which makes this right more salient to them. Perhaps, had the situation been reversed (an asylum seeker who wants to live outside London), the findings may have been different. Generally speaking, then, when age effects were found, younger rather than older young people extended more rights to asylum seekers.

Such a finding complements research that shows that 9-year-old children prefer deviant group members who advocate equality more than do 13-year-old adolescents (Mulvey, Hitti, Rutland, Abrams, & Killen, 2014). Preference for equal distribution of resources may underlie young people's support for asylum seekers' freedom to choose where to live. However, there seems to be a few years' lag in applying this preference for equality to the case of reasoning about asylum seekers.

There was mixed support for the second set of hypotheses, focused on justifications, which suggested that younger adolescents would use more outcome-based reasoning than older participants, whereas older participants were expected to invoke social conventional reasoning more than younger participants. The only age-related finding that emerged was that the youngest group of participants were more likely than older participants to focus on outcomes. Similar research finds that younger children are more likely to consider the outcomes associated with the fulfillment of children's rights (Helwig, 1997; Ruck, Peterson-Badali, & Day, 2002; Peterson-Badali & Ruck, 2008). Of central importance are the findings pertaining to the justification employed for the different scenarios to which participants responded. Consistent with social cognitive domain theory (e.g., Killen et al., 2002; Turiel, 2006) participants' social reasoning revealed the multifaceted nature of their thinking. In addition, respondents took into account the particular aspects of the situations in their reasoning. Overall, participants were more likely to invoke moral justifications (e.g., equality or respecting religious belief) when considering the asylum seekers' freedom of religious expression unspecified and freedom of religious expression involving wearing a headscarf. In contrast, participants were more likely to invoke social-conventional concerns (e.g., maintaining group norms) when considering the story-characters' access to parental emotional support and choosing where to live.

The relation between reasoning and endorsement of rights provide further evidence of the multifaceted nature of young people's thinking about rights. Across the vignettes participants were more likely to invoke moral reasoning in situations where they endorsed or supported the rights of the asylum seeker story characters. In contrast, participants employed social-conventional reasoning in situations where they did not favor or support the asylum seekers' rights. Interestingly, these findings are similar to what has been reported in the available research on children's intergroup exclusion (e.g., Killen et al., 2002) where young people employ moral justifications when rejecting the exclusion of minority group children and invoke social-conventional reasoning to condone such exclusion. Given the similarity when reasoning about exclusion and rights, future research should examine individual differences to see if those who extend fewer rights to others are also more likely to condone exclusion. Such findings could have implications for intergroup relations.

As Abrams and Killen (2014) underscore, exclusion can have negative lifelong ramifications for those excluded. Moreover, children who exclude may grow into adults who perpetuate negative out-group biases. For some cases, prejudice toward non-U.K. native residents and confusion about the legal status of nonnative immigrants probably influenced decisions to condemn the rights of asylum seekers. Thijs et al. (2014) find that multiculturalism in the classroom was negatively related to Dutch majority children's outgroup bias towards Turkish–Dutch children. Incorporating multiculturalism in U.K. classrooms might increase the rights that U.K. citizens are willing to endorse for asylum seekers, who are legal immigrants. Such interventions may increase cultural openness, which is linked to defending an immigrant in a name-calling situation (Abbott & Cameron, 2014). Given the current campaign against illegal immigration in the United Kingdom (The Guardian, 2013), there may be confusion about legal immigrants' status and increased prejudice. Interventions are needed to combat exclusion given its negative lifelong consequences.

In sum, the current findings demonstrate that young people extend fewer rights with age and the justifications provided vary based on the context or situation in which the right is embedded. In addition, they extend fewer rights when they view situations through a social conventional lens and more when they conceive of issues from a moral viewpoint. To that end, social programs and interventions designed to improve intergroup relations concerning the rights of out-group members would benefit by framing such issues from a moral perspective.

References

Abbott, N., & Cameron, L. (2014). What makes a young assertive bystander? The effect of intergroup contact, empathy, cultural openness, and in-group bias on assertive bystander intervention intentions. *Journal of Social Issues*, *70*(1), 167–182.

Abrams, D., & Killen, M. (2014). Social exclusion of children: Developmental origins of prejudice. *Journal of Social Issues*, *70*(1), 1–11.

Cameron, L. & Rutland, A., (2008). An integrative approach to changing children's intergroup attitudes. In S. R. Levy & M. Killen (Eds.), *Intergroup attitudes and relations in childhood through adulthood* (pp. 191–203). New York, NY: Oxford University Press.

Cherney, I. (2010). Mothers', fathers', and their children's perceptions and reasoning about nurturance and self-determination rights. *International Journal of Children's Rights*, *18*, 1–21.

Heinze, J. E., & Horn, S. E. (2014). Do adolescents' evaluations of exclusion differ based on gender expression and sexual orientation. *Journal of Social Issues*, *70*(1), 63–80.

Helwig, C. C. (1997). The role of agent and social context in judgments of speech and religion. *Child Development*, *68*, 484–495.

Helwig, C. C. (1998). Children' conceptions of fair government and freedom of speech. *Child Development*, *69*, 518–531.

Home Office. (2007). *Life in the UK: A guide to citizenship*. Norwich: Her Majesty's Stationery Office.

Killen, M., Lee-Kim, J., McGlothlin, H., Stangor, C. (2002). How children and adolescents evaluate gender and racial exclusion. *Monographs for the Society for Research in Child Development*, *67*(4, Serial No. 271).

Killen, M., Rutland, A., & Ruck, M. (2011). Promoting equity, tolerance, and justice: Policy implications. *Social Policy Report: Society for Research in Child Development*, *25*, 1–33.

Lunney, G. H. (1970). Using Analysis of Variance with dichotomous data: An empirical study. *Journal of Educational Measurement*, *7*, 263–269.

Lynch, M. A., & Cunninghame, C. (2000). Understanding the needs of young asylum seekers. *Archives Diseases of Childhood*, *83*, 384–387.

MØller, S. J., & Tenenbaum, H. (2011). Danish majority children's reasoning about exclusion based on gender and ethnicity. *Child Development*, *82*, 520–532.

MORI. (2003). *British views of immigration*. London: MORI.

Mulvey, K. L., Hitti, Al., Rutland, A. F., Abrams, D., & Killen, M. (2014). When do children dislike ingroup members?: Resource allocation from individual and group members. *Journal of Social Issues*, *70*(1), 29–46.

Osborn, H. (18 March 2008). London most expensive city. Retrieved on 18 July 2012 from http://www.guardian.co.uk/money/2008/mar/18/consumeraffairs.renting.

Neff, K. D., & Helwig, C. (2002). A constructivist approach to understanding the development of reasoning about rights and authority within cultural contexts. *Cognitive Development*, *17*, 1429–1450.

Peterson-Badali, M., & Ruck, M. D. (2008). Studying children's perspectives on self-determination and nurturance rights: Issues and challenges. *Journal of Social Issues*, *64*(4), 749–769. doi: 10.1111/j.1540-4560.2008.00587.x

Pew Global Attitudes. (2006). The Great Divide: How Westerners and Muslims View Each Other. Retrieved on August 19, 2011 from http://pewglobal.org/2006/06/22/the-great-divide-how-westerners-and-muslims-view-each-other/.

Ruck, M. D., Abramovitch, R., & Keating, D. (1998). Children's and adolescents' Understanding of rights: Balancing nurturance and self-determination. *Child Development*, *64*, 404–417.

Ruck, M. D., & Horn, S. S. (2008). Charting the landscape of children's rights. *Journal of Social Issues*, *64*(4), 685–700. doi: 10.1111/j.1540-4560.2008.00584.x

Ruck, M. D., Peterson-Badali, M., & Day, D. (2002). Adolescents' and mothers' understanding of children's rights in the home. *Journal of Research on Adolescence*, *12*(3), 373–398.

Ruck, M. D., Tenenbaum, H., & Sines, J. (2007). Brief report: British adolescents' views about the rights of asylum-seeker children. *Journal of Adolescence*, *30*, 687–693.

Ruck, M. D., Tenenbaum, H. R., & Willenberg, I. (2011). South African mixed-race children's and mothers' judgments and reasoning about children's nurturance and self-determination rights. *Social Development*, *20*(3), 431–643.

Smetana, J. G. (2006). Social domain theory: Consistencies and variations in children's moral and social judgments. In M. Killen & J. G. Smetana (Eds.), *Handbook of moral development* (pp.119–154). Mahwah, NJ: Erlbaum.

Tenenbaum, H. R., & Ruck, M. D. (2012). British adolescents' and young adults' understanding and reasoning about the religious and non-religious rights of asylum-seeker youth. *Child Development*, *83*, 1102–1115.

Thijs, J., Verkuyten, M., & Grundel, M. (2014). Ethnic classroom composition and victimisation: The moderating role of attitudes. *Journal of Social Issues*, *70*(1), 134–150.

Turiel, E. (2006). The development of morality. In W. Damon & N. Eisenberg (Eds.), *Handbook of child psychology: Social, emotional and personality development* (6th ed., Vol. 3, pp. 863–932). New York: Wiley.

United Nations (UN) General Assembly. (1989, November 17). *Adoption of a convention on the rights of the child*. New York: Author.

Verkuyten, M., & Slooter, L. (2007). Tolerance of Muslim beliefs and practices: Age related differences and context effects. *International Journal of Behavioral Development*, *31*, 467–477.

Verkuyten, M., & Slooter, L. (2008). Muslim and non-Muslim adolescents' reasoning about freedom of speech and minority rights. *Child Development*, *79*, 514–528.

Verkuyten, M., & Steenhuis, A. (2005). Preadolescents' understanding and reasoning about asylum seeker peers and friendships. *Applied Developmental Psychology*, *26*, 660–679.

MARTIN D. RUCK is an Associate Professor in the Departments of Psychology and Urban Education at the Graduate Center of the City University of New York. His work examines the overall process of cognitive socialization—at the intersection of race, ethnicity, and class—in terms of children's and adolescents' thinking about human rights and exclusion.

HARRIET TENENBAUM is Reader at the University of Surrey (UK). She is interested in children's cognitive, social, and emotional development in relationships. She is the editor of the *British Journal of Educational Psychology*.

Do Adolescents' Evaluations of Exclusion Differ Based on Gender Expression and Sexual Orientation?

Justin E. Heinze[*]
University of Michigan

Stacey S. Horn
University of Illinois-Chicago

Previous research focused on sexual prejudice has shown that lesbian and gay adolescents are at greater risk of peer harassment and victimization than their straight counterparts. Peer victimization such as exclusion, however, may also be related to conventional expectations adolescents hold about their social environment. This study examined adolescents' (N = 1069) attitudes and reasoning about the exclusion of peers based on sexual orientation and gender nonconformity. Results indicate that although participants reported it was more acceptable to exclude their gay or lesbian, as opposed to straight, peers, gender nonconformity was also a distinguishing factor. Whereas mannerism and activity nonconforming gay targets were rated less positively than similarly nonconforming straight targets, straight appearance nonconforming targets were not evaluated differently than gay appearance nonconforming targets. Further, the types of reasoning adolescents used to justify their exclusion judgments varied by sexual orientation and gender nonconformity of the target.

With the onset of puberty, harassment related to sexuality and gender expression becomes more prevalent and is often directed at same-sex peers (Craig, Peplar, Connolly, & Henderson, 2001; Horn, 2006a, 2007; Pascoe, 2011; Poteat, Kimmel, & Wilchins, 2011). As children move into adolescence, gender roles become more salient and limiting, while adherence to these norms becomes much more important (Pascoe, 2011). Even as individuals are trying to figure

---

[*]Correspondence concerning this article should be addressed to Justin Heinze, Department of Health Behavior and Health Education, 1415 Washington Heights, SPH I, Rm 3703, University of Michigan, Ann Arbor, MI 48109 [e-mail: jheinze@umich.edu].

This research was supported in part by a research grant to the first author from the Wayne F. Placek fund of the American Psychological Foundation.

out their own sexual and gender identity in adolescence, they are also policing their peers regarding this process. Adolescents may perceive exclusion as a legitimate way to socially sanction individuals whose personal attributes or identity expressions fall outside of what is considered acceptable according to social norms regarding gender and sexuality. Further, recent research on harassment and victimization related to sexual orientation suggests that adolescents' perception of appropriate gender norms regarding dress, physical appearance, and mannerisms influence their judgments about how to treat their peers as much as, or perhaps even more than, their attitudes about sexual orientation (Blashill & Powlishta, 2009; Horn, 2007; Pascoe, 2011). Building upon this previous research, the purpose of this study was to investigate the ways in which gender nonconformity and sexual orientation relate to adolescents' social reasoning about peer group exclusion. To frame our research questions and investigate these issues, we utilize two related theories of social cognitive development: social cognitive domain theory, as well as social reasoning development theory recently proposed by Killen and colleagues (Rutland, Killen, & Abrams, 2010; Killen & Rutland, 2011).

Social Cognitive Domain Theory

A growing body of research on children and adolescents' reasoning about peer group exclusion suggests that in evaluating issues of exclusion, individuals draw upon their knowledge of fairness and individual rights, their understanding of groups as social systems based on consensually agreed upon norms, conventions, and identities, as well as their sense of autonomy and personal choice (Horn, 2003; Killen, 2007; Killen, Lee-Kim, McGlothlin, & Stangor, 2002; Mulvey, Hitti, Rutland, Abrams, & Killen, 2014). The central premise of social cognitive domain theory (Turiel, 1983) is that evaluative social judgments are multifaceted and draw from a number of conceptual frameworks or domains rather than a single structure of sociomoral reasoning. Three basic conceptual frameworks or domains are posited by domain theory: morality, societal convention, and the personal. Concepts of morality address issues of human welfare, rights, and fairness and are constructed out of the child's early social interactions around events, such as unprovoked hitting and hurting, that have intrinsic effects upon another person (Turiel, 1983). Morality (defined in terms of justice, welfare, rights) can be distinguished from concepts of social conventions, which are the consensually determined standards of conduct particular to a given social group. Whereas morality and convention deal with aspects of interpersonal regulation, concepts of personal issues refer to actions that comprise the private aspects of one's life, such as the contents of a diary, and issues of preference and choice (e.g., friends, music, hairstyle) rather than right or wrong. Nucci (1996) proposed that desire for control over the personal domain emerges from the need to establish boundaries between the self and others, and is critical to the establishment of individual autonomy and identity.

In extending social cognitive domain theory to intergroup contexts, Killen and colleagues suggest that domain reasoning is influenced by individuals' group membership and identification (Killen, 2007; Rutland et al., 2010). The interplay between the self and the group is argued to influence exclusionary attitudes and behavior in that the demands of group cohesion and promotion can legitimate social conventions as a justification for exclusion, especially if the situation is ambiguous or complex.

Research utilizing these approaches provides evidence that individuals of all ages draw upon these domains of social knowledge in reasoning about exclusion. How these domains of knowledge get coordinated and applied to issues of peer group inclusion/exclusion changes, however, as children move into adolescence (Horn, 2003, 2006b; Killen et al., 2002). Many adolescents view exclusion that is based solely on one's social group membership in a particular race, gender or peer group as wrong from a moral viewpoint (it is unfair or hurtful; Horn, 2003). Adolescents, however, are more likely than children to evaluate excluding someone from a peer group or friendship group as all right (Killen, 2007) and more frequently justify these judgments by making appeals to group functioning, group norms, or personal choice (Horn, 2003; Rutland et al., 2010). These results suggest that as children get older they have an increased knowledge of the conventional features of groups (group identity, group functioning) that are legitimately necessary to the organization and maintenance of groups, as well as an expanded understanding of issues that are up to the individual to decide (Nucci, 1996).

There is some preliminary evidence that social norms regarding gender and gender roles are related to children and adolescents' evaluations of exclusion based on gender. Killen and her colleagues found that gender exclusion is less often evaluated as wrong than exclusion based on race (Killen et al., 2002). Children and adolescents were also more likely to rely on conventions regarding gender in justifying exclusion. Applying a similar framework to exclusion based on sexual orientation, Horn (2006a) found that ninth-graders were less likely than older adolescents to evaluate exclusion of lesbian or gay peers as wrong and used more conventional and personal reasoning in justifying their decisions. Less understood are the ways in which social norms regarding gender expression in terms of appearance and mannerisms influence adolescents' evaluations of exclusion, and whether those evaluations are related to sexual orientation.

Social Norms, Gender, Sexual Orientation, and Peer Harassment

Social norms regarding gender and sexuality are particularly salient in adolescence (Craig et al., 2001; Pascoe, 2011). Heterosexuality is the prevailing norm in the majority of middle and high schools in the United States and adolescents are socialized, both informally and formally, toward heterosexual behaviors and relationships (Mandel & Shakeshaft, 2000). Harassment based on sexuality becomes much more salient in adolescence due to normative biological development (puberty), as well as developmental changes within the peer group structure (Craig et al., 2001). Moreover, research with adolescents on homophobia and anti-gay prejudice suggests that anti-gay attitudes are in place by early adolescence (Baker & Fishbein, 1998; Mandel & Shakeshaft, 2000; Poteat, Espelage, & Koenig, 2009) and that individuals who hold conventional beliefs about gender roles are more likely to be prejudiced and less likely to befriend a gay or lesbian person (Poteat et al., 2009). Interestingly, anti-gay language and harassment, while in part related to regulating peers' sexual orientation, is in large part used by adolescents to regulate each other's gender and gender expression (Horn, 2006b; Pascoe, 2011; Poteat et al., 2011). Individuals who fall outside the range of what is considered acceptable for their gender in terms of mannerisms, appearance, or activities can be targets of ridicule, teasing, and harassment from their peers (Horn, 2006b; Pascoe, 2011).

Despite the greater risk of victimization faced by adolescents who deviate from either gender or sexuality norms, relatively little work has focused on the interaction between sexual orientation and gender nonconformity, particularly as it relates to social exclusion. Previous work is mixed as to which individual characteristic (sexual orientation versus gender nonconformity) increase adolescents' vulnerability to negative evaluations, social exclusion and peer harassment. In adult samples, Schope and Eliason (2004), for example, found few differences in negative evaluations of gay and lesbian targets that were related to the targets' femininity or masculinity, and instead suggested that the targets' sexual orientation was the basis for negative reaction. In contrast, Blashill and Powlishta (2009) found that negative evaluations of gay males were related to both sexual orientation and gender role adherence, with gender roles having a more consistent effect. Whether there is additional risk associated with being both homosexual and gender nonconforming remains unclear. A young gay male who participates in stereotypically feminine activities, for example, may be at greater risk for harassment or exclusion than a gay male who adheres to masculine norms. Similarly, a heterosexual male who exhibits a gender nonconforming appearance may be at as much risk for peer sanction and harassment as a similar student who identifies as gay.

Even less research has examined what forms of gender nonconformity are related to greater rebuke from peers. Studies have shown that gay men are perceived to be more feminine and lesbian women more masculine than straight men and women, respectively (Fingerhut & Peplau, 2006; Lehavot & Lambert, 2007). Consequently, adolescents may hold stereotypic expectations about their lesbian or gay peers ("He's gay, so he doesn't like sports"). Such beliefs may mean adolescents are more tolerant of certain forms on nonconformity (e.g., cross-gender activities), but not others (e.g., acting or dressing like the opposite sex). One reason this may be the case, is that adolescents perceive certain types of gender transgressions as more deviant, and therefore as more of a risk to the "in-group" than others.

Recent research on intergroup dynamics and deviance evidences that individuals who deviate from the implicitly agreed upon norms of their in-group are viewed more negatively by their peers than out-group members who adhere to the in-group norms (Abrams, Rutland, & Cameron, 2003; Killen, Rutland, Abrams, Mulvey, & Hitti, 2012). Further, including the deviant in-group member is less favorable than excluding an out-group member who adheres to the groups norms, in part because the deviant in-group member is viewed as more of a risk to the coherence and maintenance of the group than the deviant out-group member (Killen et al., 2012). Thus, adolescents may view certain types of gender deviance (e.g., appearance, mannerisms) as more threatening to the construction and maintenance of gender roles and norms during this developmental period than other types of gender deviance (e.g., choice of activities).

Investigating these issues can further our understanding of how social norms about specific personal characteristics or identity expression influence reasoning about social exclusion. In addition, schools can be unsafe and inhospitable places for lesbian, gay, bisexual, transgender, and gender nonconforming young people due to social exclusion, ostracism, and harassment. Increasing our understanding of these issues can inform efforts to create safer schools for all young people.

Overview of the Study and Hypotheses

In this study, we investigated whether and how sexual orientation and different types of gender nonconformity were related to adolescents' judgments and reasoning about social exclusion of their peers. To investigate these questions we asked adolescents to respond to a series of scenarios about excluding individuals who varied in terms of their sexual orientation (heterosexual, gay, or lesbian) and nonconformity in gender expression (gender nonconforming in forms of appearance, mannerisms or activity). Adolescents were asked to evaluate whether they thought excluding someone from a peer group based on his/her sexual orientation and gender expression was wrong and to provide a reason for their evaluation. Consistent with previous research (Schope & Eliason, 2004), we expected that adolescents would evaluate social exclusion of gay or lesbian peers as less wrong than straight peers. Further, we expected that type of gender nonconformity would be related to adolescents' judgments with exclusion of appearance nonconforming targets viewed as least wrong.

We also expected that an individual's sexual orientation and gender expression would be related to differences in reasoning about why excluding a target would be wrong or all right. Based on previous work suggesting early adolescents view decisions about friendships and peer groups in personal and conventional terms (Killen et al., 2002), we expected that adolescents would use more conventional and personal reasons in justifying their evaluations about excluding peers who were gay, lesbian, and gender nonconforming. In contrast, we anticipated greater use of moral and personal reasons for judgments about straight peers.

Method

Participants and Procedures

One thousand sixty-nine adolescents (female, $n = 639$; male, $n = 430$) attending two different schools participated in the study. The sample consisted of 9th-grade (194 male, 288 female, mean age $= 15.0$) 10th-grade (111 male, 166 female, mean age $= 15.8$) 11th-grade (72 male, 122 female, mean age $= 16.8$), and 12th-grade (53 male, 61 female, mean age $= 17.8$) students. The largest proportion of students was European American (29.7%), followed by Asian American (27.4%), Latino (19.4%), and African American (14.5%). Relatively few students identified as bicultural, Middle-Eastern or Native American (5.9%, 2.9%, and 0.3%, respectively). Students attended either an urban college preparatory high school (School A) located within a large Midwestern city ($n = 575$), or a larger suburban high school (School B) located just outside of the same city ($n = 494$). Further, we excluded 17 participants because they identified as other than heterosexual.

Participants completed the questionnaire in their required advisory period, English, health, or social studies class. Participants were presented a 2 × 3 series of scenarios depicting individuals who were gay or straight, and gender nonconforming in appearance, mannerisms, or choice of extracurricular activity (Horn, 2007). For example, "Ashley is a straight female high school student. She plays on the school volleyball team. She is a 'B' student. She dresses differently from most of the other girls at school. For example she has a crew cut, and never wears make-up or dresses." Participants were asked to evaluate whether or not they thought it was wrong (*judgment*) for the students to exclude the target individual and to provide a reason for why (*justifications*). Participants were randomly assigned to read stories about either male or female targets. The six scenarios were counterbalanced to account for order of presentation.

Measures

Exclusion treatment judgments. Participants evaluated whether they thought it was right or wrong for individuals to exclude the target. Judgments were assessed on a five-point Likert scale (1 = *completely wrong*; 3 = *neither right nor wrong*; 5 = *completely all right*).

Exclusion treatment justifications. In addition to an evaluation judgment, for each story we asked participants to choose, from a set of eleven responses, the reasons that best reflected their opinion for why they thought the action (exclusion) was right or wrong. The responses used were developed from pilot interviews and informed by social cognitive domain theory (Turiel, 1983), and prior work on sexual prejudice (Herek, 1994). In addition to moral ("It is unfair/hurtful to him"), conventional ("He dresses or acts the way a [guy] in our society should") and personal ("Who you hand out with is a matter of personal choice) domain categories, we also included as response options types of reasoning that have been related to sexual prejudice in social psychological research (e.g., that the "gay" person might hit on them, that homosexuality is disgusting; see Heinze & Horn, 2009, for a complete list). Participants could choose more than one response. Scores were calculated as the proportion of a participants' response that fell into each justification type. Log-linear transformations were conducted on the proportional scores to adjust for nonnormality (Winer, Brown, & Michels, 1991).

Results

Given previous research reporting differences in individuals' gender role attitudes for females and males, as well as differences in prejudice toward lesbians versus gay men (Schope & Eliason, 2004), we ran and report separate analyses based on the gender of the target. Because significant school differences related to adolescents sexual prejudice have been reported elsewhere (Horn & Szalacha, 2009), we controlled for school in all analyses.

Exclusion Judgments

To investigate the relationship between exclusion judgments, sexual orientation and gender expression, we conducted two 2 (sexual orientation: gay/lesbian, straight) × 3 (gender expression: appearance nonconforming, mannerisms nonconforming, activity nonconforming) × 4 (grade: freshman, sophomore, junior, senior) × 2 (participant gender: male, female) repeated measures ANCOVAs with sexual orientation and gender identity as repeated measures (one for male targets and one for female targets).

Male targets. Whereas main effects for sexual orientation and gender expression did not emerge, the hypothesized interaction between sexual orientation and gender expression did occur for male targets $F(2, 1088) = 3.61, p < .05$ $\eta^2 = .01$. Follow-up tests of simple effects supported our hypotheses regarding type of gender nonconformity. Overall, for gay targets, participants were significantly more likely to say it would be OK to exclude their appearance ($M = 2.48$, $SE = .05$) and mannerism ($M = 2.47, SE = .05$) nonconforming peers, than their activity nonconforming peers ($M = 2.37$, $SE = .05$; $t(570) = 2.58$, $p < .01$; $t(567) = 2.07$, $p < .05$, respectively). A similar pattern emerged for straight targets, with adolescents indicating it was more acceptable to exclude appearance ($M = 2.49$, $SE = .05$) and mannerism ($M = 2.38$, $SE = .05$) nonconforming peers relative to activity nonconformers ($M = 2.23$, $SE = .05$; $t(568) = 4.38$, $p < .001$; $t(561) = 1.96$, $p = .05$, respectively). Notably, the difference between appearance and mannerism nonconforming straight targets was also significant ($t(559) = 2.21$, $p < .05$).

Further, participants evaluated excluding gay targets who were nonconforming in mannerisms or activities as less wrong than straight targets who were nonconforming in these same ways ($t(561) = 2.75$, $p < .01$; $t(567) = 2.52$, $p < .05$, respectively). Interestingly, there was no difference between gay and straight appearance nonconforming targets suggesting that this type of nonconformity is viewed as equally negative for both gay and straight males.

Although no overall grade differences were found in exclusions judgments, judgments did differ significantly by gender of the participant. Male adolescents in this sample were more likely to agree that it would be OK to exclude their peers, across all scenarios, ($M = 2.65$, $SE = .07$) than their female counterparts ($M = 2.16$, $SE = .06$, $p < .01$).

Female targets. When the scenarios depicted females targets, a main effect emerged for sexual orientation $F(1, 525) = 13.78$, $p < .001$ $\eta^2 = .03$. Overall, participants indicated that it would be more OK to exclude their lesbian peers ($M = 2.38$, $SE = .04$) compared to their straight counterparts ($M = 2.26$, $SE = .04$, $p < .001$). Gender nonconformity was not a significant predictor of exclusion for lesbian targets.

As with male targets, a significant between-subjects effect based on participant gender was obtained ($F(1, 525) = 17.53$, $p < .001$ $\eta^2 = .03$) with male adolescents ($M = 2.52$, $SE = .09$) saying it was more OK to exclude lesbian targets, in general, compared to females (M $= 2.13$, $SE = .09$, $p < .01$). Grade differences also emerged with freshman ($M = 2.44$, $SE = .06$) saying, in general, it would be more OK to exclude their lesbian peers than sophomores ($M = 2.13$, $SE = .09$, $p < .05$). Differences between other grades were not significant.

Exclusion Justifications

To investigate the relationship between participants' justifications for why exclusion was right or wrong, we conducted a 2 (sexual orientation: gay/lesbian, straight) × 3 (gender expression: appearance nonconforming, mannerisms nonconforming, activity nonconforming) × 11 (justification: affirms norms, fairness, hit on me, human equality, negates norms, personal choice, God's law, it's unnatural/disgusting, people need to belong, religious human equality, might think they're gay) repeated measures ANCOVA with sexual orientation, gender expression and justification as repeated measures. To reduce the complexity of the analysis and because significant differences on judgments were obtained, we controlled for participant grade and participant gender by including them with school as covariates.

Male targets. A main effect for justification ($F(10, 5,850) = 2.70$, $p < .01$ $\eta^2 = .01$) emerged. The main effect was qualified by two significant two-way interactions between justification type and gender expression ($F(20, 11,700) = 5.52$, $p < .001$ $\eta^2 = .01$), and between justification type and target sexual orientation ($F(10, 5,850) = 6.10$, $p < .001$ $\eta^2 = .01$). The hypothesized three-way interaction between justification type by gender expression and target sexual orientation ($F(20, 11,700) = 1.74$, $p < .05$ $\eta^2 = .003$) also emerged.

As seen in Table 1, participants tended to use justifications for straight non-conforming targets that appeal to the moral domain issues of fairness and not harming others (fairness, human equality, need to belong, religious human equality). In contrast, when justifying the exclusion of gay targets, participants were more likely to use conventional (God's law) reasoning or stereotypic assumptions about gay people (might hit on me, it's unnatural/disgusting).

The type of gender nonconformity further qualified differences in the use of justifications across sexual orientation. Table 2 highlights the hypothesized interaction. Participants used moral justifications less frequently (human equality), and conventional or stereotypic justifications more frequently (negates norms, God's Law, it's unnatural/disgusting), for straight targets whose appearance did not conform to expected gender norms compared to straight targets whose mannerism or choice of activity were nonconforming. When the appearance nonconforming target was gay, participants reported a higher use of the negation of norms. Participants also used more stereotypic justifications to justify the exclusion of activity nonconforming gay targets compared to mannerism nonconforming targets.

Female targets. The analysis revealed a main effect for justification for the female target scenarios ($F(10, 5,590) = 3.47$, $p < .001$ $\eta^2 = .01$). The main effect was qualified by a two-way interactions between justification and sexual orientation ($F(10, 5,590) = 2.50$, $p < .01$ $\eta^2 = .004$). The hypothesized three-way interaction between justification type, gender expression and sexual orientation was not significant.

Justifications for the exclusion of female targets differed based on the target's sexual orientation. Similar to male targets, participants tended to use more moral justifications for straight nonconforming targets, and more conventional or stereotypic justifications for lesbian nonconforming targets (see Table 1).

Table 1. Proportion of Justification Type by Sexual Orientation

	Sexual orientation	Affirms norms	Fairness	Might hit on them	Human equality	Negates norms	Personal choice	God's law	Unnatural/ disgusting	Need to belong	Religious human equality	Might think they're gay
Male targets	Straight	0.04***	0.18*	0.02***	0.18***	0.03	0.25	0.01***	0.02**	0.10*	0.09**	0.03
	Gay	0.03	0.17	0.04	0.16	0.04	0.25	0.03	0.03	0.09	0.08	0.03
Female targets	Straight	0.04**	0.21	0.01***	0.19***	0.03	0.23	0.01***	.02**	0.10***	0.10**	0.01***
	Lesbian	0.03	0.20	0.03	0.17	0.02	0.24	0.03	0.03	0.09	0.09	0.02

Note. Values represent the nontransformed mean proportion of justification responses. Asterisks denote significant justification differences within justification category and target sexual orientation. *$p < .05$. **$p < .01$. ***$p < .001$.

Table 2. Proportion of Justification Type by Gender Expression and Sexual Orientation for Male Targets

	Gender expression	Affirms norms	Fairness	Might hit on them	Human equality	Negates norms	Personal choice	God's law	Unnatural/ disgusting	Need to belong	Religious human equality	Might think they are gay
Straight target	Appearance	0.02[a]	0.17	0.02	0.16[a]	0.06[a]	0.25	0.02[a]	0.03[a]	0.10	0.09	0.02
	Mannerisms	0.03[b]	0.18	0.02	0.18[b]	0.03[b]	0.26	0.01[b]*	0.02[b]	0.09	0.10	0.03
	Activities	0.06[c]	0.18	0.02	0.19[b]	0.02[c]	0.25	0.01[b]	0.01[b]	0.10	0.10	0.02
Gay target	Appearance	0.02	0.16	0.04	0.16	0.05[a]	0.25	0.03	0.04	0.09	0.08	0.03
	Mannerisms	0.02	0.17	0.04	0.16	0.04[b]	0.25	0.03	0.03	0.09	0.09	0.02[a]
	Activities	0.03	0.16	0.04	0.17	0.04	0.25	0.03	0.03	0.09	0.09	0.03[b]

Note. Values represent the nontransformed mean proportion of justification responses. Different lettered (a, b, c) superscripts denote significant ($p < .05$) justification difference within justification category and target sexual orientation.
*$p < .10$.

Discussion

The purpose of this study was to examine adolescents' attitudes about exclusion of gender nonconforming, heterosexual, gay or lesbian peers, as well as their reasoning behind their decisions. Earlier work has argued that children's and adolescents' reasoning about exclusion is multifaceted, domain specific and influenced by group identification (Rutland et al., 2010). Whereas exclusion based solely on race or gender, for example, is typically rejected on moral grounds (Killen & Stangor, 2001), potential threats to group identity lead to more conventional rationalizations for exclusion (Rutland et al., 2010). Exclusion, then, serves as a regulatory mechanism within an intragroup context or a differentiation mechanism in an intergroup context. This study extends the social reasoning developmental perspective to instances of sexuality and gender expression-based exclusion and the role that conventional and moral reasoning play when evaluating exclusion of both gay and straight gender nonconforming peers.

Previous work on sexual orientation, gender nonconformity and peer victimization has argued that sexual orientation and gender nonconformity are independent pieces of information when making a decision about exclusion (Blashill & Powlishta, 2009; Schope & Eliason, 2004). Consistent with these findings, participants in our sample did generally report that it was more acceptable to exclude their gay or lesbian, as opposed to straight, peers. Our study expands on this previous research, however, by also providing evidence that gender nonconformity in appearance, especially for males, is a salient factor in adolescents' decisions about their peer interactions, regardless of sexual orientation. Certain types of gender nonconformity for males may be perceived as more deviant and more of a threat to the in-group, thus resulting in greater censure from peers, regardless of whether the individual is gay OR straight. Interestingly, this did not seem to be the case for girls who deviate from prescribed gender roles in any way.

At a time when both group conformity and physical appearance are especially salient (Carlson-Jones & Crawford, 2006), appearance nonconformity in males was particularly susceptible to adolescents evaluating exclusion as OK. Straight male appearance nonconforming targets were not evaluated differently than gay appearance nonconforming targets suggesting that social norms regarding masculine appearance affect gay and straight males' peer interactions and relationships equally and is viewed by adolescents as the most deviant type of transgression of masculine gender norms. Deep-seeded gender socialization, which begins in childhood (Martin & Ruble, 2002), may explain why exclusion of males who do not follow conventions for gendered appearance is evaluated as more legitimate, regardless of their sexuality. Maintaining the distinction between masculinity and femininity through exclusion may be a way to address threats to the in-group (i.e., "maleness") that transgressing masculine norms for appearance and dress may pose. In contrast, because females typically have relatively greater flexibility in gender role adherence (Schope & Eliason, 2004), participants may have felt less of a need to regulate the actions of their female peers who transgress feminine gender norms.

Similar to previous research by Horn (2006a, 2007) and Poteat, Espelage, and Koenig (2009), this study provides additional evidence that adolescents use exclusion to regulate each other's personal expressions. More specifically, the type of reasoning adolescents used to justify their exclusion judgments varied based on the type of gender nonconformity the target expressed. When male targets were straight and appearance nonconforming, participants used conventional justifications more often for their judgments, whereas they used more moral reasoning for judgments regarding straight mannerism or activity nonconformers. This finding is interesting considering that, overall, participants were more likely to use appeals to conventions when considering why excluding a gay target (disregarding gender conformity) would be OK. When the appearance nonconforming target was gay, however, participants more frequently resorted to stereotypic justifications. This pattern of results may be linked to adolescents' stereotypes of gay men as more "naturally" feminine coupled with their underlying assumptions regarding the lack of normality of nonheterosexual forms of sexuality for males.

It is important to note that exclusion judgments across sexual orientation and gender nonconformity were below the neutral value, indicating that adolescents, overwhelmingly, believed that excluding a peer based on these attributes was wrong. Moreover, consistent with previous work on exclusion (Killen & Rutland, 2011), respondents most often cited moral justifications for why exclusion was wrong. That said, differences in participant judgments and reasoning provide additional evidence that gay and lesbian adolescents face increased levels of social exclusion and prejudice because of their sexuality. In addition, the results extend previous research on exclusion and harassment related to sexual orientation by demonstrating that adolescents' judgments and reasoning about exclusion were also related to gender expression, particularly for males. Young men, and gay men in particular, appear to have even less flexibility in their gender expression lest they draw negative reprisal from their peers. In addition, straight males who violate norms regarding gender appearance faced prejudicial attitudes similar to their gay counterparts. Interventions focused on expanding adolescents' notions of what constitutes normative expressions of masculinity (and femininity) would benefit adolescents of all sexes and help to create a school environment that supports all individuals' identity expressions (see e.g., Pahlke, Bigler, & Martin, 2014).

Limitations and Future Directions

Several design concerns potentially limit the extent to which our findings inform research on sexual orientation, gender conformity and exclusion. First, the absence of gender conforming conditions, which would serve as an important reference category, prohibits potentially interesting comparisons. Our results suggest certain types of nonconformity can lead to less tolerant judgments of peers than others; it is unclear, however, whether gay or lesbian gender conforming targets would be rated similarly based solely on their sexual orientation. It could be the case that gender conforming gay or lesbian targets are evaluated as more acceptable than certain (or all) nonconforming straight targets. Further, the nonconforming scenarios were not pretested to assess the degree to which participants evaluated the characters as nonconforming. Depending on the individual, the manipulation of appearance, mannerism or activity may have been viewed as normative. Previous work utilizing these scenarios, however, has noted differences in the extent to which adolescents view different characters as acceptable (Horn, 2003), supporting our view that adolescents would consider the characters as nonconforming.

Second, the use of a single item rating to measure participants' judgment of the scenarios may have masked more discriminating components of exclusion. For example, adolescents may consider exclusion of nonconfirming peers to be more appropriate in certain contexts compared to others (Horn, 2003; Killen & Stangor, 2001). Further whereas our justification choices were informed by pilot studies and previous research, we did not include a self-report option for respondents. A more qualitative approach for collecting exclusion justifications may reveal multifaceted or complex reasoning around exclusion (e.g., reasoning that references multiple domains; is context and/or person specific; etc.). Future research could expand on the present findings by including design features that allow respondents to provide open-ended responses.

In addition, a particularly small number of participants identified as gay or lesbian and were thus excluded from the study because preliminary analyses suggest that they evaluated these issues differently than their peers who identified as heterosexual. Given that adolescence is a significant developmental period regarding sexuality, however, we recognize that a larger proportion of students may be exploring, questioning, or experimenting with nonheterosexual identities than identified as such on the survey, in part due to the stigma and sanction attached to these identities. Due to the nature of the method and the fact that we asked only one question about sexual identity (as opposed to additional questions about same-sex attractions or behaviors) our sample of "heterosexually identified" adolescents may have included students who were in the process of exploring same-sex sexuality or who identify as lesbian, gay, or bisexual but did not want to identify this way on a survey. In addition, because we did not ask individuals about their own gender identities or expressions, the sample may also have included young people who identify as transgender or are nonconforming in their own gender expression.

Though our results emphasize the interaction between sexual orientation and gender expression, it is likely that justification use is also influenced by participant age and gender. Researchers have noted age-related changes in adolescents' reasoning about issues of exclusion (Horn, 2003; Killen et al., 2002; Mulvey et al., 2014). Whereas Killen and colleagues have found an increase in the use of conventional and personal reasoning with age (up to 7th grade), in a study of 9th- and 11th-grade adolescents' reasoning regarding exclusion, Horn (2003) found a decrease in the use of conventional reasoning with age. This suggests that adherence to social norms in making decisions about peer interactions peaks in middle adolescence. Though further analysis of gender and age effects was beyond the scope of this article, future research should explore these relationships.

Finally, our research is cross-sectional, which limits the extent to which we can tie our current findings to individual development. Future research should consider repeated measurements of the same individuals as they mature from children to young adults. This type of research would allow us to better understand how developmental changes in social cognition interact with individuals' social judgments regarding their nonheterosexual and gender nonconforming peers during this dynamic period of development.

Implications

Within the United States (and globally), victimization of lesbian and gay young people at school is prevalent and has dire consequences for young peoples' overall health, development, academic engagement and achievement, and well-being (see Russell, Kosciw, Horn, & Saewyc, 2010). The results of this study provide evidence, however, that this type of harassment does not affect only students who identify as lesbian or gay, but rather young people, particularly males, who fall outside of the prescribed expectations for "appropriate" masculine appearance, mannerisms, or identity expressions regardless of their sexual orientation.

These results have tremendous implications for advocacy work in schools related to creating safer environments for all young people regardless of sexual orientation or gender identity/expression in that they suggest that the entire school community, whether or not any students at the school are out as lesbian or gay, is affected by misogynistic and homophobic harassment. In fact, in his work on uncovering the correlates of the most deadly school shootings in the United States (e.g., Columbine), Michael Kimmel (2003) provides evidence that in almost every case he examined, the young men who perpetrated the shootings faced repeated and insidious gay bating and gay bashing at the hands of their peers, yet to date, none of the shooters in those cases identified as gay. Furthermore, in most of these cases the young men report that educators or their peers did little to stop this type of harassment or victimization from happening. The results of our study provide compelling evidence for advocates seeking to enact strategies and policies that reduce this type of harassment in schools.

In addition, the results of this study provide further support that bullying and harassment are often based on bias and discrimination and that antibullying laws and policies should not only be enumerated (i.e., list protected identity categories covered by the legislation) but also that sexual orientation and gender identity and/or expression should be included within the list of protected categories. The results of our study suggest that young people use exclusion related to expectations regarding gendered appearance as a way to regulate intra- and intergroup interactions and are less likely to view this type of exclusion as unfair or hurtful. Including sexual orientation and gender identity/expression as protected categories within state level anti-bullying legislation and school-level policies sends a strong message to everyone within that state or school that these types of behaviors are wrong and that they are wrong because they are harmful to the educational and developmental well-being of individuals within those contexts. Our research provides evidence that including protections related to sexual orientation and/or gender identity/expression in schools will protect straight identified students who are victimized in these ways, and may also protect the entire school community by reducing the types of victimization that lead young people to engage in retaliatory violence against the community.

Schools should be places that young people experience as safe and supportive, but also in which young people can engage in finding solutions to contemporary and relevant problems, discuss complex and controversial issues, and interact and learn with others who are different from themselves. Because adolescents' social interactions with their peers, including social exclusion, require young people to coordinate knowledge from multiple domains of social reasoning, these types of conversations can serve to facilitate young peoples' navigation and constructed understandings of these issues ultimately helping them to understand how and when their interactions with each other may be hurtful and harmful to others.

References

Abrams, D., Rutland, A., & Cameron, L. (2003). The development of subjective group dynamics: children's judgments of normative and deviant in-group and out-group individuals. *Child Development*, *74*(6), 1840–1856.

Abrams, D., & Rutland, A. (2008). The development of subjective group dynamics. In S. R. Levy, M. Killen (Eds.), *Intergroup attitudes and relations in childhood through adulthood* (pp. 47–65). New York, NY: Oxford University Press.

Alfieri, T., Ruble, D., & Higgins, T. (1996). Gender stereotypes during adolescence: Developmental changes and the transition to junior high school. *Developmental Psychology*, *32*, 1129–1137.

Baker, J., & Fishbein, H. (1998). The development of prejudice towards gays and lesbians by adolescents. *Journal of Homosexuality*, *36*, 89–100.

Blashill, A. J., & Powlishta, K. K. (2009). The impact of sexual orientation and gender role on evaluations of men. *Psychology of Men and Masculinity*, *10*, 160–173.

Carlson-Jones, D., & Crawford, J. K. (2006). The peer appearance culture in adolescence: Gender and body mass variations. *Journal of Youth and Adolescence*, *35*, 257–269.

Carr, C. L. (1998). Tomboy resistance and conformity: Agency in social psychological gender theory. *Gender & Society, 12*, 528–553.

Craig, W. M., Peplar, D., Connolly, J., & Henderson, K. (2001). Developmental context of peer harassment in early adolescence: The role of puberty and the peer group. In J. Juvonen & S. Graham (Eds.), *Peer harassment in school: The plight of the vulnerable and victimized* (pp. 242–262). New York: Guilford Press.

Fingerhut, A. W., & Peplau, L. A. (2006). The impact of social roles on stereotypes of gay men. *Sex Roles, 55*(3-4), 273–278.

Heinze, J. E., & Horn, S. S. (2009). Intergroup contact and beliefs about homosexuality in adolescence. *Journal of Youth and Adolescence, 38*, 937–951.

Herek, G. M. (1994). Assessing heterosexuals' attitudes toward lesbians and gay men: A review of empirical research with the ATLG scale. In B. Greene, G. M. Herek (Eds.), *Lesbian and gay psychology: Theory, research, and clinical applications* (pp. 206–228). Thousand Oaks, CA: Sage Publications, Inc.

Horn, S. S. (2003). Adolescents' reasoning about exclusion from social groups. *Developmental Psychology, 39*, 71–84.

Horn, S. S. (2006a). Heterosexual students' attitudes and beliefs about same-sex sexuality and the treatment of gay, lesbian, and gender non-conforming youth. *Cognitive Development, 21*, 420–440.

Horn, S. S. (2006b). Group status, group bias, and adolescents' reasoning about the treatment of others in school contexts. *International Journal of Behavioral Development, 30*, 208–218.

Horn, S. S. (2007). Adolescents' acceptance of same-sex peers based on sexual orientation and gender expression. *Journal of Youth and Adolescence, 36*, 363–371.

Horn, S. S., & Szalacha, L. A. (2009). School differences in heterosexual students' attitudes about homosexuality and prejudice based on sexual orientation. *European Journal of Developmental Sciences, 3*, 66–81.

Killen, M. (2007). Children's social and moral reasoning about exclusion. *Current Directions In Psychological Science, 16*, 32–36.

Killen, M., Lee-Kim, J., McGlothlin, H., & Stangor, C. (2002). How children and adolescents evaluate gender and racial exclusion. *Monograph of the Society for Research in Child Development, 67* (4, Serial No. 271).

Killen, M., & Rutland, A. (2011). *Children and exclusion: Morality, prejudice, and group identity.* New York: Wiley/Blackwell Publishers.

Killen, M., Rutland, A., Abrams, D., Mulvey, K. L., & Hitti, A. (2012). Development of intra- and intergroup judgments in the context of moral and social conventional norms. *Child Development, 84*, 1063–1080.

Killen, M., & Stangor, C. (2001). Children's reasoning about inclusion and exclusion in gender and race peer group contexts. *Child Development, 72*, 174–186.

Kimmel, M. (2003). Adolescent masculinity, homophobia, and violence: Random school shootings, 1982-2001. *American Behavioral Scientist, 46*, 1439–1458.

Lehavot, K., & Lambert, A. J. (2007). Toward a greater understanding of antigay prejudice: On the role of sexual orientation and gender role violation. *Basic and Applied Social Psychology, 29*, 279–292.

Mandel, L., & Shakeshaft, C. (2000). Heterosexism in middle schools. In N. Lesko (Ed.), *Masculinities at school*. Thousand Oaks, CA: Sage.

Martin, C. L., & Ruble, D. (2002). Cognitive theories of early gender development. *Psychological Bulletin, 128*, 903–933.

Mulvey, K. L., Hitti, A., Rutland, A., Abrams, D., & Killen, M. (2014). When do children dislike ingroup members? Resource allocation from individual and group perspectives. *Journal of Social Issues, 70*(1), 29–46.

Nucci, L. (1996). Morality and the personal sphere of actions. In E. Reed, E. Turiel, & T. Brown (Eds.), *Values and knowledge* (pp. 41–60). Hillsdale, NJ: Lawrence Erlbaum

Pahlke, E., Bigler, R. S., & Martin, C. L. (2014). Can fostering children's ability to challenge sexism improve critical analysis, internalization, and enactment of inclusive, egalitarian peer relationships? *Journal of Social Issues, 70*(1), 115–133.

Pascoe, C. J. (2011). *Dude, you're a fag: Masculinity and sexuality orientation in high school*. Los Angeles, CA: University of California Press.

Poteat, V. P., Espelage, D. L., & Koenig, B. W. (2009). Willingness to remain friends and attend school with lesbian and gay peers: Relational expressions of prejudice among heterosexual youth. *Journal of Youth and Adolescence, 38*, 952–962.

Poteat, V. P., Kimmel, M. S., & Wilchins, R. (2011). The moderating effects of support for violence beliefs on masculine norms, aggression, and homophobic behavior during adolescence. *Journal of Research on Adolescence, 21*(2), 434–447.

Russell, S. R., Kosciw, J. G., Horn, S. S., & Saewyc, E. (2010). Safe schools policy for LGBT students. *Society for Research in Child Development Social Policy Report, 24*, 1–25.

Rutland, A., Killen, M., & Abrams, D. (2010). A new social-cognitive developmental perspective on prejudice: The interplay between morality and group identity. *Perspectives on Psychological Science, 5*, 280–291.

Schope, R. D., & Eliason, M. J. (2004). Sissies and tomboys: Gender role behaviors and homophobia. *Journal of Gay & Lesbian Social Services: Issues in Practice, Policy & Research, 16*, 73–97.

Thorne, B. (1993). *Gender play: Girls and boys in school*. New Brunswick, NJ: Rutgers University Press.

Turiel, E. (1983). *The development of social knowledge: Morality and convention*. Cambridge, England: Cambridge University Press.

Winer, B. J., Brown, D. R., & Michels, K. M. (1991). *Statistical principles in experimental design*. New York: McGraw-Hill.

JUSTIN HEINZE, is a Research Investigator in the Department of Health Behavior and Health Education at the University of Michigan. He earned his PhD in educational psychology from the University of Illinois at Chicago in 2011 and a BA and MA from the University of Michigan. His primary research interests include belonging motivation and developmental transitions in adolescence and emerging adulthood. He is also interested in the formation of social judgments that lead to social exclusion/ostracism or prejudicial behavior, and how valence in social climate affects individuals' mental and physical health.

STACEY S. HORN, is a Professor of Educational Psychology in the Department of Educational Psychology. She received her PhD from the University of Maryland in Human Development. Dr. Horn is interested in peer groups and intergroup relations; stereotypes, prejudice, and discrimination related to sexual orientation and gender identity, as well as the relationships among institutional structures and adolescents' social and moral reasoning. Stacey is on the editorial boards for the *Journal of Youth and Adolescence, International Journal of Behavioral Development,* and the *Journal of Gay and Lesbian Youth*. Her research has been published in journals such as *Developmental Psychology*, the *International Journal of Behavior and Development, Cognitive Development*, and the *Journal of Youth and Adolescence*.

Of Affect and Ambiguity: The Emergence of Preference for Arbitrary Ingroups

Yarrow Dunham[*]
Yale University

Jason Emory
University of California, Merced

What cognitive and affective processes underlie the all-too-human tendency toward group-based affiliation and exclusion? Using a paradigm in which children are randomly assigned to previously unfamiliar and meaningless "minimal" social groups, we investigate the developmental origins of the tendency to prefer and positively evaluate the actions of social ingroup members. Using a procedure derived from evaluative priming as well as children's verbal descriptions of intergroup encounters, we show that 6-year olds but not 3-year olds manifest robust ingroup preference. These results suggest that the mechanisms underlying the wide range of human social group affiliations undergoes a striking increase in generality between ages 3 and 6, perhaps driven by a shift from an individual-level to a group-level or "sociocentric" orientation.

Decisions about whom to affiliate with or exclude cluster into identifiable collectives. The forms of such collectives are dizzying, from ethnic and racial groups through religious, linguistic, and national distinctions, to identities defined via ideologies or political movements. This variety stands in stark contrast with other primates, who appear to be attentive to just a small set of social categories (namely kinship, gender, and band; Wilson & Wrangham, 2003). Thus, our species places great importance on culturally defined forms of social affiliation, and uses membership (or lack thereof) as an important heuristic governing how to understand and treat others. Why are we so given to group-based social reasoning?

One clue comes from social psychology, where it has long been known that merely dividing social space into "us" and "them" can produce intergroup bias. For

---

[*]Correspondence concerning this article should be addressed to Yarrow Dunham, Yale University, Kirtland Hall, New Haven, CT [e-mail: yarrow.dunham@yale.edu].

example, people manifest preferences for previously unfamiliar and meaningless groups to which they have been arbitrarily assigned ("minimal groups"; Brewer, 1979; Tajfel, 1971), and this tendency emerges by age 5 (Dunham, Baron, & Carey, 2011). Whereas explanations for this phenomenon have varied, there is general agreement that it is grounded in some form of self-involvement, for example, a motivation to positively distinguish the ingroup (Tajfel & Turner, 1986) or a lower level process by which self-related positivity spreads to groups associated with the self (Gramzow & Gaertner, 2005). Thus, simply belonging to a group leads us to prefer it, planting the seed for potential differential or exclusionary treatment. Could this be one of the psychological mechanisms supporting bias against culturally familiar groups?

One way to answer this question is to characterize children's reactions to minimal social groups, and ask how they relate to children's well-studied responses to "maximal" groups such as race or gender. If there are close parallels across these two kinds of groups, we can conclude that a determinant of real-world bias is the basic tendency to prefer ingroups, even when minimally defined (Dunham, 2011). Thus, the current research investigates when the tendency to prefer minimal ingroups emerges, and whether the initial form of such preference is a positive evaluation of the ingroup, a negative evaluation of the outgroup, or both.

Prior work has demonstrated that children show minimal group preferences by age 5 (Dunham et al., 2011), including sensitivity to subtle aspects of the groups such as relative status (Bigler, Brown, & Markell, 2001), group size (Brown & Bigler, 2002), and within-group fairness norms (Mulvey, Hitti, Rutland, Abrams, & Killen, 2014). If preference for minimal groups is the result of basic associative processes that transfer self-related positivity to anything associated with the self (Gramzow & Gaertner, 2005), we might expect these preferences to emerge as early as children can comprehend group membership. However, if we look broadly across the developmental intergroup literature, there appears to be a substantial increase in the range of social categories children show interest in between the ages of about 3 and 6. Infants and children under age 3 show social preferences for gender (LaFreniere, Strayer, & Gauthier, 1984), age (Shutts, Banaji, & Spelke, 2010), and linguistic (Kinzler, Dupoux, & Spelke, 2007) ingroups, but it is not until a few years later that preference for other culturally salient social categories such as race, ethnicity, and nationality emerge (Aboud, 1988; Barrett, 2007; Brand, Ruiz, & Padilla, 1974; Cristol & Gimbert, 2008; Shutts et al., 2010; see also Huckstadt & Shutts, 2014). Race is a particularly interesting case because infants can discriminate between faces belonging to different racial groups (Kelly et al., 2005) and can categorize along racial lines in habituation paradigms (Anzures, Quinn, Pascalis, Slater, & Lee, 2009). Thus, the absence of racial preferences in younger preschoolers cannot be attributed to simple perceptual difficulties.

One intriguing possibility is that children undergo a shift from a more "individualistic" to a more "sociocentric" mode of reasoning (Aboud, 1988), i.e., increasing comfort with a range of individual relationships could free children to attend to the myriad ways in which individuals cluster into groups. A useful heuristic might be to pay attention to any group that is consistently pointed out by cultural elders (e.g., Bigler & Liben, 2007), including groups based on a novel distinction such as shirt color. This possibility predicts that the minimal group effect might emerge between ages 3 and 6, and this is one of the central hypotheses that we explored here.

Our second question concerns the initial form of minimal group preference. Is it primarily positivity toward the ingroup, negativity toward the outgroup, or both? Addressing this question will clarify the consequences of minimal group preference: Does it lead to affiliation with ingroups or exclusion of outgroups? To address this question, it is crucial to employ nonrelative measures of attitude that allow an independent assessment of ingroup positivity and outgroup negativity. With respect to real-world groups like race, it has been argued that ingroup positivity is distinct from and perhaps developmentally prior to outgroup derogation (Aboud, 2003; Brewer, 1999). Since we are exploring the possibility that those biases are built on the same mechanism underlying minimal group preference, we predicted that children's bias in the minimal group setting would be driven primarily by increased ingroup liking.

In selecting appropriate measures, we build on recent work on automatic or "implicit" forms of attitude. It is now well-understood that many forms of bias are not accessible to introspective access (e.g., Greenwald & Banaji, 1995), taking the form of lower level semantic associations, such as positive associations with ingroups, which then exert downstream pressure on a wide range of intergroup behaviors (e.g., Greenwald, Poehlman, Uhlmann, & Banaji, 2009). Taking this insight seriously requires supplementing self-report measures with attempts to measure the implicit constructs, an approach still relatively rare in developmental research (see Olson & Dunham, 2010, for a review). In this study, we contribute a new measure that is suitable for children younger than have previously been investigated.

Second, fitting with this issue's focus on social exclusion, we sought to move beyond simple measures of preference by attempting to document how group-centered biases influence other aspects of intergroup functioning. Here we ask whether group membership affects how children interpret otherwise ambiguous intergroup interactions. Social psychologists have long pointed out that ambiguity is a likely place for bias to intrude. For example, in a now classic study, Duncan (1976) showed that White Americans were more likely to judge otherwise identical scenes involving one person bumping into another as hostile when the "bumper" was African America and the "bumpee" was White American. Thus, despite situational constancy, different social targets were judged in quite different ways.

Do these sorts of interpretive biases extend to the minimal social groups employed here? This question is important because ambiguous interactions between groups are commonplace; if children interpret ingroup and outgroup members differently in such situations, they would in essence be creating subjectively compelling but entirely illusory "evidence" in favor of the superiority of the ingroup ("they've behaved more positively!"). This could adversely affect potentially ameliorative processes such as intergroup cooperation (e.g., Chizhik, Shelly, & Toryer, 2009), and could provide the motivation and justification for systematic exclusion of outgroup members.

In summary, we investigated the developmental emergence of the preference for minimal ingroups and examine whether it is characterized by ingroup positivity, outgroup negativity, or both, using a self-report, an implicit, and an interpretive measure of intergroup bias. Experiment 1 focuses on 6-year olds, developing and validating a novel implicit measure and establishing the general procedure that will be adapted for use with younger children in Experiment 2.

Experiment 1

Methods

Participants. Thirty-seven 6-year olds (mean age = 6.2 [SD = .6], girls = 21) of diverse racial-ethnic background (16 Hispanic, 15 White, and 6 other) were recruited from an elementary school in central California. Parental consent was secured in advance of all testing, and children provided verbal assent prior to beginning the procedure.

Procedures. Participants were tested alone in a small testing room by one of the two authors. Children were randomly assigned to either a green or orange group by drawing a colored token from a bag, were told that this indicated their group membership, and were then given a green or orange shirt to make membership salient. Children were then seated in front of a laptop computer and completed the measures described in the next section. At the completion of the study, as a manipulation check, children were asked which group they belonged to; all children successfully answered this question.

Measures. Children completed the following measures in counterbalanced order.

The affect misattribution procedure (AMP). In the AMP (Payne et al., 2005), participants are asked to make dichotomous good/bad judgments regarding the meaning of unfamiliar Chinese characters. Each character is preceded by a supraliminal prime image, which participants are led to believe is a prompt indicating the next trial is about to begin. The logic of the task is that if the prime

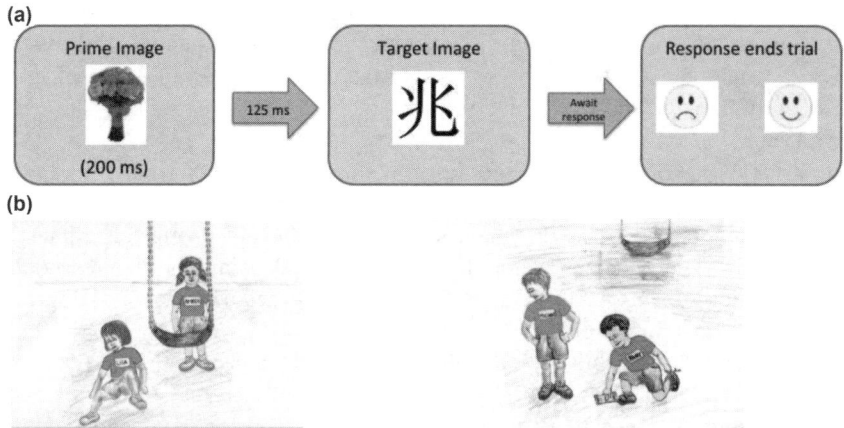

Fig. 1. (a) A schematic illustration of the insect–flower AMP. In the AMP, a prime is briefly flashed on the screen, followed by a short intertrial interval, followed by a Chinese character. Participants are asked to ignore the initial image and evaluate the target stimulus as positive or negative by pressing a key; their response ends the trial. (b) Example ambiguous situations, adapted from McGlothlin et al., 2005. Left scenario is an example of (girls, orange perpetrator), right scenario an example of (boys, green perpetrator).

images are automatically evaluated, i.e., if they automatically activate positive or negative affect, that affect will be misattributed to the valence-ambiguous Chinese characters, biasing judgments of them in the corresponding direction. In other words, valence aroused by the supraliminal prime will be "misattributed" to intuitive responses to the Chinese character, resulting in judgments that tend to match the valence of the prime image. In adults, this operates outside of conscious awareness and control, in that even participants explicitly asked to avoid the influence of the prime nonetheless show the same effect at the same magnitude (Payne et al., 2005). Thus, this measure satisfied commonly identified criteria for automatic or implicit cognition (e.g., Bargh, 1994). In our child-friendly version of the task, color photographs of prime images appeared on screen for 250 ms, followed by a 125-ms intertrial interval and then an unfamiliar Chinese character which remained on the screen until the child responded by verbally making a good or bad judgment. A schematic depiction of the task is presented in Figure 1(a). To validate this new measure for use with children, in addition to intergroup preferences, we also included an initial block of trials assessing preference for flowers over insects. Prior research has established that children of this age prefer flowers to insects when assessed at the implicit level (Baron & Banaji, 2006), we had a priori reason to anticipate that same result with the AMP. In the insect–flower version of the task, photographs of insects, flowers, and gray squares (serving as neutral primes) were employed as primes, randomly presented over 30 trials. In a second block, constituting the minimal groups version of the task, prime images were full color head and torso photographs of ingroup members or outgroup members (indicated by t-shirt color), or gray squares, randomly presented over 48 trials. Results thus turn on whether the different types of prime image differently affect the subsequent interpretation of the valence of unfamiliar Chinese characters.

Prior research on implicit attitudes in children has almost exclusively employed the Implicit Association Test (IAT; Greenwald, McGhee, & Schwartz, 1998), which relies on reaction time, task switching, and other forms of response inhibition. The substantial developments in these faculties during the preschool years (Davidson, Amso, Anderson, & Diamond, 2006) led us to doubt its appropriateness with young children. By contrast, the AMP does not rely on reaction time or task switching. In addition, unlike the IAT, which is essentially a relative measure of preference, the AMP allows independent assessments of ingroup positivity and outgroup negativity, which may differently develop in young children (Aboud, 2003).

Ambiguous situations task (AST). We modified a task previously used to investigate racial attitudes (McGlothlin & Killen, 2006; McGlothlin, Killen, & Edmonds, 2005). The task involves four scenarios depicting dyadic interactions designed to be ambiguous with respect to the nature of the interaction, with one child in a potential "perpetrator" role and the other in a potential "victim" role (children were gender-matched to the participant). For example, a child has fallen down in front of a swing, with another child standing behind the swing (Figure 1b). Did the child fall, or was she pushed by the standing child? Our version of the task, the two members of each dyad differed solely on t-shirt color, and perpetrator roles were counterbalanced across participants. Two scenarios involved an ingroup and two an outgroup perpetrator. Children were asked what happened in the picture, and what the potential perpetrator did, and their free responses were recorded for subsequent coding. Because these scenarios were made with the intention of implying potential negative behaviors (i.e., identifying perpetrators), we followed prior work with the procedure (McGlothlin et al., 2005) by basing our analysis on children's interpretations of actions as negative or neutral/positive. Approximately 50% of responses were independently coded by a graduate student rater blind to condition. Interrater reliability was high, Cohen's Kappa = .83, suggesting that children's responses were clearly interpretable.

Explicit attitude measure. To facilitate comparison with prior research, we included a self-report measure of attitude, in which photographs of six children, three from the child's ingroup and three from the child's outgroup, were presented sequentially. These were the same photographs used as primes in the AMP, though the pairing of children to group was counterbalanced as a between-participants factor. Children were asked to indicate their liking for each child on a 6-point scale pictorially represented as a range of faces going from a large frown to a large smile, and responses were averaged to produce an index of preference.

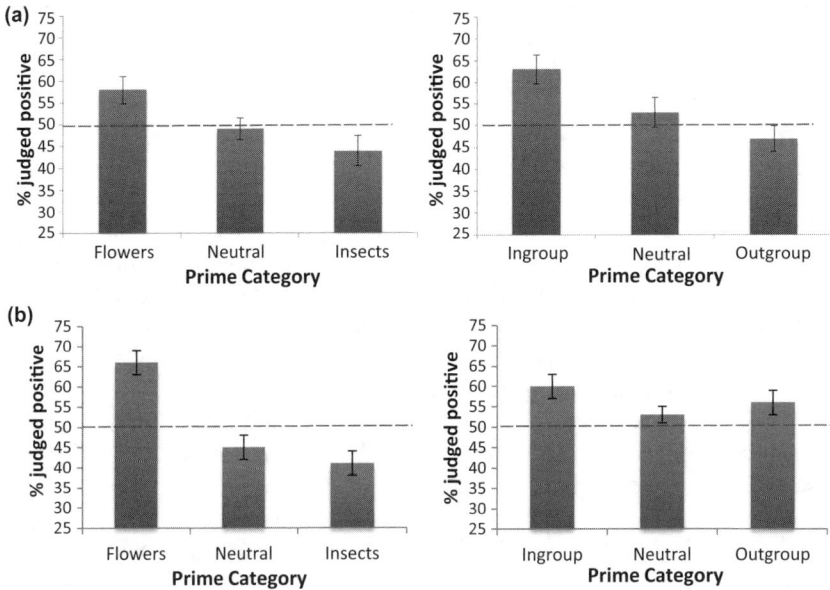

Fig. 2. (a) Interpretations of unfamiliar Chinese characters following priming with insects, flowers, and neutral gray squares (left panel) and ingroup faces, outgroup faces, and neutral gray squares (right panel) for 6-year-old children in Experiment 1. Error bars represent standard errors of the means; chance responding = 50%. (b) Interpretations of unfamiliar Chinese characters following priming with insects, flowers, and neutral gray squares (left panel) and ingroup faces, outgroup faces, and neutral gray squares (right panel) for 3–4-year-old children in Experiment 2. Error bars represent standard errors of the means; chance responding = 50%.

Results and Discussion

No differences were observed with respect to participant gender, race/ethnicity, or color of the group, so these factors were dropped from subsequent analyses.

The AMP

We begin with the insect–flower version of the task (Figure 2, panel a). On average, children interpreted 58% ($SD = 19\%$) of characters as positive when they followed pictures of flowers, which differed from chance responding, $t(36) = 2.65$, $p = .011$; participants interpreted 49% ($SD = 15\%$) as positive when they followed gray squares, which did not differ from chance, $t(36) = -.47$, $p = .64$; finally, participants interpreted only 44% ($SD = 21\%$) as positive when they followed insects, which was marginally below chance, $t(36) = -1.79$, $p = .092$. These differences were compared in an ANOVA predicting the percentage of positive responses from prime type, revealing a significant main effect of prime type, $F(2, 35) = 3.42, p = .044$. Planned contrasts revealed that responses following flower primes differed from responses following insect primes and neutral primes, both paired $t(36) > 2.1, p < .04$, insect–flower comparison $d = .44$, but responses to negative and neutral primes did not differ, paired $t(36) = 1.18, p = .25$. This pattern of results demonstrates that implicit preference for flowers over insects is driven primarily by positivity associated with flowers, but negativity associated with insects likely also contributes, given the deviation from chance responding for insect stimuli. Crucially, by replicating prior research with a different measure showing implicit flower over insect preference (Baron & Banaji, 2006), we demonstrate that the AMP yields interpretable results with children of this age.

Turning to the minimal groups AMP (Figure 2, panel a), on average, participants interpreted 63% ($SD = 18\%$) of words as positive following pictures of ingroup members, which differed from chance performance, $t(36) = 4.28, p < .001$; participants interpreted 53% ($SD = 20\%$) as positive following gray squares, and 47% ($SD = 19\%$) as positive following outgroup members, neither of which deviated from chance, both $t(36) < 1.1, p > .29$. We again compared these figures in an ANOVA, revealing a main effect of prime type, $F(2, 35 = 5.07), p = .012$, indicating that valence judgments were affected by prime category. Planned contrasts revealed that this effect was driven by an increased rate of positive responses following ingroup primes, which differed from outgroup primes, paired $t(36) = 3.22, p = .003, d = .53$, as well as neutral primes, paired $t(36) = 1.99, p = .054$. Neutral primes and outgroup primes did not yield differential effects, paired $t(36) = 1.61, p = .12$. Thus, the AMP revealed implicit positivity associated with members of the novel ingroup, but no negativity associated with members of the outgroup (for related findings with early race preferences, see Aboud, 2003; cf. Brewer, 1999).

Ambiguous Situations Task

Preliminary analyses indicated that rates of negative interpretation differed significantly depending on scenario. To capture this variation while also respecting the repeated measures aspect of the data (multiple trials per participant), data were analyzed via mixed logistic regression (trials nested within participants), predicting the probability of positive or negative judgments from prime valence and/or perpetrator group (ingroup or outgroup), and scenario. Effect sizes are odds ratios indicting the increased likelihood of favoring the ingroup.

Our analysis thus focused on whether the rate of negative interpretations differed depending on the perpetrator's group. Overall, participants made negative interpretations in 58% of scenarios, but this varied as a function of target group membership (51% for the ingroup, 64% for the outgroup), $F(1, 107) = 4.79$,

$p = .03$, with participants 2.2 times more likely to make a negative interpretation of a protagonist's behavior when that protagonist was a member of the outgroup than the ingroup (conventionally a medium effect). Thus, the interpretive bias previously observed in the context of race bias (McGlothlin & Killen, 2006) can also be observed with randomly assigned and previously unfamiliar minimal groups.

Explicit Attitude Measure

The dependent measure was a difference score representing the degree to which ingroup members were rated higher than outgroup members. While trending toward ingroup preference, this value did not approach significance, $M_{diff} = .23$ (1.5), $t(36) = .91, p = .37, d = .15$. Thus, participants did not report a preference for their ingroup. Examination of means in comparison to the scale midpoint (3.5 on the 6-point scale) revealed that both the outgroup ($M = 4.2, SD = 1.4$) and the ingroup ($M = 4.4, SD = 1.2$) were positively evaluated, both $t(36) > 3.04$, $p < .005$. Thus, children self-reported liking for all children, irrespective of group membership. Given that our photographs were of smiling, attractive same-gender age-mates, this is perhaps not unsurprising; we return to this issue in the general discussion.

Relationships between Measures

We examined correlations between the AST, the AMP, and self-report attitude. Only one correlation reached significance, between ingroup preference on the AMP and explicit preference, $r(36) = .35, p = .03$; others $|r|(36) < .14, p > .43$. This finding indicates that, despite finding no main effect of group membership on the self-report measure, self-reported attitudes were reliably related to the larger effects we found on the priming-based AMP.

In sum, Experiment 1 indicates that random assignment to arbitrary social groups produces a highly generalized form of ingroup preference in 6-year olds, such that mere exposure to members of the ingroup activates positive valence. In addition, ingroup members are less likely to be interpreted as engaging in negative actions, suggesting that initial biases could have downstream consequences by affecting how group-relevant information is internalized. At first glance this result might be simply be interpreted as an indirect measure of attitude, this interpretive bias plausibly goes further, furnishing subjectively compelling "evidence" in favor of the superiority of the ingroup. That is, if children believe that their experience provides direct evidence that ingroup members have behaved better, they are likely to believe that their biases are justified. More broadly, these findings support the claim that, by age 6, children are predisposed evaluate ingroup members more positively than outgroup members, though this tendency is less reliable when assessed through self-report.

Experiment 2

Experiment 1 provided evidence of a highly general tendency to positively evaluate arbitrary social groups in 6-year olds. We interpret this as evidence that, by this age, children are predisposed to focus on social distinctions, and attach evaluative weight to such distinctions. Given that younger children seem more restrictive in the preferences they show, for example failing to reliably show race-based preferences until sometime around age 3–4, we speculated that minimal group preferences would be weaker in younger children.

Methods

Participants. Fifty 3–4-year olds participated in Study 2 (mean age = 3.9 years (SD = .7 years), female = 35). Though predominately White and middle class, the sample included children from diverse racial and ethnic backgrounds (32 White, 3 Hispanic, 3 Black, 5 South Asian, and 7 other), and were recruited from local preschools in California and New Jersey.

Procedures and measures

Affect misattribution procedure. To accommodate the shorter attention spans of younger children, we decreased the number of trials to 30 in the minimal groups block (from 48).

Ambiguous situations task. Because we were concerned that the verbal demands of this task might be too great for younger children, we included a prompt after soliciting free responses by indicating the potential perpetrator and asking "do you think [name] did something nice or mean?" and recording children's responses. Of course, this change reduces the possibility that children will provide neutral responses, as they are prompted for a single valenced response. Except for this variant, the task was identical to that described in Experiment 1.

As a manipulation check, at the completion of the study children were asked which group they belonged to; only one child failed to answer this question correctly.

Results and Discussion

No differences were observed with respect to participant gender, race/ethnicity, or color of the ingroup, so these factors were dropped from subsequent analyses. One participant was eliminated for failing to follow instructions and one participant asked to stop the procedure prior to completing the minimal groups AMP; in addition, AMP data from participants who made solely positive or negative responses on all trials was eliminated, resulting in a usable sample of 45 participants for the Insect–Flower AMP, 42 participants from the minimal group AMP, and 47 participants for the AST.

The AMP

Beginning with the insect–flower version of the task (Figure 2, panel b), on average children interpreted 66% ($SD = 18\%$) of characters as positive when they followed pictures of flowers, which differed from chance expectations, $t(44) = 5.66$, $p < .001$; 45% ($SD = 22\%$) when they followed gray squares, which did not differ from chance, $t(45) = -1.49$, $p = .14$, and 41% ($SD = 20\%$) when they followed insects, which was reliably below chance, $t(45) = -3.25$, $p = .002$. Comparing these values via ANOVA revealed an effect of prime type, $F(2, 43 = 19.85)$, $p < .001$, indicating that responses varied as a function of prime. Planned comparisons revealed that responses following flowers were reliably different from both responses following neutral primes and insects, both paired $t(44) > 5.1$, $p < .001$, insect–flower comparison $d = .74$. However, negative and neutral primes did not significantly differ, paired $t(44) = 1.35$, $p = .19$. This pattern of results is identical to that revealed with older children in Experiment 1. Thus, younger children showed the same effects as older children in Experiment 1, responding more positively following flowers than insects. This replication with younger children provides evidence of the suitability of the AMP for children in this age range.

A different pattern emerged on the minimal groups AMP (Figure 2, panel b). The mean percentage of positive interpretations following ingroup primes was 60% ($SD = 18\%$), which differed from chance expectations, $t(41) = 3.54$, $p = .001$; positive interpretations following outgroup primes were 56% ($SD = 22\%$), which was also marginally above chance, $t(41) = 1.92$, $p = .062$; the mean percentage following neutral primes hovered around chance (53%, $SD = 16\%$), which did not differ from chance, $t(41) = 1.31$, $p = .20$. Turning to the ANOVA used to compare these figures, the analysis revealed no effect of prime type, $F(2, 40) = 2.33$, $p = .11$, thus, the rate of responding following ingroup, outgroup, and neutral primes did not differ. The primary divergence from prior findings is the trend toward more positive responses following both ingroup and outgroup primes, suggesting that for younger children, pictures of smiling children were positive irrespective of group membership. To test this possibility more formally, we collapsed across the dimension of group membership and analyzed responses following children as compared with neutral gray squares. While suggesting a small effect, $d = .27$, the results were of only marginal significance, $F(1, 41) = 3.07$, $p = .087$, but can cautiously be interpreted as showing that, for children of this age, smiling, same-gender age-mates served as positive primes irrespective of group membership.

Ambiguous situations task

We fit the same model described in Experiment 1, but the main effect of protagonist group was not significant, $F(1, 137) = 1.65, p = .20$; thus, rates of negative interpretation did not differ as a function of whether the target was in the ingroup or the outgroup. Unlike with the older children in Experiment 1, younger children's interpretations of ambiguous events were not affected by the membership of the individuals involved.

Explicit attitude measure

There was no evidence of explicit preference for the ingroup, $M = -.06$ ($SD = 1.5$), $t(49) = -.30, p = .77$. Both the outgroup ($M = 4.1, SD = 1.2$) and the ingroup ($M = 4.2, SD = 1.2$) were evaluated above the scale midpoint (3.5), $ts(49) > 3.7, ps < .001$.

Relationships between measures

The correlation between the AMP and the self-report measure was of marginal significance, $r(42) = .27, p = .087$; no other correlations approached significance, both $r > -.12, p > .27$. It is interesting that the one significant correlation in Experiment 1, between the AMP and self-report attitude, was the strongest correlation here; this suggests that even at this young age, some children may be beginning to orient toward their minimal groups, and this is registering on both self-report and implicit measures.

Overall, Experiment 2 suggests that 3–4-year-old children do not rapidly form ingroup preference with respect to novel social distinctions, despite encoding their group membership (all children but one successfully recalled their group membership). While there was the barest hint of group-based preference (in that children were most positively primed by ingroup faces), this difference was not statistically reliable, and a more parsimonious interpretation is that they are responding positively to smiling children's faces with little additional influence from group membership. It is possible that group members with neutral expressions would elicit clearer evidence of group-based priming, but this possibility indirectly supports our hypothesized individual to sociocentric shift, in that smiling faces, a canonical individual-level feature, were pervasively impactful in younger children, while a few years later smiling outgroup faces no longer served as positive primes. Thus, by age 6 individuals are not just individuals; they are also members of social groups, with clear evaluative consequences. Though differences in the task, e.g., the number of trials, make it necessary to interpret across-study comparisons with some caution, in a supplementary analysis we compared results on the AMP across the two studies in a single ANOVA predicting positive responses as a function of age and prime type. This analysis revealed a main effect of prime type, $F(2, 76) = 6.67$, $p = .002$, indicating that ingroup primes elicited more positive responses than outgroup primes, no overall effect of age, $F(1, 77) = 0.45$, $p = .51$, and a marginal interaction between age and prime type, $F(2, 76) = 2.72$, $p = .07$, suggesting that the effect of prime type differed by age. Post hoc contrasts indicated that this interaction was driven by responses to outgroup primes, which were significantly less positive in older than younger children, $t(77) = 1.98$, $p = .05$ (ingroup and neutral primes both $ps > .49$). This supports the contention of an age-related shift such that smiling outgroup children cease to serve as positive primes over the age range investigated.

General Discussion

By age 6, mere exposure to photographs of arbitrarily assigned ingroup members is sufficient to arouse positive affect, which can then be misattributed to other unfamiliar ambiguous stimuli. In addition, children of this age interpret outgroup members more negatively when viewing intergroup interactions in which they figure. Given that children did not report preference for these same ingroup members, these biases appear to operate largely outside of conscious awareness, suggesting that they are best considered part of an implicit or automatic evaluative system. This dissociation also militates against the worry that children were directly evaluating the prime images during the AMP; if so, we would have expected high concordance between the AMP and the self-report task that involved evaluating those same stimuli. Some prior research (e.g., Dunham et al., 2011) does report ingroup preference on self-report measures; we do not have a clear explanation for this discrepancy, but do note that even in that prior work the effect size was small, considerably smaller than when bias was measured implicitly. This is intriguing, as it suggests that the implicit form of intergroup bias is stronger—or at least earlier emerging—than the explicit form. Given that the implicit measure we employed here, evaluative priming, implicates a highly general cognitive process, it could underlie the emergence of entrenched intergroup biases.

However, the present data also provide evidence that these cognitive phenomena do not emerge until sometime after age 3. We have some concerns about whether the AST was too difficult for children, potentially leading to the null result with that measure, but this cannot wholly explain our findings. In particular, younger children were perfectly susceptible to affective priming more generally, given the results of the insect–flower portion of the study. In addition, other work demonstrates that children of this age are sensitive to similarities of the sort used to define groups in this work. For example, 3-year olds do use similarity to guide preference for individuals, preferring individuals with whom they share a food preference or who are similar along some visual dimensions such as hair color (Fawcett & Markson, 2010). This suggests that the cognitive components necessary to identify and affiliate with ingroups are in place. Indeed, despite showing no preference for their ingroup, 3-year olds did encode their group membership, as shown by the fact that they readily recalled their membership at the conclusion of the study.

We suggest that the decisive shift involves the expansion of habitual modes of social reasoning from individuals to collectives. This period has been characterized as "sociocentric" (Aboud, 1988), and is associated with increasing self-reported preference for a wide range of ingroups (Raabe & Beelmann, 2011). In simplest terms, having acquired substantial familiarity with the individuals in their immediate social circle, children are becoming increasingly aware of the myriad ways in which those individuals cluster into groups. Because these distinctions are so varied (e.g., based on biological phenotypes, shared beliefs, ethnic markings, invisible facts in the causal history of the individual), children at this stage may choose to be promiscuously group-focused, attaching meaning to any group distinction that is explicitly provided for them. Of course, some groups, namely those that are culturally reinforced, will gradually rise in importance and come to be more habitual modes of social perception. But it remains the case that children are sensitive to even quite minimal markers of group differentiation and that their attitudes toward them as well as their experiences of affiliation and rejection (Nesdale, Zimmer-Gembeck, & Roxburgh, 2014) shape their emerging intergroup social cognition.

Children do manifest preferences for a few social groups, namely gender, age, and language, several years before this putative sociocentric shift. Whereas it has been argued that some or all of these three categories might be supported by innate acquisition mechanisms (e.g., Kinzler, Shutts, & Correll, 2010), it seems equally plausible that these categories emerge first because they are the most salient and relevant to young children. Language is vital to communication and the internalization of cultural knowledge; adults repeatedly mark, and remark upon, gender; age often rigidly demarcates the world of the child from the world of the adult. In short, our argument is not that younger children are incapable of sociocentric reasoning, but rather that they only draw upon it when the categories in question pass a threshold of salience and relevance (for suggestions of what factors might matter, see Bigler & Liben, 2007). The current findings suggest that the threshold for treating a category relevant undergoes a pronounced shift between ages 3 and 6, with older children prepared to accept a category as socially meaningful with only the barest of evidence, namely their membership in it.

We acknowledge several limitations of this study. Most notably, it suffers from the general limitations associated with interpreting negative evidence: just because young children failed to manifest preferences for shirt-based minimal groups on the measures employed here, it would be premature to conclude that younger children are unable to form affiliations with novel groups (of other sorts, on other measures), for example if additional evidence suggested that a social distinction was meaningful. Nonetheless, negative evidence is informative when it illuminates a boundary condition not present in other contexts, in this case preferences of other sorts on the same measure (i.e., insects vs. flowers) and preferences of the same sort in older children. In the current context, for older children and adults, essentially any social distinction is sufficient to produce robust ingroup preferences; not so for their younger counterparts, who appear to require more direct evidence of the category's utility (e.g., Patterson & Bigler, 2006). Of course, a variety of cognitive, social, and developmental changes occur between the ages of 3 and 6 years. It is likely that multiple factors contribute to the increase in affiliation with ingroups evident in our results. Future work should begin to more fully explore what developmental shifts drive an increase in social group affiliation during these years.

Group Affiliation as a Social Issue

The findings reported here suggest that "mere membership" in a previously unfamiliar "minimal" social group is sufficient to bias interpretations of behavior among children as young as 6 years old. Simply put, by this age children are more likely to grant ingroup members the benefit of the doubt when presented with the possibility that an ingroup member was engaged in wrongdoing, and are more likely to ascribe blame to an outgroup member in the very same situation. These findings suggest that similar tendencies observed in adults have a long developmental history, and indeed, could grow stronger over developmental time as children form richer representations of groups that are themselves influenced by these biases. It is important to note that these biases bear a striking similarity to well-known social problems such as social profiling and disparities in criminal penalties, in which one element of the problem is the cloud of increased suspicion that hangs over members of some stigmatized social categories. The fact that these discriminatory tendencies emerge most pervasively at the automatic or implicit level poses an additional problem, because it suggests that they can occur despite our best intentions. A crucial problem for future research therefore concerns the steps that can be taken to reduce or eliminate the forms of intergroup bias described here, and ideally to circumvent their formation in childhood.

In closing, our guiding assumption is that understanding the basic cognitive processes underlying intergroup reasoning will ultimately contribute to efforts to positively intervene on the lives of children. Our findings suggest that over the late preschool years children begin to more reflexively affiliate with social groups, and that this could drive increasing attention to group differences. More importantly, the perception of those differences is itself biased in ingroup-favoring ways, arming children with persuasive but ultimately unfounded beliefs about the superiority of the ingroup. These beliefs are plausible inputs into the decision processes which culminate in social exclusion, discrimination, and prejudice.

References

Aboud, F. E. (1988). *Children and prejudice.* Oxford: Basil Blackwell.
Aboud, F. E. (2003). The formation of in-group favoritism and out-group prejudice in young children: Are they distinct attitudes? *Developmental Psychology, 39*(1), 48–60. doi: 10.1037/0012-1649.39.1.48
Anzures, G., Quinn, P. C., Pascalis, O., Slater, A. M., & Lee, K. (2009). Categorization, categorical perceptions, and asymmetry in infants' representation of face race. *Developmental Science,* 1–12. doi: 10.1111/j.1467-7687.2009.00900.x
Bargh, J. A. (1994). The four horsemen of automaticity. In R. S. Wyer & T. K. Srull (Eds.), *Handbook of social cognition: Basic processes* (pp. 3–37). Mahwah: Lawrence Erlbaum.
Baron, A. S., & Banaji, M. R. (2006). The development of implicit attitudes: Evidence of race evaluations from ages 6 and 10 and adulthood. *Psychological Science, 17*(1), 53–58. doi: 10.1111/j.1467-9280.2005.01664.x
Barrett, M. (2007). *Children's knowledge, beliefs and feelings about nations and national groups.* Hove, England: Psychology Press.
Bigler, R. S., Brown, C. S., & Markell, M. (2001). When groups are not created equal: Effects of group status on the formation of intergroup attitudes in children. *Child Development, 72,* 1151–1162. doi: 10.1111/1467-8624.00339
Bigler, R. S., & Liben, L. S. (2007). Developmental intergroup theory: Explaining and reducing children's social stereotyping and prejudice. *Current Directions in Psychological Science, 16*(3), 162–166. doi: 10.1111/j.1467-8721.2007.00496.x
Brand, E., Ruiz, R., and Padilla, A. (1974). Ethnic identification and preference: A review. *Psychological Bulletin, 81*(11), 860–890. doi: 10.1037/h0037266
Brewer, M. B. (1979). In-group bias in the minimal intergroup situation: A cognitive-motivational analysis. *Psychological Bulletin, 86,* 307–324. doi: 10.1037/0033-2909.86.2.307
Brewer, M. B. (1999). The psychology of prejudice: Ingroup love or outgroup hate? *Journal of Social Issues, 55*(3), 429–444. doi: 10.1111/0022-4537.00126
Brown, C. S., & Bigler, R. S. (2002). Effects of minority status in the classroom on children's intergroup attitudes. *Journal of Experimental Child Psychology, 83*(2), 77–110. doi: 10.1016/S0022-0965(02)00123-6
Chizhik, A. W., Shelly, R. K., & Toryer, L. (2009). Intergroup conflict and cooperation: An introduction. *Journal of Social Issues, 65*(2), 251–259. doi: 10.1111/j.1540-4560.2009.01599.x
Cristol, D., & Gimbert, B. (2008). Racial perceptions of young children: A review of literature post-1999. *Early Childhood Education Journal, 36*(2), 201–207. doi: 10.1007/s10643-008-0251-6
Davidson, M. C., Amso, D., Anderson, L. C., & Diamond, A. (2006). Development of cognitive control and executive functions from 4 to 13 years: Evidence from manipulations of memory, inhibition, and task switching. *Neuropsychologia, 44*(11), 2037. doi: 10.1016/j.neuropsychologia.2006.02.006
Duncan, B. L. (1976). Differential social perception and attribution of intergroup violence: Testing the lower limits of stereotyping of Blacks. *Journal of Personality and Social Psychology, 34*(4), 590–598. doi: 10.1037/0022-3514.34.4.590
Dunham, Y. (2011). An angry = outgroup effect. *Journal of Experimental Social Psychology, 47,* 668–671. doi: 10.1016/j.jesp.2011.01.003
Dunham, Y., Baron, A. S., & Carey, S. (2011). Consequences of "minimal" group affiliations in childhood. *Child Development, 82*(3), 793–811. doi: 10.1111/j.1467-8624.2011.01577.x
Fawcett, C. A. & Markson, L. (2010). Similarity predicts liking in 3-year-old children. *Journal of Experimental Child Psychology, 105,* 345–358. doi: 10.1016/j.jecp.2009.12.002

Gramzow, R. H. & Gaertner, L. (2005). Self-esteem and favoritism toward novel in-groups: The self as an evaluative base. *Journal of Personality and Social Psychology*, 88(5), 801–815. doi: 10.1037/0022-3514.88.5.801

Greenwald, A. G., & Banaji, M. R. (1995). Implicit social cognition: Attitudes, self-esteem, and stereotypes. *Psychological Review*, 102(1), 4–27. doi: 10.1037/0033-295X.102.1.4

Greenwald, A. G., McGhee, D. E., & Schwartz, J. L. K. (1998). Measuring individual differences in implicit cognition: The Implicit Association Test. *Journal of Personality and Social Psychology*, 74, 1464–1480. doi: 10.1037/0022-3514.74.6.1464

Greenwald, A. G., Poehlman, T. A., Uhlmann, E., & Banaji, M. R. (2009). Understanding and using the Implicit Association Test: III. Meta-analysis of predictive validity. *Journal of Personality and Social Psychology*, 97(1), 17–41. doi: 10.1037/a0015575

Huckstadt, L. & Shutts, K. (2014). How young children evaluate people with and without disabilities. *Journal of Social Issues* 70(1), 99–114. Special Issue on Social Exclusion in Children.

Kelly, D. J., Quinn, P. C., Slater, A. M., Lee, K., Gibson, A., Smith, M., Ge, L., & Pascalis, O. (2005). Three-month-olds, but not newborns, prefer own-race faces. *Developmental Science*, 8, 31–36. doi: 10.1111/j.1467-7687.2005.0434a.x

Kinzler, K. D., Dupoux, E., & Spelke, E. S. (2007). The native language of social cognition. *The Proceedings of the National Academy of Sciences of the United States of America*, 104, 12577–12580. doi: 10.1073/pnas.0705345104

Kinzler, K. D., Shutts, K., & Correll, J. (2010). Priorities in social categories. *European Journal of Social Psychology*, 40, 581–592. doi: 10.1002/ejsp.739

LaFreniere, P., Strayer, F. F., & Gauthier, R. (1984). The emergence of same-sex preferences among preschool peers: A developmental ethological perspective. *Child Development*, 55, 1958–1965. doi: 10.2307/1129942

McGlothlin, H., & Killen, M. (2006) Intergroup attitudes of European American children attending ethnically homogeneous schools. *Child Development*, 77, 1375–1386. doi: 10.1111/j.1467-8624.2006.00941.x

McGlothlin, H., Killen, M., & Edmonds, C. (2005). European-American children's intergroup attitudes about peer relationships. *British Journal of Developmental Psychology*, 23, 227–249. doi: 10.1348/026151005x26101

Nesdale, D., Zimmer-Gembeck, M. J., & Roxburgh, N. (2014). Peer group rejection in childhood: Effects of rejection ambiguity, rejections sensitivity, and social acumen. *Journal of Social Issues* 70(1), 12–28. Special Issue on Social Exclusion in Children.

Mulvey, K. L., Hitti, A., Rutland, A., Abrams, D., & Killen, M. (2014). When do children dislike ingroup members? Resource allocation from individual and group perspectives. *Journal of Social Issues* 70(1), 29–46. Special Issue on Social Exclusion in Children.

Olson, K. R. & Dunham, Y. D. (2010). The development of implicit social cognition. In B. Gawronski & B. K. Payne (Eds.), *Handbook of implicit social cognition: Measurement, theory, and applications*. New York: Guilford.

Patterson, M. M., & Bigler, R. S. (2006). Preschool children's attention to environmental messages about groups: Social categorization and the origins of intergroup bias. *Child Development*, 77(4), 847–860. doi: 10.1111/j.1467-8624.2006.00906.x

Payne, B. K., Cheng, C. M., Govorun, O., & Stewart, B. D. (2005). An inkblot for attitudes: Affect misattribution as implicit measurement. *Journal of Personality and Social Psychology*, 89, 277–293. doi: 10.1037/0022-3514.89.3.277

Raabe, T. & Beelmann, A. (2011). Development of ethnic, racial, and national prejudice in childhood and adolescence: A multinational meta-analysis of age differences. *Child Development*, 82(6):1715–1737. doi: 0.1111/j.1467-8624.2011.01668.x

Shutts, K., Banaji, M. R., & Spelke, E. S. (2010). Social categories guide young children's preferences for novel objects. *Developmental Science*, 13, 599–610. doi: 10.1111/j.1467-7687.2009.00913.x

Tajfel, H. (1971/2001). Experiments in intergroup discrimination. In M. A. Hogg & D. Abrams (Eds.), *Intergroup relations: Essential readings* (pp. 178–187). New York, NY: Psychology Press. doi: 10.1038/scientificamerican1170-96

Tajfel, H., & Turner, J. C. (1986). The social identity theory of intergroup behaviour. In S. Worchel & W. G. Austin (Eds.), *Psychology of intergroup relations* (pp. 7–24). Chicago, IL: Nelson-Hall.

Wilson, M. L, & Wrangham, R. W. (2003). Intergroup relations in chimpanzees. *Annual Review of Anthropology, 32*, 363–392. doi: 10.1146/annurev.anthro.32.061002.120046

YARROW DUNHAM is trained in cognitive development and social cognition, and focuses on intergroup social processes across the lifespan. After completing his doctorate at Harvard University, he was an assistant professor at the University of California, Merced, and a Research Scholar at Princeton University. He is currently an assistant professor of psychology and cognitive science at Yale University.

JASON EMORY is an advanced graduate student in social and health psychology at the University of California, Merced. He is interested in the social psychology of intergroup relations and applications of social psychology to public health campaigns.

How Young Children Evaluate People With and Without Disabilities

Lauren K. Huckstadt and Kristin Shutts*
University of Wisconsin-Madison

How do preschool-age children evaluate people with disabilities, and does social contact make children more positive toward those who are different from them? To answer these questions, typically developing (TD) 3- to 5-year-old children completed tasks designed to measure their social preferences for, and judgments about the actions of, unfamiliar individuals with and without disabilities. Participants preferred pictures of TD children over children in wheelchairs, but did not prefer children who were described with disabilities over those who were described with mildly negative facts. In a third task, participants evaluated actions that violated norms more negatively than those that did not, regardless of whether the actors had a disability. Children's participation in inclusion programs did not appear to affect their responses. We consider possible explanations for children's responses—including the absence of social contact effects—in the discussion.

Social group biases emerge early in development. For example, studies of preschool-age children reveal that girls tend to favor girls, boys to tend favor boys, and white children tend to favor white children (e.g., Lam, Guerrero, Damree, & Enesco, 2011; Shutts, Roben, & Spelke, 2013). Whereas the literature on early gender and race attitudes is extensive (for reviews, see Aboud, 1988; Ruble, Martin, & Berenbaum, 2006), there is a paucity of research on preschool-age children's reactions to other dimensions of human variation. Yet investigating the full range of children's social biases is important: Such research can illuminate the nature of

---

*Correspondence concerning this article should be addressed to Kristin Shutts, Psychology Department, University of Wisconsin-Madison, 1202 West Johnson Street, Madison, WI 53706 [e-mail: kshutts@wisc.edu].

The authors thank Kelsey Dewey and Marissa Johnson for their assistance with data management, Casey Lew-Williams for his advice on the vignettes, and Caitlin Kirihara for drawing the cartoons used in the norm violation task. This research was supported by a grant to LKH from the College of Letters & Science Honors Program at UW-Madison, by UW-Madison research funds to KS, and by a core grant to the Waisman Center from NICHD (P30-HD03352).

children's interpersonal experiences with peers and provide suggestions for how to ameliorate prejudice and stereotyping early in development.

This article considers 3- to 5-year-old children's evaluations of people who are often the target of negative attitudes later in life (e.g., Nosek et al., 2007)—namely, those with disabilities. One in six children in the United States has a developmental disability (Boyle et al., 2011) and most students with disabilities attend schools with typically developing (TD) peers (U.S. Department of Education, 2012). Thus, in addition to expanding the scope of research on early social biases, studying children's disability attitudes addresses a topic of increasing relevance to children with and without disabilities.

Previous Research

Sociometric studies indicate that TD children favor TD peers over peers with disabilities. For example, Nabors (1996, 1997) asked preschool-age children in inclusive childcare settings to provide liking ratings for each of their peers and generate names of preferred and nonpreferred playmates. Analyses showed that peers with disabilities received lower preference ratings and fewer playmate nominations compared with TD peers. Several other sociometric studies have reported similar findings with TD preschoolers and older children (e.g., Diamond, Le Furgy, & Blass, 1993; Gerber, 1977; Goodman, Gottlieb, & Harrison, 1972; Guralnick, Connor, Hammond, Gottman, & Kinnish, 1996; Guralnick & Groom, 1987; Ochoa & Olivarez, 1995; Scheepstra, Nakken, & Pijl, 1999).

Sociometry can shed light on the nature of relationships among peers and identify attributes that are correlated with preferences and close friendships. However, when children are asked to consider known peers, they may rely on a multitude of factors besides an individual's disability status to guide their responses (e.g., manner of dress, observations of others' preferences, outcomes of previous social interactions). In order to understand whether children use disability status per se to evaluate other people, it is useful to present participants with controlled stimuli they have never before encountered.

A meta-analysis of results from studies featuring controlled stimuli (e.g., pictures or descriptions of unfamiliar children) found that TD school-age children tend to hold negatively biased attitudes toward people with disabilities (Nowicki & Sandieson, 2002), but research using controlled stimuli to assess younger children's social evaluations is relatively sparse. Nevertheless, there are reasons to hypothesize that preschool-age participants in the present research will evaluate TD children more favorably than children with disabilities. First, many researchers have argued that visually salient distinctions support social biases (e.g., Aboud, 1988; Bigler & Liben, 2007; Sigelman, Miller, & Whitworth, 1986), and some disabilities are visually apparent. Second, preschool-age children make positive social inferences about people who appear to be competent (Brosseau-Liard & Birch,

2010) and tend to view unfamiliar individuals with disabilities as less competent than TD individuals (Diamond & Hestenes, 1996; Diamond, Hestenes, Carpenter, & Innes, 1997). Finally, a handful of studies have shown that TD preschoolers say they like and would prefer to play with unfamiliar TD individuals over unfamiliar individuals with disabilities (Cohen, Nabors, & Pierce, 1994; Nabors & Keyes, 1995; Popp, Fu, & Warrell, 1981; Sigelman et al., 1986).

Working under the hypothesis that social contact can ameliorate bias (Allport, 1954), some researchers have focused on comparing the attitudes of children at schools with inclusion programs to the attitudes of children attending noninclusion schools. The findings from research with school-age children are mixed (Cameron & Rutland, 2006; Esposito & Reed, 1986): Some studies have shown positive effects of inclusive settings on school-age children's attitudes toward those with disabilities (e.g., Favazza & Odom, 1996; Nikolaraizi et al., 2005—Greek sample; Voeltz, 1980), while others have shown null or negative effects (e.g., Maras & Brown, 2000; Nikolaraizi et al., 2005—American sample; Sandberg, 1982). Very little research has compared the attitudes of preschool-age children in inclusion and noninclusion schools, although studies by Diamond and colleagues indicate that TD preschool-age children in inclusion schools are more likely to think that individuals with disabilities will be socially accepted by other people (Diamond & Carpenter, 2000; Diamond et al., 1997).

This Study

The primary goal of the present research was to contribute to the modest literature on preschool-age children's evaluations of people with disabilities, and test whether young children are more positively disposed toward TD individuals on a range of measures. Our participants were 3- to 5-year-old children from four different preschools. Participants completed three different tasks at two different time-points: the beginning of the school year (as a baseline assessment) and later in the school year (to examine change over time).

Two tasks probed children's social preferences by asking how interested participants were in befriending unfamiliar children with and without disabilities. One preference task ("vignette preference") assessed participants' willingness to befriend children with different disabilities. Disabilities were conveyed verbally, but not visually, because young children are not sensitive to visual indicators of cognitive disabilities (e.g., features of Down syndrome: Diamond & Hestenes, 1996) and because some disabilities (e.g., autism) are difficult to convey with pictures. To assess the strength of children's ratings, we also asked participants to evaluate targets described with mildly negative (but not disability) facts. A second task ("visible preference") focused only on physical disabilities and used visual information to convey disability status: Participants saw photographs of children who did and did not use wheelchairs.

A third task asked children to judge how acceptable it would be for someone with a disability to violate a social norm because of his/her disability. Participants saw cartoon scenes in which a TD child and a child with a visual impairment played a novel game in a way that deviated from the rest of a social group. Previous research provides evidence that children are sensitive to violations of social norms (e.g., Rakoczy, Warneken, & Tomasello, 2008; Smetana, 1981). In this study, we created a new measure to test whether children consider an individual's disability status when evaluating norm violations.

Beyond assessing children's social evaluations of those with and without disabilities, a secondary goal of the present research was to examine whether contact and familiarity might affect children's assessments. To do this, we tested participants from preschools with and without formal inclusion programs. Children in inclusion preschools spend their days with peers who have disabilities, and are therefore highly familiar with such individuals (Hanline, 1993; Okagaki, Diamond, Kontos, & Hestenes, 1998). Additionally, teachers in inclusion preschools are typically supportive of contact between peers with different abilities, and can facilitate classroom-wide activities that involve all children. Both familiarity (Cameron, Alvarez, Ruble, & Fuligni, 2001) and authority-supported contact (Allport, 1954; Pettigrew, 1998) could lead children in inclusion programs to be more favorable toward individuals with disabilities.

Method

Participants

Participants were 69 TD 3- to 5-year-old children living in the Midwestern region of the United States. Thirty-one participants attended one of two preschools with formal inclusion programs. Remaining participants attended one of two preschools without inclusion programs. Most participants completed all three tasks in a session, but some only contributed data for one or two tasks. See Table 1 for information about sample sizes and participant demographics at Times 1 and 2. Children with disabilities were invited to participate in this study; of those whose parents returned consent forms, none were able complete the tasks.

Participants from inclusion and noninclusion schools were similar in socioeconomic status. According to parental report, the most common household income bracket for families of participants in both kinds of schools was $100,000–125,000/year. Most parents (>90% of mothers and fathers) had a college degree.

Settings. About one third of students in targeted classrooms at one inclusion preschool had disabilities, while about 20% of students in targeted classrooms at the other inclusion preschool had disabilities or were being referred for diagnosis. Diagnosed disabilities included Down syndrome, Rhett syndrome, myotonic

Table 1. Information about Participants at Times 1 and 2

	Time 1		Time 2	
	Inclusion	Noninclusion	Inclusion	Noninclusion
Number of participants	31	37	28	37
Gender	11 F, 20 M	19 F, 18 M	9 F, 19M	19 F, 18 M
Mean age (years)	4.32	4.19	4.66	4.54
Age range (years)	3.03–5.09	3.10–5.22	3.65–5.34	3.48–5.59
Race/ethnicity	74% white	84% white	71% white	84% white
N for vignette preference	31	37	28	37
N for visible preference	31	37	28	36
N for norm violation	30	30	28	35

Note. All 28 "inclusion" children who participated at Time 2 also participated at Time 1. Three of the "inclusion" children who participated at Time 1 were absent at Time 2. Of the 37 "noninclusion" children who participated at Time 2, 36 had participated at Time 1. One "noninclusion" child was absent at Time 1, but present for testing at Time 2.

dystrophy, cerebral palsy, sensory processing disorder, autism spectrum disorder, ADHD, Williams syndrome, Noonan's syndrome, and significant cognitive and/or language delays. At the two preschools without dedicated inclusion programs, children with disabilities were less numerous: In one, 6% of children in classrooms where we tested had individualized education programs (IEPs) for speech or social skills development. In the other preschool, 7% of children in targeted classrooms had IEPs for speech, language, or social skills development, and one child was in the process of being evaluated for a diagnosis.

Procedure

An experimenter tested all participants individually in a quiet room at their preschool. Children had two opportunities to participate in the study. Testing for "Time 1" occurred in September and early October (at the beginning of the fall session), and testing for "Time 2" occurred in January and early February (at the mid-point of the year). Children completed the same three measures in the same order at both time-points: vignette preference, visible preference, and norm violation. Each testing session lasted approximately 15 minutes.

Vignette preference. The experimenter told participants that they would meet some new children and be asked to say how much they would like to be friends with each child. She then explained how participants could use a 3-point "smiley face" scale to indicate their choices. There was a happy face ("really would like to be friends with"), a neutral face ("sort of would want to be friends with"), and a frowning face ("really would not like be friends with"). Practice trials ensured that participants understood how to use the scale.

On each of 12 test trials, the experimenter presented a photograph of a child's face, provided a verbal description, and solicited a scale rating. Half of trials presented descriptions that conveyed one of six different disabilities: visual impairment, hearing impairment, physical disability, autism spectrum disorder, ADHD, or cognitive disability. Vignettes used by Smith and Williams (2004) inspired some of the disability descriptions in this study. Remaining trials presented mildly negative facts that contained no disability information; these trials served as a baseline against which we could compare the strength of participants' evaluations of children with disabilities. Table 2 lists all 12 descriptions used in the task.

Trials that presented disability facts were interspersed with trials that presented mildly negative facts. Female participants saw faces of white preschool-age girls throughout the task, while male participants saw faces of white preschool-age boys. The order of facts and the pairings of particular faces with particular facts were counterbalanced across participants. Thus, approximately half of participants saw a particular face paired with a disability fact, while half saw that same face paired with a mildly negative fact. Additionally, across participants different faces were paired with each of the disability and mildly negative facts.

Visible preference. On each of four unique trials, the experimenter presented participants with a photograph of a child in a wheelchair alongside a photograph of a child who was not in a wheelchair (Figure 1a). Participants were asked to rate (one at a time) how much they would like to be friends with each child using the scale from the first task.

Participants always rated the child on the left first, but whether the child in the wheelchair appeared on the left or the right was counterbalanced within and across participants. Pair order also varied across participants. Photographs within a pair were matched for attractiveness, age, hair color, and race (all were white), and participants only saw children of their own gender.

Norm violation. On each of three unique trials, participants saw a cartoon picture of seven children seated around a table (see Figure 1b). Six of the children appeared to be TD, while one wore glasses and did not have visible pupils. The experimenter pointed to and described three different "target" children: She introduced two TD target children with mildly negative facts (similar to those used in the vignette preference task), and noted that the child with glasses had a visual impairment (i.e., "This kid's eyes don't work so he can't see anything"). Previous research has shown that preschool-age children understand that people with visual impairments cannot see (Diamond et al., 1997). She then checked participants' memory for the facts associated with each target child (e.g., "Which kid's eyes

Table 2. Results and Text for Individual Items in the Vignette Preference Task at Times 1 and 2

	Time 1	Time 2
Disability vignettes		
Visual impairment	0.12	0.12
Hearing impairment	0.12	0.11
Physical disability	0.12	0.15
Autism spectrum disorder	0.29***	−0.14
ADHD	0.26**	0.09
Cognitive disability	0.12	−0.06
Typical vignettes		
Item A	0.27***	0.15
Item B	0.13	0.28*
Item C	0.15	0.14
Item D	0.22*	0.20
Item E	−0.04	−0.18
Item F	0.07	0.26*

Note. Asterisks represent the results of one-sample t-tests comparing each mean to the mid-point of the scale (i.e., "0"). ***$p < .005$, **$p < .01$, *$p < .05$.
Visual Impairment: This kid's eyes don't work and she can't see very much. Even if she has her eyes open she can't see because it's like being in the dark.
Hearing Impairment: This kid's ears don't work very well and she can't hear very much. If someone is talking, she can't hear it.
Physical Disability: This kid can't move her legs so she can't use them to walk around. She doesn't have any feelings in her legs so she can't run or walk.
Autism Spectrum Disorder: This kid doesn't really understand what others are thinking and feeling. If someone was happy or sad, she might not understand.
ADHD: This kid gets excited really quickly and can only sit still for a few minutes at a time. She gets out of her seat a lot and does things without thinking about them.
Cognitive Disability: This kid takes a long time to learn things and she forgets what people say to her a lot. Sometimes she doesn't understand or remember how to do things in class.
Item A: This kid dropped her pencil on the way to school today.
Item B: This kid fell off her bike last week.
Item C: This kid forgot to bring her lunch yesterday.
Item D: This kid missed the bus to school today.
Item E: This kid spilled food on her shirt last night.
Item F: This kid pressed the wrong button on the computer game.

don't work?"). Participants correctly identified the child with the disability 100% of the time.

Next the experimenter explained that all the children were playing a game where the goal was to discover what kind of animal was in a box by looking through tubes. She noted that the child with the visual impairment could not play the game in this manner because of his/her disability. Participants then saw how each of the children played the game. Five of the seven children—including one of the TD targets—played the game by looking through the tube. However,

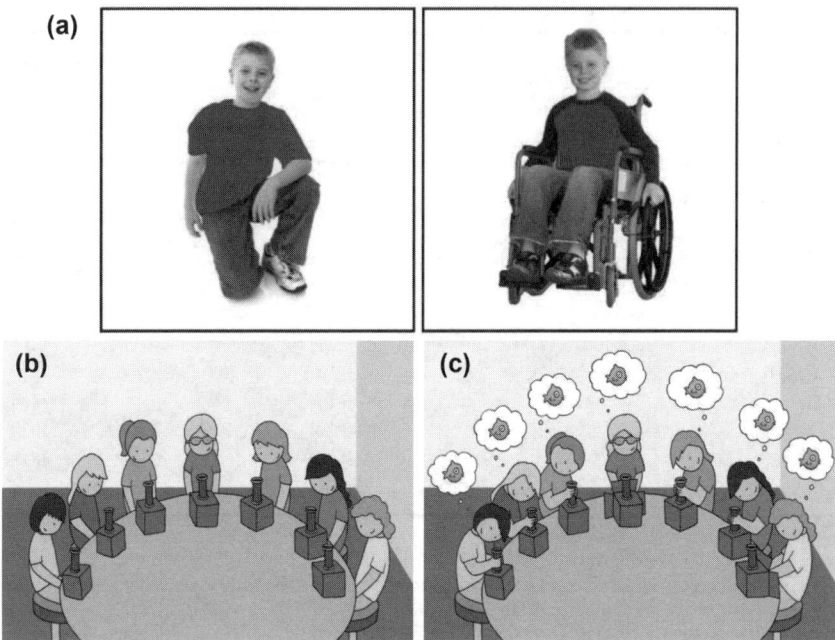

Fig. 1. Example displays from the visible preference (a) and norm violation tasks (b and c).

two of the children (the other TD target and the child with the visual impairment) reached inside the box in order to determine the identity of the animal. All children achieved the same outcome (e.g., discovered that a fish was in the box).

Children's methods were depicted in the cartoon (Figure 1c), and were also noted by the experimenter. Participants were then asked to use a smiley-face scale to indicate how "OK" it was that each of the target children played the game the way they did (happy face = "really OK"; neutral face = "sort of OK"; sad face = "really not OK").

Each kind of target (i.e., typical-conform, typical-violate, disability-violate) appeared once in each of the three positions (leftmost, middle, or rightmost seat at the table) across the three trials. Across participants we varied: the order in which participants rated the targets on every trial; the order in which participants saw the different kinds of targets in each position across trials (e.g., some saw the visually impaired child in the leftmost position on the first trial, while others saw him/her in the middle or rightmost position on the first trial); and the pairings of particular mildly negative facts with particular TD targets (e.g., whether "bumped his toe" went with a target who conformed to or violated the norm). Female participants saw female cartoons and male participants saw males.

Results

For each trial, a score of "–1" was assigned if a participant pointed to the frowning face; a score of "0" was assigned if a participant pointed to the neutral face; and a score of "1" was assigned if a participant pointed to the smiling face.

Vignette Preference

We generated two scores for each participant at both Time 1 and Time 2. The "disability vignette score" was the average of ratings given to the six children described with a disability fact. The "typical vignette score" was the average of ratings given to the six children described with a mildly negative fact. At Time 1, the mean disability vignette and typical vignette scores for the whole sample were 0.17 and 0.13, respectively. Participants' Time 1 responses to the disability vignettes differed from the mid-point of the scale (mid-point = 0; $t(67) = 2.69$, $p = .009$), while participants' Time 1 responses to the typical vignettes were only marginally different from the mid-point ($t(67) = 1.92$, $p = .06$). At Time 2, the mean disability vignette and typical vignette scores for the whole sample were 0.05 and 0.14, respectively. Participants' Time 2 responses to the disability vignettes did not differ from the mid-point of the scale ($t < 1$), but participants' Time 2 responses to the typical vignettes did ($t(64) = 2.12$, $p = .04$).

Mean responses for each of the different disability and typical vignettes at Times 1 and 2 are displayed in Table 2. For responses to the disability vignettes, an ANOVA with trial type (visual impairment, hearing impairment, physical disability, autism spectrum disorder, ADHD, and cognitive disability) and time as within-subjects factors revealed no significant effects. For responses to the typical vignettes, an ANOVA with trial type (Item A, Item B, Item C, Item D, Item E, and Item F) and time as within-subjects factors revealed only a main effect of trial type ($F(5, 274.81) = 4.25, p = .002$; Greenhouse–Geisser correction). According to pair-wise comparisons with Bonferroni correction, children treated all typical vignette trial types the same except for "Item E" (Table 2). Children rated faces associated with Item E more negatively than those associated with Items A, B, D, and F.

An ANOVA with vignette type (disability, typical) and time (Time 1, Time 2) as within-subjects factors, and participant gender and school type (inclusion, noninclusion) as between-subjects factors, revealed no significant main effects or interactions (all $p > .11$). Participants were equally wiling to befriend children who were associated with disability vignettes and mildly negative facts, and this did not differ according to school type, gender, or testing time.

All the "mildly negative" vignettes described individuals who committed specific actions (e.g., dropping a pencil). The mental disability vignettes similarly described specific actions (e.g., getting out of one's seat; forgetting what people say), but the physical disability vignettes did not. To test whether participants gave higher ratings to individuals who were described without specific actions (i.e., individuals with physical disabilities), we repeated the ANOVA considering only physical disability vignette ratings. This analysis revealed that participants gave similar ratings to targets associated with mildly negative (nondisability) facts and targets associated with physical disability descriptions ($p = .65$).

Visible Preference

Following the logic of the previous task, we generated a "visible disability score" and a "visible typical score" for each participant at Times 1 and 2 by averaging across trials. At Time 1, the mean visible disability and visible typical scores were both above the mid-point of the scale (mid-point = 0; $M_{\text{Disability}} = 0.24$, $t(67) = 3.08$, $p = .003$; $M_{\text{Typical}} = 0.31$, $t(67) = 4.01$, $p < .001$). At Time 2, the mean visible disability and visible typical scores were also above the mid-point of the scale ($M_{\text{Disability}} = 0.16$, $t(63) = 2.20$, $p = .03$; $M_{\text{Typical}} = 0.39$, $t(63) = 6.18$, $p < .001$). An ANOVA with person type (disability, typical) and time (Time 1, Time 2) as within-subjects factors, and participant gender and school type (inclusion, noninclusion) as between-subjects factors, revealed only a main effect of person type ($F(1,59) = 8.75$, $p = .004$). Regardless of school type, gender, or testing time, participants expressed a greater desire to befriend children who appeared to be TD over those who appeared to have a physical disability.

Norm Violation

We generated three scores for each participant at Times 1 and 2: "typical-conform" (the average of ratings given to normative actions performed by TD children), "typical-violate" (the average of ratings given to nonnormative actions performed by TD children), and "disability-violate" (the average of ratings given to nonnormative actions performed by children with visual impairments). Mean "typical-conform" scores for Times 1 and 2 were 0.52 and 0.67, respectively; both of these scores were significantly greater than the mid-point of the scale according to one-sample t-tests ($t(59) = 7.45$, $p < .001$; $t(62) = 11.55$, $p < .001$; respectively). Mean "typical-violate" scores for Times 1 and 2 were –0.23 and –0.38, respectively; both of these scores were significantly less than zero ($t(59) = 2.93$, $p = .005$; $t(62) = 5.05$, $p < .001$; respectively). Finally, mean "disability-violate" scores for Times 1 and 2 were –0.18 and –0.28, respectively; both of these scores were also significantly less than zero ($t(59) = 2.12$, $p = .04$; $t(62) = 3.21$, $p = .002$, respectively).

An ANOVA with person type (typical-conform, typical-violate, disability-violate) and time (Time 1, Time 2) as within-subjects factors and school type (inclusion, noninclusion) and participant gender as between-subjects factors indicated only one significant finding: a main effect of person type ($F(2,100) = 44.51, p < .001$). LSD post-hoc tests revealed that participants rated "typical-conform" children's actions more positively than "typical-violate" or "disability-violate" children's actions (both $p < .001$). Participants' evaluations of nonnormative actions performed by TD and visually impaired children did not differ ($p = .24$).

Discussion

Summary and Conclusions

This study suggests nuanced conclusions about the extent to which TD preschool-age children use disability status to guide their social preferences and judge others' actions. Results from the visible preference task confirm previous research showing that young TD children tend to prefer individuals without visible physical disabilities over those portrayed with adaptive equipment (e.g., Cohen et al., 1994; Popp et al., 1981; Sigelman et al., 1986). Additionally, in the norm violation task, participants rated the actions of visually impaired targets as "not OK", even though the experimenter highlighted targets' visual impairments and noted that they could not play the game according to the norm because of their disabilities. Both findings provide evidence for some degree of bias or insensitivity regarding disability status on the part of TD children.

Three further findings, however, suggest that TD children do not hold extremely negative views of individuals with disabilities. First, even though participants indicated that they would be more interested in befriending targets without disabilities in the visible preference task, the average preference ratings for targets in wheelchairs were not below the mid-point of the scale at Time 1 or Time 2. In other words, while participants were not very positive about befriending children in wheelchairs, they were also not very negative about the prospect of doing so. Second, in the vignette preference task, children's ratings for targets with disabilities were near the mid-point of the scale, as were their ratings of individuals described with mildly negative (nondisability) facts. The fact that participants' preferences for individuals with disabilities were largely equivalent to their preferences for individuals associated with common, incidental facts could be taken as evidence that young children's disability attitudes are not markedly negative. Nevertheless, one could also argue that it is unfair to judge individuals with disabilities—whose behaviors or limitations may be beyond their control (e.g., someone who cannot see because of a visual impairment)—similarly to those who commit acts that may be within their control (e.g., forgetting to bring lunch). Third, while participants were not forgiving of norm violations committed by individuals with disabilities, they were similarly harsh when judging TD individuals who violated norms.

Limitations and Suggestions for Future Research

It is worth noting some of the limitations of the present research. First, our sample size was small, especially for analyses probing effects of school type on children's responses. Second, most participants in the study were from high socioeconomic backgrounds and all participants attended well-funded, high-quality preschools; it is unclear whether the effects we observed would generalize to other populations. Third, the vignette preference task may not be an appropriate measure of preschool-age children's attitudes toward those with disabilities. We presented children with vignettes, reasoning that it would difficult—if not impossible—to convey some disabilities (e.g., ADHD) with static images. Nevertheless, young children may not have understood the content we presented, given limitations on their language comprehension and theory of mind skills. Future research might present children with simplified verbal descriptions or use dynamic video clips to convey content.

The present findings raise several additional suggestions and questions for future research on young children's evaluations of individuals with disabilities. One important question is why children begin to use disability status to evaluate unfamiliar people. There are many possible explanations, including in-group favoritism (e.g., Dunham & Emory, 2014), exposure to the biases of adults (e.g., Castelli, De Dea, & Nesdale, 2008), or emerging beliefs about the competence of individuals with and without disabilities (Diamond et al., 1997). An additional possibility raised by the present research is that children's bias stems from their dislike of apparent norm violations. The norm violation task provided clear evidence that children disapprove of behavior that is "wrong" (see also Abrams, Rutland, Ferrell, & Pelletier, 2008). Perhaps young children come to view people with disabilities as individuals who commit—or are likely to commit—norm violations. Future research might probe the attitudes of children with disabilities; examine correlations between the preferences of adults and children over time; and test for relations between children's attitudes toward, and inferences about, people with disabilities.

Further research is also necessary to probe the effects of inclusive preschool programs on young children's social evaluations. We found no evidence for effects of schooling environment—i.e., inclusion vs. noninclusion—on children's evaluations of individuals with disabilities in the present research. One possibility is that our measures and sample sizes were not sensitive enough to detect differences between children in inclusion and noninclusion schools. Additionally, the presence of a few children with disabilities in the "noninclusion" preschools may have made the social contexts more similar than we expected. Finally, inclusive settings may positively affect aspects of TD children's social and cognitive development that were not measured in this work (Peck, Carlson, & Helmstetter, 1992). Future research on effects of inclusion might seek larger sample sizes, include participants with a wider range of exposure to individuals with disabilities, aim to recruit children from (rare) schools where no one has a disability, and present a greater array of tasks to participants.

Two further reasons for the lack of school effects in our study are worthy of consideration. First, children may not represent "people with disabilities" as a social category comprised of individuals who are similar to one another. There are many kinds of disabilities, and even the "same" disability can manifest differently from one individual to another. Children may not think that a person with autism and a person in a wheelchair—or even two people with cognitive disabilities—have much in common with one another. If young children do not see individuals with disabilities as deeply (or even superficially) similar to one another, then any positive (or negative) experiences children have with particular children in their school may not generalize to other children with disabilities. It would therefore be interesting to borrow methods that have been used to study children's social categories (e.g., gender, race, and ethnicity: Diesendruck & haLevi, 2006; Rhodes & Gelman, 2009; Shutts et al., 2013) in order to investigate how children reason about individuals with disabilities.

A second point to consider is that while children in inclusion settings have *more* contact with individuals with disabilities, their experiences may not be uniformly positive. Thus, our data may reflect a mixture of feelings that are possible when children interact with individuals who differ from them along some dimension. In future research, it could be useful to measure individual children's experiences in inclusion contexts (e.g., whether a TD child has a close friendship with a child who has a disability) in order to probe connections between contact and attitudes more closely. It would also be fruitful to manipulate or study how inclusion is implemented in particular classrooms and schools in order to understand how different kinds of contact affects preschool-age children's attitudes (see Maras & Brown, 2000, for such an approach with older children).

Implications

In addition to contributing to our understanding of children's social cognitive development, research on children's disability attitudes has important practical implications. The present findings, together with previous research, suggest that young children may be less interested in interacting with people who have disabilities, and may not be forgiving about adaptations and accommodations for disabilities (e.g., alternate ways of completing a task in school). Thus, parents and teachers may need to facilitate social interactions between children with and without disabilities, provide children with tools for thinking about accommodations for their peers, and help children recognize bias and exclusion (see Pahlke, Bigler, & Martin, 2014). Social exclusion and bullying have obvious negative impacts on the targets of those behaviors, but biased attitudes and behaviors also deny TD children the opportunity to develop close relationships with diverse individuals. A deeper understanding of why and how children develop biased attitudes could eventually illuminate strategies regarding how best to support all children as they interact with people who have different talents and abilities.

References

Aboud, F. (1988). *Children and prejudice*. Cambridge, MA: Basil Blackwell.
Abrams, D., Rutland, A., Ferrell, J. M., & Pelletier, J. (2008). Children's judgments of disloyal and immoral peer behavior: Subjective group dynamics in minimal intergroup contexts. *Child Development, 79*, 444–461.
Allport, G. W. (1954). *The nature of prejudice*. Reading, MA: Addison-Wesley.
Boyle, C. A., Boulet, S., Schieve, L. A., Cohen, R. A., Blumberg, S. J., Yeargin-Allsopp, M., Visser, S., & Kogan, M. D. (2011). Trends in the prevalence of developmental disabilities in US children, 1997–2008. *Pediatrics, 127*, 1034–1042.
Bigler, R., & Liben, L. (2007). Developmental intergroup theory: Explaining and reducing children's social stereotyping and prejudice. *Current Directions in Psychological Science, 16*, 162–166.
Brosseau-Liard, P. E., & Birch, S. A. J. (2010). "I bet you know more and are nicer too!": What children infer from others' accuracy. *Developmental Science, 13*, 772–778.
Cameron, J. A., Alvarez, J. M., Ruble, D. N., & Fuligni, A. J. (2001). Children's lay theories about ingroups and outgroups: Reconceptualizing research on prejudice. *Personality and Social Psychology Review, 5*, 118–128.
Cameron, L., & Rutland, A. (2006). Extending contact through story reading in school: Reducing children's prejudice toward the disabled. *Journal of Social Issues, 62*, 469–488. doi: 10.1111/j.1540-4560.2006.00469.x
Castelli, L., De Dea, C., & Nesdale, D. (2008). Learning social attitudes: Children's sensitivity to the nonverbal behaviors of adult models during interracial interactions. *Personality and Social Psychology Bulletin, 34*, 1504–1513.
Cohen, R., Nabors, L. A., & Pierce, K. A. (1994). Preschoolers' evaluations of physical disabilities: A consideration of attitudes and behaviors. *Journal of Pediatric Psychology, 19*, 103–111.
Diamond, K. E., & Carpenter, C. (2000). The influence of inclusive preschool programs on children's sensitivity to the needs of others. *Journal of Early Intervention, 23*, 81–91.
Diamond, K. E., & Hestenes L. L. (1996). Preschool children's conceptions of disabilities: The salience of disability in children's ideas about others. *Topics in Early Childhood Special Education, 16*, 458–475.
Diamond, K. E., Hestenes, L. L., Carpenter, E. S., & Innes, F. K. (1997). Relationships between enrollment in an inclusive class and preschool children's ideas about people with disabilities. *Topics in Early Childhood Special Education, 17*, 520–536.
Diamond, K., Le Furgy, W., & Blass, S. (1993). Attitudes of preschool children toward their peers with disabilities: A year-long investigation in integrated classrooms. *The Journal of Genetic Psychology, 154*, 215–221.
Diesendruck, G., & haLevi, H. (2006). The role of language, appearance, and culture in children's social category-based induction. *Child Development, 77*, 539–553.
Dunham, Y. D., & Emory, J. (2014). Of affect and ambiguity: The emergence of preference for arbitrary ingroups. *Journal of Social Issues, 70*(1), 81–98
Esposito, B. G., & Reed, T. M. (1986). The effect of contact with handicapped persons on young children's attitudes. *Exceptional Children, 53*, 224–229.
Favazza, P. C., & Odom, S. L. (1996). Use of the acceptance scale to measure attitudes of kindergarten-age children. *Journal of Early Intervention, 20*, 232–249.
Gerber, P. J. (1977). Awareness of handicapping conditions and sociometric status in an integrated pre-school setting. *Mental Retardation, 15*, 24–25.
Goodman, H., Gottlieb, J., & Harrison, R. H. (1972). Social acceptance of EMRs integrated into nongraded elementary school. *American Journal of Mental Deficiency, 76*, 412–417.

Guralnick, M. J., & Groom, J. M. (1987). The peer relations of mildly delayed and nonhandicapped preschool children in mainstreamed playgroups. *Child Development, 58,* 1556–1572.

Guralnick, M. J., Connor, R. T., Hammond, M., Gottman, J. M., & Kinnish, K. (1996). The peer relations of preschool children with communication disorders. *Child Development, 67,* 471–489.

Hanline, M. F. (1993). Inclusion of preschoolers with profound disabilities: An analysis of children's interactions. *Journal of the Association for Persons with Severe Handicaps, 18,* 28–35.

Lam, V., Guerrero, S., Damree, N., & Enesco, I. (2011). Young children's racial awareness and affect and their perceptions about mothers' racial affect in a multiracial context. *British Journal of Developmental Psychology, 29,* 842–864.

Maras, P., & Brown, R. (2000). Effects of different forms of school contact on children's attitudes toward disabled and non-disabled peers. *British Journal of Educational Psychology, 70,* 337–351.

Nabors, L. (1996). Are preschool children with special needs being accepted by their typically developing peers in inclusive child care programs? *Physical & Occupational Therapy in Pediatrics, 16,* 55–71.

Nabors, L. (1997). Playmate preferences of children who are typically developing for their classmates with special needs. *Mental Retardation, 35,* 107–113.

Nabors, L., & Keyes, L. (1995). Preschoolers' reasons for accepting peers with and without disabilities. *Journal of Developmental and Physical Disabilities, 7,* 335–355.

Nikolaraizi, M., Kumar, P., Favazza, P., Sideridis, G., Koulousiou, D., & Riall, A. (2005). A cross-cultural examination of typically developing children's attitudes toward individuals with special needs. *International Journal of Disability, Development and Education, 52,* 101–119.

Nosek, B. A., Smyth, F. L., Hansen, J. J., Devos, T., Lindner, N. M., Ranganath, K. A., Smith, C. T., Olson, K. R., Chugh, D., Greenwald, A. G., & Banaji, M. R. (2007). Pervasiveness and correlates of implicit attitudes and stereotypes. *European Review of Social Psychology, 18,* 36–88.

Nowicki, E. A., & Sandieson, R. (2002). A meta-analysis of school-age children's attitudes towards person with physical or intellectual disabilities. *International Journal of Disability, Development, and Education, 49,* 243–265.

Ochoa, S. H., & Olivarez, A. (1995). A meta-analysis of peer rating sociometric studies of pupils with learning disabilities. *The Journal of Special Education, 29,* 1–19.

Okagaki, L., Diamond, K. E., Kontos, S. J., & Hestenes, L. L. (1998). Correlates of young children's interactions with classmates with disabilities. *Early Childhood Research Quarterly, 13,* 67–86.

Pahlke, E., Bigler, R. S., Martin, C. L. (2014). Can fostering children's ability to challenge sexism improve critical analysis, internalization, and enactment of inclusive, egalitarian peer relationships? *Journal of Social Issues, 70*(1), 115–133.

Peck, C. A., Carlson, P., & Helmstetter, E. (1992). Parent and teacher perceptions of outcomes for nonhandicapped children enrolled in integrated early childhood programs: A statewide study. *Journal of Early Intervention, 16,* 53–63.

Pettigrew, T. F. (1998). Intergroup contact theory. *Annual Review of Psychology, 49,* 65–85.

Popp, R. A., Fu, V. R., & Warrell, S. E. (1981). Preschool children's recognition and acceptance of three physical disabilities. *Child Study Journal, 11,* 99–114.

Rakoczy, H., Warneken, F., & Tomasello, M. (2008). The sources of normativity: Young children's awareness of the normative structure of games. *Developmental Psychology, 44,* 875–881.

Rhodes, M., & Gelman, S. A. (2009). A developmental examination of the conceptual structure of animal, artifact, and human social categories across two cultural contexts. *Cognitive Psychology, 59,* 244–274.

Ruble, D. N., Martin, C. L., & Berenbaum, S. A. (2006). Gender development. In W. Damon & N. Eisenberg (Eds.), *Handbook of child psychology* (6th ed., Vol. *3*, pp. 858–931). New York: Wiley.

Sandberg, L. D. (1982). Attitudes of handicapped elementary school students toward school-aged trainable mentally retarded students. *Education and Training of the Mentally Retarded, 17,* 30–34.

Scheepstra, A. J. M., Nakken, H., & Pijl, S. J. (1999). Contact with classmates: the social position of pupils with Down's syndrome in Dutch mainstream education. *European Journal of Special Needs Education, 14*, 212–220.
Shutts, K., Roben, C. K. P., & Spelke, E. S. (2013). Children's use of social categories in thinking about people and social relationships. *Journal of Cognition and Development, 14*, 35–62.
Sigelman, C. K., Miller, T. E., & Whitworth, L. A. (1986). The early development of stigmatizing reactions to physical differences. *Journal of Applied Developmental Psychology, 7*, 17–32.
Smetana, J. G. (1981). Preschool children's conceptions of moral and social rules. *Child Development, 52*, 1333–1336.
Smith, L. A., & Williams, J. M. (2004). Children's understanding of the causal origins of disability. *Journal of Cognition and Development, 5*, 383–397.
U. S. Department of Education, National Center for Education Statistics. (2012). *Digest of Education Statistics*, 2011.
Voeltz, L. M. (1980). Children's attitudes toward handicapped peers. *American Journal of Mental Deficiency, 84*, 455–464.

LAUREN HUCKSTADT, received her BA from the University of Wisconsin-Madison in 2012. She is currently a special education teacher at The Soulsville Charter School in Memphis, TN.

KRISTIN SHUTTS, received her PhD from Harvard University in 2006. She is currently an assistant professor of psychology at the University of Wisconsin-Madison.

Journal of Social Issues, Vol. 70, No. 1, 2014, pp. 115–133
doi: 10.1111/josi.12050

Can Fostering Children's Ability to Challenge Sexism Improve Critical Analysis, Internalization, and Enactment of Inclusive, Egalitarian Peer Relationships?

Erin Pahlke[*]
Whitman College

Rebecca S. Bigler
University of Texas at Austin

Carol Lynn Martin
Arizona State University

Elementary school-age children (N = 137, 70 boys, ages 4–10) were randomly assigned to receive one of two types of lessons aimed at increasing the inclusiveness of peer relations and improving children's ability to identify bias in media. Children in the pro-social condition were taught to identify and respond to undesirable/unfair social behaviors (e.g., teasing), whereas children in the pro-egalitarian condition were taught to respond to these same behaviors, with additional attention to gender bias (e.g., teasing about gender role nonconformity). After five lessons, children completed immediate and 6-month delayed measures of egalitarian attitudes, intergroup liking, responses to hypothetical peers' sexist remarks, and ability to identify sexism in media. The lessons did not differentially affect children's gender egalitarian attitudes and intergroup liking. As expected, however, children in the pro-egalitarian condition were better able to identify

---

[*]Correspondence concerning this article should be addressed to Erin Pahlke, Department of Psychology, Whitman College, 345 Boyer Avenue, Walla Walla, WA 99362 [e-mail: pahlke@whitman.edu].

We thank Barbara Porter and the teachers, parents, and students affiliated with St. Francis School for their gracious cooperation. We also thank Amy Hayes, Sarah McKenney, Yamanda Wright, and the members of the Gender and Racial Attitudes Lab who helped with data collection. This project was supported in part by funding from the T. Denny Sanford School of Social and Family Dynamics as part of the Lives of Girls and Boys Enterprise http://livesofgirlsandboys.org

115

sexism in media and to respond to peers' sexist comments than were children in the pro-social condition.

Children learn cultural gender stereotypes very early in childhood, and peers and media represent significant sources of this knowledge (Blakemore, Berenbaum, & Liben, 2009). Peers provide gender-stereotypic messages, pressuring each other via verbal (e.g., teasing) and nonverbal (e.g., exclusion) means to adopt traditional rather than egalitarian gender role attitudes and behaviors (e.g., Kowalski, 2007; McGuire, Martin, Fabes, & Hanish, 2007). Entertainment programs targeted at children are also often riddled with highly gender-stereotyped content (e.g., Leaper, Breed, Hoffman, & Perlman, 2002). Ironically, even programming characterized by pro-social morals (e.g., inclusion) often promotes gender bias and exclusion. Every December, for example, children in the U.S. gather in front of television sets to watch the classic movie *Rudolph the Red-Nosed Reindeer* (1964). The Rudolph story is focused on the moral that excluding someone on the basis of appearance (an unusual nose) is wrong, and yet the story's reindeer training session also illustrates another form of social exclusion—one based on gender: only male reindeer are allowed to train for and eventually pull Santa's sleigh. The exclusion based on gender is unremarked upon and implicitly treated as acceptable. Reducing children's tendency to engage in—and increasing their tendency to overtly challenge—all types of social exclusion is important. However, gender exclusion, because it is a form of intergroup (rather than interpersonal) exclusion and is bolstered by cultural gender stereotypes and prejudice (Killen, Sinno, & Margie, 2007), is likely to be especially difficult to redress.

Preparing children to recognize and combat gender stereotypic messages is particularly important because of the negative outcomes associated with gender bias and exclusion. Children who feel atypical of their gender and pressured to conform to gender norms show high rates of psychological distress (Egan & Perry, 2001). Youth whose behaviors or mannerisms are gender atypical, including LGBTQ students, are especially vulnerable to victimization and harassment at school (Heinz & Horn, 2014; Russell, Kosciw, Horn, & Saewyc, 2010). To combat exclusion requires tackling the many contributors to the behavior. For instance, children use gender stereotypes to rationalize the exclusion of children from work and play settings (e.g., Killen, Lee-Kim, McGlothlin, & Stangor, 2002). Children also tend to have less positive and more negative views of other-gender peers (Zosuls et al., 2011), which may cause them discomfort with, and avoidance of, other-gender peers, even to the point of social exclusion. Furthermore, children have exposure to many examples of stereotyping and sexism in the media (Leaper et al., 2002).

The primary purpose of this study was to examine the efficacy of a newly developed intervention program, grounded in social cognitive theories (Martin,

2000; Rutland, Killen, & Abrams, 2010), aimed at countering gender stereotyping (i.e., assignment of characteristics on the basis of gender) and prejudice (i.e., favoring one's own or disliking of the other gender) among children. Specifically, the intervention focused on increasing children's ability to (i) detect sexism in the media and (ii) challenge sexist comments by their peers. Sexism refers to attitudes and behaviors that exhibit or foster gender stereotyping or prejudice. We compare the efficacy of using egalitarian lessons with the kinds of programs that are much more common within schools—ones with lessons that focus on interpersonal (rather than intergroup) bias and encourage broadly pro-social (rather than pro-egalitarian) behavior.

Media and Peer Influence on Gender Role Development

Children now watch more television per day than at any time in history and spend almost 8 hours per day using electronic media (Rideout, Foehr, & Roberts, 2010). Such media are rife with gender stereotypic messages (Leaper et al., 2002). Females are significantly underrepresented and portrayed in narrow, stereotypic ways within movies and television aimed at child audiences (Smith & Cook, 2008). The entertainment industry has responded to the increasing pressure to depict females in less stereotypic roles (e.g., "*Brave*" 2012). Nonetheless, depictions of gender nonconformity remain rare and thus, it is vital that children are able to independently construct and apply a critical "sexism" lens when viewing media.

Children also learn many gendered behaviors and stereotypes from their peers (Martin & Fabes, 2001) via instructive comments (e.g., "*Only boys like race cars*," Kowalski, 2007), peer modeling, reinforcement, and punishment (e.g., Blakemore et al., 2009). These behaviors have consequences. For instance, children in classrooms with more "gender enforcers" (i.e., children who monitor gender appropriate behavior among others) show higher levels of gender segregation than children in classes with fewer gender enforcers (McGuire et al., 2007). For these reasons, it is vital that intervention also targets children's responses to peers' sexism.

Intervention Programming: Using Theory to Enact Change

For children to show substantial and lasting reductions in gender stereotyping and prejudice, they need to consciously detect and actively critique the sexist messages that they encounter. Little work, however, has addressed the question of how young children might be taught such skills. In a classic paper, Bem (1983) recommended fostering "sexism schemas" in young children. Specifically, she suggested that parents explicitly acknowledge others' beliefs about the links between gender and various attributes (e.g., boys should not cry) and label these beliefs as incorrect (or silly). We hoped that by teaching children about sexism and giving them practice using this information to critique media and to challenge peers' sexist comments, we would empower them to confront gender stereotyping and prejudice in their daily lives.

Whereas few educational programs have attempted to prepare children to actively challenge the sexist messages that they encounter, intervention programs are commonly aimed at increasing pro-social behaviors and decreasing bullying (Tofi, Farrington, & Baldry, 2008). Such programs typically target interpersonal, rather than intergroup, biases. Although some of these programs successfully reduce antisocial behavior, they are likely to leave gender biases in place. Educators may prefer this general, pro-social approach because of concerns about the possible negative impacts of discussing gender differences and sexism with children. Teachers' concerns may, however, be overblown; interventions that have taught children about discrimination, for example, produce increases in nonbiased responding and small or nonsignificant elevations in negative affect (e.g., Hughes, Bigler, & Levy, 2007; Pahlke, Bigler, & Green, 2010).

Perhaps the most common gender-related intervention is the inclusion of counter-stereotypic models (e.g., female astronauts) in curricula. Reviews of the intervention literature, however, suggest these programs are often unsuccessful (Bigler, 1999), in part because of reliance on passive learning. To be successful, active learning is important (Lambert & McCombs, 1998). That is, building an egalitarian school climate requires that children detect peers' sexism and then actively confront problem behaviors. In a constructivist, active-learning based intervention closely aligned to the one used here, Lamb, Bigler, Liben, and Green (2009) taught children the term "sexism" and gave children opportunities to practice retorts to peers' sexist comments. Children who learned about sexism were later more likely to challenge peers' sexist comments than were children who did not learn about sexism. The study did not, however, target media and the lessons left children's gender attitudes unchanged. Thus, in the current study, we built upon prior work by providing children both with opportunities to practice the skills of responding to peers and actively critiquing media as part of the lessons.

A final important theoretical issue concerns age-related changes in children's ability to detect and confront sexism. Although children are adept at making moral judgments about fairness (Smetana, 2006), the ability to detect, analyze, and respond to gender stereotyping and prejudice in daily life is likely to be highly challenging for young children in particular. Young children are especially likely to rigidly endorse gender stereotypes (Blakemore et al., 2009). They may also struggle to abstract and integrate the relevant information concerning gender norms and fairness from the complex contexts that are typical of media and peer settings (Rutland et al., 2010). Thus there was reason to believe that our lessons may be more effective among older than younger elementary school-age children. However, Killen and colleagues (2002) have consistently reported that older children are more likely than younger children to use gender stereotypes as the basis for rationalizing differential treatment based on gender. Indeed, young children often use the mere existence of gender-differentiated outcomes (without regard to contextual factors) as evidence of gender discrimination (Brown, Bigler, & Chu, 2010). There was, therefore, also reason to believe that our lessons concerning sexism would be effective among both younger and older students.

This Study

We sought to teach elementary school children to identify and respond to sexism in both peer relationships and media. We assessed whether children who receive lessons on fairness within gender contexts (*pro-egalitarian condition*) respond differently than their peers who receive lessons that are focused on pro-social behaviors within interpersonal contexts (*pro-social condition*). We hypothesized that the pro-egalitarian lessons would be more effective than the pro-social lessons at reducing children's preferences for their own gender, as well as increasing their egalitarian attitudes and their ability to detect and explicitly challenge sexism within both media and peer contexts.

Method

Participants

Participants were 137 students (70 boys, 67 girls) enrolled in an elementary school in the Southwest of the United States. The school is private, but draws from a heterogeneous population. Because the lessons were implemented as part of the school's educational programming, parental consent was not relevant for participation in the curriculum, and all children enrolled in kindergarten through fourth grade received lessons. Parental consent was, however, needed for all research-related individual testing. Of the potential pool of 158 children, 21 children's parents did not consent to the administration of measures, leaving a sample of 137. The final sample reflected the school's racial/ethnic diversity; the participants were 65% European American, 13% African American, 14% Asian/East Indian, 2% Latino, and 6% biracial.

Children in ten classrooms participated in the study (two classrooms each in grades K, 1, 2, 3, and 4). One classroom at each grade was randomly assigned to either the pro-egalitarian ($n = 69$; 39 boys, 30 girls) or pro-social ($n = 68$; 31 boys, 37 girls) condition. Because of the school's commitment to implementing a school-wide curriculum to increase inclusiveness and prevent bullying, there was no control group in which children received no lessons. Thus, we focused on comparing the effectiveness of the two forms of intervention (i.e., pro-egalitarian and pro-social conditions). At the start of the study, children ranged in age from 4 years, 9 months to 10 years, 4 months ($M = 7$ years, 6 months, $SD = 1$ year, 6 months).

Procedure

Children in kindergarten through second grade met individually with a trained experimenter and completed measures of egalitarian attitudes and intergroup liking. Children in third and fourth grade completed these measures as a group in their classrooms. Next, children were given one of two types of lessons aimed at preparing them to identify and respond to exclusionary, unfair behavior in media and peer relationships. Children in the pro-social condition were taught to identify and respond to undesirable social behaviors (teasing, manipulation, etc.) in peer relationships and media. Children in the pro-egalitarian condition were taught to identify and respond to these same behaviors, with additional specific attention to the role of gender. In both conditions, children participated in five 30-minute lessons. Within two weeks of completing the lessons, children completed posttest measures of the same constructs assessed at pretest, as well as measures of their responses to hypothetical peer behaviors, expected values and costs of same- and other-gender interactions, and identification of undesirable behaviors depicted in media. Finally, possible long-term changes in children's attitudes and behaviors were assessed at a delayed posttest six months after the intervention.

Treatment Conditions

Pro-social condition. Children completed lessons based on the same general themes used in the pro-egalitarian condition, but the content was not specifically related to gender. Children participated in interactive lessons designed to enable them to identify, analyze, and respond effectively to six forms of undesirable social behavior: (1) peer exclusion, (2) trait-based stereotyping, (3) role-based stereotyping, (4) biased comparative judgments, (5) unequal relationships, and (6) ridiculing of relationships.

Lessons were led by one of the two first authors and were given to the entire class (12–16 children). The lessons were prefaced with a brief presentation about bullying (e.g., definition and consequences) and stereotyping and prejudice (e.g., definitions). Next, the five lessons (one for each type of undesirable social behavior except in the case of stereotyping, which included both trait- and role-based stereotyping in one lesson; see above for list of behaviors) were presented. For each type of behavior, children practiced identifying the presence of the behavior within vignettes and then were taught a phrase (or phrases) for challenging that particular form of bias. Children practiced it along with the researcher until each child could repeat the phrase verbatim (i.e., each child was asked to repeat the statement). Children were taught the following phrases: lesson 1: "You can't say that you [they] can't play!" *(peer exclusion)*, lesson 2: "There's no such thing as a —." (e.g., "There's no such thing as a first graders' only backpack") *(trait-based stereotyping)* and "Not true, nothing limits you!" *(role-based stereotyping)*, lesson 3: "Give it a rest, no group is best!" (*biased comparative judgments*), lesson 4: "Don't you dare! That's not fair!" (*unequal relationships*), and lesson 5: "Being friends with everyone is cool!" (*ridiculing of relationships*). Students then practiced identifying the target forms of undesirable behavior in clips taken from children's media (i.e., movies, television shows, and commercials targeted at children). To do this, children were shown film clips and asked, "What's the problem here?" Children watched two to four video excerpts per lesson, one of which was identical across conditions and between one and three that varied across conditions. So, for example, children in the pro-social condition saw a clip of general exclusion in the television show *The Simpsons*, whereas children in the pro-egalitarian condition (explained below) saw an excerpt depicting gender exclusion in the television show *Arthur*.

Pro-egalitarian condition. Children completed lessons based on the same general themes used in the pro-social condition, but gender was highlighted. Thus, children were given five interactive lessons designed to enable them to identify, analyze, and respond effectively to six forms of sexism: (1) gender-based exclusion, (2) trait-based gender stereotyping, (3) role-based gender stereotyping, (4) gender-biased comparative judgments, (5) unequal gender relationships, and (6) ridiculing of cross-gender relationships. These lessons drew from and expanded upon those used by Lamb et al. (2009).

The lessons began with brief presentations about bullying (e.g., definition and consequences) and gender stereotyping and prejudice (e.g., definitions). Each of the five lessons then taught children one form of sexism and a phrase (or phrases) for challenging that particular form of bias: lesson 1) "You can't say that boys [girls] can't play!" (*gender-based exclusion*), lesson 2) "There's no such thing as a girls' [boys'] —." (*trait-based gender stereotyping*) and "Not true, gender doesn't limit you!" (*role-based gender stereotyping*), lesson 3) "Give it a rest, no group is best!" (*gender-biased comparative judgments*), lesson 4) "Don't you dare! That's not fair!" (*unequal gender relationships*), and lesson 5) "Being friends with everyone is cool!" (*ridiculing of cross-gender relationships*). Students then practiced identifying the forms of sexism in clips taken from children's media. Specifically, children were shown film clips and asked, "What's the problem here?"

Pretest Measures

Egalitarian attitudes. Children completed the activity subscale of the Preschool Occupation, Activity, and Trait-Attitude Measure (POAT-AM; Liben, Bigler, Shechner, & Arthur, 2006). Children rated whether a series of masculine, feminine, and gender-neutral activities should be engaged in by "only boys," "only girls," or "both boys and girls." The proportion of "both boys and girls" responses to masculine and feminine activities was summed, with higher scores indicating more egalitarian (i.e., less stereotypic) views ($\alpha = 0.77$).

Intergroup liking. To assess global intergroup liking, children were asked "How do you feel about girls?" and "How do you feel about boys?" To assess context-dependent intergroup liking, children were asked, "How do you feel about girls in your class?" and "How do you feel about boys in your class?" Children responded to each question on a 7-point scale from 1 (Don't like at all) to 7 (Like a lot) with corresponding graphic depictions of emotions (i.e., emoticons). The corresponding global and context-dependent responses were highly correlated ($r > .48$) and thus summary scores were created, one for liking of males, one for liking of females.

Immediate Posttest Measures

Egalitarian attitudes. Children completed the occupation subscale of the POAT-AM (Liben et al., 2006). We used the occupation subscale (rather than the activity subscale used at pretest) because responses on the two subscales are highly correlated, and the pretest and immediate posttest were close enough together that we worried that children would remember the items. Children rated whether a series of traditionally masculine, feminine, and gender-neutral occupations should be performed by "only men," "only women," or "both men and women." The proportion of "both men and women" responses to traditionally gender-typed occupations was summed, with higher scores indicating more egalitarian views ($\alpha = 0.84$).

Intergroup liking. The intergroup liking items given at pretest were re-administered.

Hypothetical responses to sexist peers. Children's self-reported responses to peers' hypothetical sex-typed remarks were assessed using a shortened, modified version of the Sexist Peer Vignette measure, developed by Lamb et al. (2009). Children were asked how they would respond to seven hypothetical situations. The situations included cases of the six explicitly taught forms of sexism (1) gender-based exclusion, (2) trait-based gender stereotyping, (3) role-based gender stereotyping, (4) gender-biased comparative judgments, (5) unequal cross-gender friendships, and (6) ridiculing cross-gender friendships, as well as an instance of (7) the use of gender to label and organize children (which was addressed by Lamb et al.'s sexism lessons but was not addressed here). For each situation, children were asked (yes or no) whether they would (i) explicitly agree with the sexism (e.g., "Agree that Sarah's new short haircut is a boy's haircut"),

(ii) implicitly agree with the sexism but challenge the peer based on the unfair or antisocial nature of the remark (e.g., "Tell the classmate that it is not nice to make fun of Sarah's hair, even if it is too short"), or (iii) explicitly challenge the sexism (e.g., "Tell Sarah and the classmate that there's no such thing as a boy's haircut; anyone can have short hair"). Children were allowed to endorse multiple responses.

Expectancies for interacting with other-gender peers. Children's expectancies for interacting with other-gender peers were assessed using a scenario developed by Zosuls et al. (2011). Participants were asked to imagine that they faced the possibility of joining a group of other-gender peers playing a fun game, and then asked about potential benefits (three items; e.g., "Do you think you would have fun playing with the girls/boys?") and potential costs (six items; e.g., "Do you think other kids would tease you for playing with the girls/boys?") associated with playing with other-gender peers. Both scales were reliable (benefits $\alpha = 0.79$; costs $\alpha = 0.83$).

Media criticisms. Children's ability to identify antisocial/unfair and sexist scenarios in the media was assessed through a task developed specifically for this study. Children watched five short (2–3 minutes) video clips from popular movies that depicted a subset of the forms of sexism discussed in the gender lessons (i.e., gender-based exclusion, trait- and role-based gender stereotyping, and unequal gender relationships). One additional clip depicted counter-stereotypic behavior, allowing us to detect claims of sexism when none was apparent. The use of existing media increased the ecological validity of the task (i.e., such segments are typical of those encountered by children), but simultaneously made it impossible to tightly control the types of sexist messages depicted. (So, for example, some clips depicted more than one form of sexism simultaneously.) We strove instead for a variety of depictions of sexist behavior (live and cartoon, implicit and explicit, targeted at males and females, etc.; see Table 1). After each clip, the child was asked, "Is there a problem?" and "Why?" Children's responses were recorded.

Children's open-ended responses to the six videos were then coded as reflecting one of four categories: (1) perceived inappropriate antisocial/unfair behavior, (2) perceived inappropriate sexist behavior, (3) perceived appropriate sexist behavior, or (4) something unrelated to unfairness or sexism. Responses could receive more than one code. Two coders independently categorized all responses, and they were reliable ($\kappa = 0.85$). Discrepant responses were discussed until agreement was reached. Two versions of the task were developed so that children could view different videos at the immediate and delayed posttests. Versions were counterbalanced across condition.

Table 1. Content of Videos Used in the Media Criticism Measure Administered at Immediate and Delayed Posttest and Percentage of Children Who Identified the Content as Problematic

Content	Video A	Problematic	Video B	Problematic
Implicit gender-based exclusion	Exclusion of females from reindeer training, *Rudolph the Red-Nosed Reindeer*	60.8	Exclusion of boys from a classmate's party, *MVP*	83.7
Gender stereotyping of roles/traits	Fairy godmothers, *My Simple Wish*	55.5	Elves, *Rudolph the Red-Nosed Reindeer*	10.9
Explicit (verbally stated) gender-based exclusion	Boys but not girls allowed to hunt, *Caddie Woodlawn*	89.8	Women but not men allowed onto lifeboats, *Titanic*	65.7
Unequal gender relationships	Woman told she must obey a man, *King and I*	86.9	Father overrules a mother's decision, *My Dog Skip*	93.3
Gender stereotyping and unequal gender relationships	Man saves a woman from dragon, *Sleeping Beauty*	27.8	Man saves a woman from prison, *El Dorado*	60.9
Counter-stereotypic behavior*	Dad cooking, *My Dog Skip*	16.6	Dad cleaning, *Mr. Mom*	27.0

Note. *These clips served as "reverse-coded" items in that they contained counter-stereotypic (rather than sexist) content and thus egalitarian attitudes should have associated with the response "no" to the question of whether the clip contained a problem.

Delayed Posttest Measures

Egalitarian attitudes. Children's attitudes were assessed by re-administering the occupations subscale of the POAT-AM ($\alpha = 0.85$).

Intergroup liking. The items given at pre- and immediate posttest was re-administered.

Hypothetical responses to sexist peers. The Sexist Peer Vignette measure was re-administered. The task difficulty was increased, however, by asking children to provide open-ended responses rather than asking for their rating of experimenter-provided responses. Children's responses were then coded into one of four categories: (1) agreeing with the sexist remark (e.g., "I'd say the same thing"), (2) ignoring the sexist remark (e.g., "I wouldn't do anything"), (3) objecting to the unfair/antisocial nature of the remark (e.g., "I'd say that I don't like people being mean to each other"), or (4) challenging the sexism inherent in the remark (e.g., "I'd tell him that there is no such thing as a 'girl's thing'"). Two coders independently categorized the statements, and they were reliable ($\kappa = 0.86$). Discrepant responses were discussed until agreement was reached.

Expectancies for interacting with other-gender peers. Children again completed the outcome expectancies measures. Scales were reliable (i.e., benefits $\alpha = 0.80$; costs $\alpha = 0.85$).

Media criticisms. Children's ability to identify antisocial/unfair and sexist material was assessed by re-administering the media criticism task using different media clips than they had been shown at the immediate posttest.

Results

Overview

Data analysis included three steps. First, we examined whether children in the two conditions were equivalent on pretest measures of gender stereotyping and prejudice. Second, we tested our hypotheses that children in the pro-egalitarian condition would (i) endorse more egalitarian attitudes (e.g., fewer gender stereotypes), (ii) view other-gender interactions more positively, (iii) more effectively respond to hypothetical peers' sexist comments, and (iv) identify more cases of sexism in media than children in the pro-social condition at the immediate posttest. Third, we tested our prediction that intervention effects would continue to be evident at the delayed posttest. In all analyses, we tested for variations in responding across condition (pro-egalitarian, pro-social), participant gender (boy, girl), and participant age (younger, older). Children were divided into younger ($M = 6.23$ years, $SD = 0.80$) and older ($M = 8.82$ years, $SD = 0.82$) groups based on a median split for age.

Pretest

Egalitarian attitudes. A 2 (condition) × 2 (gender) × 2 (age) ANOVA indicated no significant main effects or interactions involving condition.

Intergroup liking. A 2 (condition) × 2 (gender) × 2 (age) X 2 (peer gender: same, other) mixed model ANOVA, with the last variable as a repeated measure, indicated a significant interaction of condition, gender, and peer gender, $F(1, 118) = 4.62$, $p = .03$. Simple effects analyses indicated a significant interaction of condition and peer gender for girls, $F(1, 58) = 7.10$, $p = .01$, but not boys. Ratings of male peers did not differ among girls in the pro-egalitarian and pro-social condition, Ms (SDs) = 3.89 (1.83) versus 4.63 (1.45); however, ratings of female peers were higher among girls in the pro-egalitarian than the pro-social condition, Ms (SDs) = 6.34 (0.73) versus 5.78 (0.93), d = 0.66. For this reason, analyses examining the effects of condition on children's intergroup liking (reported below) include pretest scores as a control.

Immediate Posttest

Egalitarian attitudes. A 2 (condition) × 2 (gender) × 2 (age) ANOVA indicated no significant main effects or interactions.

Intergroup liking. Participants' ratings of their liking of same- and other-gender peers served as the dependent variables in a 2 (condition) × 2 (gender) × 2 (age) × 2 (peer gender: same, other) × 2 (time: pretest, immediate posttest) mixed model ANOVA, with the latter two variables as repeated measures. Importantly, results indicated no significant main effects or interactions involving condition and time, indicating that changes in children's liking of same- and other-gender peers did not differ between the pretest and immediate posttest as a function of the type of lessons they heard. Instead, results revealed several main effects and interactions involving other variables. They are not presented here but are available upon request.

Hypothetical responses to sexist peers. We used three 2 (condition) × 2 (gender) × 2 (age) ANOVAs to examine the effects of condition on children's reports of each type of responses: (1) explicit agreement with peer's sexist remark, (2) challenging the antisocial nature of the peer's remark, and (3) challenging the sexism of the peer's remark. With respect to *agreement*, results indicated main effects of gender, $F(1, 120) = 5.56, p = .02$, and age, $F(1, 120) = 19.23, p < .001$. Boys were more likely than girls to say they would agree with the sexism, Ms (SDs) = 2.02 (1.58) and 1.31 (1.14), $d = 0.53$, and younger children were more likely than older children to say they would agree with the sexism, Ms (SDs) = 2.21 (1.43) and 1.06 (1.14), $d = 0.89$. Condition was unrelated to rates of agreement with the sexism. Interestingly, however, of the 26 children who had a score of zero (indicating that they would not explicitly agree with the exhibited sexism in *any* of the seven cases), 6 were from the pro-social condition and 20 were from the pro-egalitarian condition. With respect to challenging the *antisocial* nature of the remark, results indicated only a main effect of age, $F(1, 117) = 16.02, p < .001$. Younger children were more likely than older children to report that they would challenge the peer using a pro-social response, Ms (SDs) = 4.64 (1.54) and 3.37 (1.97), $d = 0.72$. With respect to challenging the *sexist* nature of the remarks, results indicated no significant effects.

Expectancies for interactions with other-gender peers. Participants' ratings of the expected benefits and costs associated with other-gender interactions served as the dependent variables in a 2 (condition) × 2 (gender) × 2 (age) × 2 (expectancy: benefits, costs) mixed model ANOVA, with the last variable as a repeated measure. Results indicated a main effect of expectancy, $F(1, 122) = 45.21$, $p < .001$. Children were more likely to expect benefits than costs associated with other-gender interactions, Ms (SDs) = 3.51 (1.20) and 2.29 (1.06), $d = 1.08$. This main effect was subsumed by a marginally significant interaction of expectancy and condition, $F(1, 122) = 2.56$, $p = .09$. Children in the pro-egalitarian condition ($M = 3.74$, $SD = 1.14$) were more likely than children in the pro-social condition ($M = 3.29$, $SD = 1.21$) to expect benefits associated with other-gender interactions, $t(129) = 2.15$, $p = .03$. Children in the pro-egalitarian ($M = 2.22$, $SD = 1.10$) and pro-social ($M = 2.37$, $SD = 1.01$) conditions were equally likely to expect costs associated with other-gender interactions, $t(129) = 0.81, p = .42$.

Media criticisms. In the first 2 (condition) × 2 (gender) × 2 (age) ANOVA, the dependent variable was the proportion of media clips that children identified as including *antisocial/unfair* behavior. Results indicated no significant main effects or interactions. In the second ANOVA, the dependent variable was the percentage of media clips that children identified as including *sexist* behavior. Results indicated significant effects of condition, $F(1, 111) = 4.07$, $p = .046$, and age, $F(1, 111) = 5.90$, $p = .02$. Children in the pro-egalitarian condition identified issues related to sexism in a larger proportion of the videos than did children in the pro-social condition, Ms (SDs) = 0.29 (0.21) and 0.22 (0.18), $d = 0.36$. Older children also identified issues related to sexism in a larger proportion of the videos than did younger children, Ms (SDs) = 0.30 (0.21) and 0.21 (0.17), $d = 0.36$. Inspection of the responses from children in the two conditions to the counter-stereotypic clip indicated only a single claim related to sexism; a fourth grader in the pro-egalitarian condition noted that there was a problem "because the mom is somewhere else and the dad has to stay home and cook." Thus, children in the pro-egalitarian condition's higher scores did not stem from indiscriminate claims of gender bias.

Delayed Posttest

Egalitarian attitudes. As was true at immediate posttest, a 2 (condition) × 2 (gender) × 2 (age) ANOVA indicated no significant main effects or interactions.

Intergroup liking. Children's ratings of their liking of same- and other-gender peers served as the dependent variables in a 2 (condition) × 2 (gender) × 2 (age) × 2 (peer gender: same, other) × 2 (time: pretest, delayed posttest) mixed model ANOVA, with the latter two variables as repeated measures. As was true at immediate posttest, results indicated no significant main effect or interactions involving condition.

Hypothetical responses to sexist peers. In the first 2 (condition) × 2 (gender) × 2 (age) ANOVA, the dependent variable was the proportion of scenarios to which children responded by objecting to the *antisocial* nature of the remark. Results differed from those at immediate posttest, which showed only a main effect of age. Results indicated a significant interaction of condition and gender, $F(1, 110) = 4.41, p = .04$. Simple effects indicated that there was a significant main effect of condition among boys, $F(1, 57) = 4.37, p = .04$, but not girls. Boys in the pro-social condition objected to the unfair/antisocial nature of the remarks in a greater proportion of the scenarios than did boys in the pro-egalitarian condition, Ms (SDs) = 0.52 (0.26) and 0.38 (0.24), $d = .56$.

In the second ANOVA, the dependent variable was the proportion of scenarios to which children responded by challenging the *sexism* inherent in the remark. In contrast to the absence of significant effects at immediate posttest, results indicated a main effect of condition, $F(1, 110) = 4.26, p = .04$. Children in the pro-egalitarian condition used antisexism responses in a greater proportion of the scenarios than did children in the pro-social condition, Ms (SDs) = 0.37 (0.26) and 0.29 (0.24), $d = .32$. Results also indicated main effects of gender, $F(1, 110) = 4.97, p = .03$, and age, $F(1, 110) = 8.25, p = .005$. Girls challenged a greater proportion of the sexist scenarios with antisexism responses than did boys, Ms (SDs) = 0.39 (0.23) and 0.27 (0.26), $d = 0.09$, and older children challenged a greater proportion of the sexist scenarios with antisexism responses than did younger children, Ms (SDs) = 0.40 (0.23) and 0.26 (0.25), $d = 0.58$.

Expectancies for interactions with other-gender peers. Participants' ratings of the expected benefits and costs associated with other-gender interactions served as the dependent variables in a 2 (condition) × 2 (gender) × 2 (age) × 2 (expectancy: benefits, costs) mixed model ANOVA, with the last variable as a repeated measure. As was true at immediate posttest, results indicated a main effect of expectancy, $F(1, 110) = 77.96, p < .001$; children expected more benefits than costs associated with other-gender interactions, Ms (SDs) = 3.60 (1.00) and 2.19 (1.09). This main effect was subsumed by an interaction of expectancy and condition, $F(1, 110) = 5.42, p = .02$. Children were more likely to expect benefits associated with other-gender interactions in the pro-egalitarian ($M = 3.74$, $SD = 1.14$) than pro-social condition ($M = 3.29, SD = 1.21$), $t(117) = 1.97$, $p = .05$. Views of costs did not differ across conditions.

Media criticisms. In the first 2 (condition) × 2 (gender) × 2 (age) ANOVA, the dependent variable was the proportion of media clips that children identified as including *antisocial/unfair* behavior. As was true at immediate posttest, results indicated no significant effects. In the second ANOVA, the dependent variable was the proportion of media clips that children identified as including *sexist* behavior. Also replicating immediate posttest findings, results indicated significant effects of condition, $F(1,96) = 8.05$, $p = .01$, and age, $F(1,96) = 8.95$, $p = .004$. Children in the pro-egalitarian condition identified issues related to sexism in a larger proportion of the videos than did children in the pro-social condition, Ms (SDs) = 0.16 (0.16) and 0.08 (0.12), $d = 0.57$. Older children also identified issues related to sexism in a larger proportion of the videos than did younger children, Ms (SDs) = 0.16 (0.18) and 0.09 (0.10), $d = 0.48$. Inspection of participants' responses to the counter-stereotypic clip indicated no child identified the clip as sexist. Thus children in the pro-egalitarian condition's higher scores did not stem from indiscriminate claims of gender bias.

Discussion

We examined the efficacy of lessons focused on promoting egalitarianism versus pro-sociality for (i) reducing children's gender stereotyping and prejudice, (ii) increasing children's ability to detect sexism in the media, and (iii) increasing children's ability to challenge sexist comments by their peers. The goal was to provide empirical data relevant to broadening theoretical models and to assist educators in designing appropriate educational programs and policies related to sexism. The most striking result was the support of our hypothesis that those children who received pro-egalitarian lessons would be more capable of identifying cases of sexism in the media clips than those children who received pro-social lessons. Both types of lessons provided information and training about unfairness within social interactions, and both types of lessons could be expected to enhance children's ability to identify antisocial problems and sexism in videos. However, the pro-social lessons, which relied on a general approach to train children to recognize antisocial problems, did not result in children being successful at recognizing gender-biased behaviors. In contrast, children in the pro-egalitarian training, in which specific types of sexist behavior were clearly described, had an advantage over other children in recognizing sexism in children's media at both the immediate and delayed posttest. Unfortunately, even children in the pro-egalitarian training recognized sexism in only a small proportion of the video clips and, furthermore, responses varied considerably across clips (see Table 1). Illustrative were children's responses to a scene from *Rudolph* in which boys and girls performed a holiday song for Santa. The gender-segregated groups were dressed stereotypically, with boys in blue pants and girls in pink skirts, but only five children (all in the pro-egalitarian condition) noted the treatment of gender as problematic ("All the men were in one group and all the women were in the other group"). The remaining children saw no problem at all (e.g., one girl even noted, "There's no problem. The girls have nice dresses!").

A second striking result was that children in the pro-egalitarian condition were more likely than children in the pro-social condition to construct antisexism challenges to their peers' sexist remarks, even when assessed several months after the original lessons. Interestingly, children in the two conditions were equally likely to report that they would challenge sexist remarks at the immediate posttest, when the experimenter provided such responses. However, when required to construct the challenge on their own, children in the pro-egalitarian condition were more likely to respond with an antisexist comment than their peers in the pro-social condition. These findings are consistent with Bem's (1983) ideas about the effectiveness of training children to develop sexism schemas. Even young children appear able to learn sexism schemas and apply them, at least within some situations. Given the need to create school climates that are supportive of gender nonconforming students (see Heinz & Horn, 2014), the conclusion that effective strategies for confronting sexism can be taught is important and suggests that intervention programs of this kind should be implemented broadly.

The findings related to gender stereotyping and peer liking add to the growing body of literature that suggests that learning about discrimination does *not* negatively impact children (e.g., Hughes et al., 2007). Many educators avoid discussing sexism in their classes because of concerns about potential negative consequences. In this study, however, children who heard gender-specific lessons were no more likely than their peers who heard gender-blind lessons to endorse gender stereotypes, prefer same-gender peers, or dislike other-gender peers. These findings suggest that discussing gender with children to highlight biases and discrimination (as in the message, "There's no such thing as a boy's backpack") does not have the same negative consequences as using gender to routinely label individuals (e.g., "Good morning boys and girls") or highlighting the differences between boys and girls (e.g., "Girls like to play with dolls and boys don't"). Developmental Intergroup Theory (Bigler & Liben, 2006) identifies the negative consequences of these latter forms of gender-highlighting: making gender salient and focusing on differences between boys and girls often increases children's stereotypes and in-group biases. In contrast, discussing gender in the context of lessons about bias and discrimination appears to prepare children to recognize and confront sexism while not inflating their stereotypes or ingroup biases.

Given that children in the pro-egalitarian condition were exposed to gender-focused lessons, it is somewhat surprising that they did not endorse fewer gender stereotypes or express increased liking of other-gender peers than children in the pro-social condition. Stereotypes and in-group favoritism are very difficult to change (see Bigler, 1999; Martin, 2000), however. More intensive and long-term exposure to lessons may be required.

In contrast to the other-gender peer liking measure, positive expectancies about other-gender peers were differentially affected by the interventions.

Children in the pro-egalitarian condition were more likely than children in the pro-social condition to perceive greater benefits to interacting with other-gender peers. The expectancy measure assessed children's beliefs about both the benefits and costs of interacting in a variety of situations with other-gender peers, and only the benefits of interacting were different for children trained in pro-social versus pro-egalitarian lessons. Few studies have explored children expectancies for other-gender interactions but when these have been examined, overall children are less positive and more negative in expectancies for interactions with other-gender peers than for same-gender interactions (Zosuls et al., 2011)—a finding that is consistent with research concerning perceptions of out-group members (Dunham & Emory, 2014). Thus, improving expectancies for interactions with other-gender peers should be a feature of future gender-based interventions.

Although the data reported here are optimistic about the value of lessons designed to foster sexism schemas among children, several limitations should be noted. First, caution should be exercised when generalizing the results. This study was conducted in a private school with a commitment to reducing bullying. Second, it is possible that our measures were not sensitive enough to detect all of the effects of the intervention. At the immediate posttest, children were asked only for their ratings of experimenter-provided responses to sexist vignettes. At the delayed posttest, we added a more challenging, open-ended measure of responding to such vignettes. We suspect that this difference between the immediate and delayed posttests led to the inconsistent age effects and may have masked some of the intervention effects. Third, we lacked a true control group. Comparing children who received pro-egalitarian training to those who received pro-social training set the bar high for detecting positive change.

Despite these limitations, these results suggest promising directions for educational policy and programming. Findings suggest that children who receive pro-egalitarian lessons are better able to identify sexism in the media and to construct responses to peers' sexist comments than are children who receive pro-social lessons. In other words, children who learn about sexism explicitly—and are given the opportunity to practice identifying and responding to sexism—are better prepared to confront gender bias than are children who learn about general exclusion. Schools are faced with mounting legal and societal pressures to reduce gender bias and bullying in the classroom. These aims are particularly important given research regarding students' perceptions of gender atypical peers and the benefits of inclusive peer norms (Heinz & Horn, 2014) and thus we hope that schools will consider including pro-egalitarian lessons, like the ones utilized in the current study, in their curricula.

References

Bem, S. L. (1983). Gender schema theory and its implications for child development: Raising gender-aschematic children in a gender-schematic society. *Signs, 8*, 598–616.

Bigler, R. S. (1999). The use of multicultural curricula and materials to counter racism in children. *Journal of Social Issues, 55*, 687–705. doi: 10.1111/0022-4537.00142

Bigler, R. S., & Liben, L. S. (2006). A developmental intergroup theory of social stereotypes and prejudice. In R. V. Kail (Ed.), *Advances in child development and behavior* (Vol. 34, pp. 39–89). San Diego: Elsevier.

Blakemore, J. E. O., Berenbaum, S. A., & Liben, L. S. (2009). *Gender development*. New York: Taylor & Francis.

Brown, C. S., Bigler, R. S., & Chu, H. (2010). An experimental study of the correlates and consequences of perceiving oneself to be the target of gender discrimination. *Journal of Experimental Child Psychology, 107*, 100–117.

Dunham, Y., & Emory, J. (2014). Of affect and ambiguity: The emergence of preference for arbitrary ingroups. *Journal of Social Issues, 70*(1), 81–98.

Egan, S., & Perry, D. G. (2001). Gender identity: A multidimensional analysis with implications for psychosocial adjustment. *Developmental Psychology, 37*, 451–463.

Heinz, J. E., & Horn, S. S. (2014). Do adolescents' evaluations of exclusion differ based on gender expression and sexual orientation? *Journal of Social Issues, 70*(1), 63–80.

Hughes, J. M., Bigler, R. S., & Levy, S. R. (2007). Consequences of learning about historical discrimination among European American and African American children. *Child Development, 78*, 1689–1705.

Killen, M., Sinno, S., & Margie, N. G. (2007). Children's experiences and judgments about group exclusion and inclusion. In R. V. Kail (Ed.), *Advances in child development and behavior* (pp. 173–218). New York: Elsevier.

Killen, M., Lee-Kim, J., McGlothlin, H., & Stangor, C. (2002). How children and adolescents evaluate gender and racial exclusion. *Monographs for the Society for Research in Child Development* (Serial No. 271, Vol. 67, No. 4). Oxford, England: Blackwell Publishers.

Kowalski, K. (2007). The development of social identity and intergroup attitudes in young children. In O. N. Saracho & B. Spodek (Series Eds.), *Contemporary perspectives on social learning in early childhood education* (pp. 51–84). Charlotte, NC: Information Age.

Lamb, L. M., Bigler, R. S., Liben, L. S., & Green, V. A. (2009). Teaching children to confront peers' sexist remarks: Implications for theories of gender development and educational practice. *Sex Roles, 61*, 361–382.

Lambert, N. M., & McCombs, B. L. (Eds.) (1998). *How students learn: Reforming schools through learner-centered instruction*. Washington: American Psychological Association.

Leaper, C., Breed, L., Hoffman, L., & Perlman, C. A. (2002). Variations in the gender-stereotyped content of children's television cartoons across genres. *Journal of Applied Social Psychology, 32*, 1653–1662.

Liben, L. S., Bigler, R. S., Shechner, T., & Arthur, A. E. (2006). Preschoolers' sex-typing of self and others: Toward coordinated lifespan measures. *Poster presented at the Gender Development Research Conference*, San Francisco, California.

Martin, C. L. (2000). Cognitive theories of gender development. In T. Eckes & H. M. Trautner (Eds.), *The developmental social psychology of gender* (pp. 91–121). Mahwah, NJ: Erlbaum.

Martin, C. L., & Fabes, R. A. (2001). The stability and consequences of same-sex peer interactions. *Developmental Psychology, 37*, 431–446.

McGuire, J., Martin, C. L., Fabes, R. A., & Hanish, L. D. (2007). The role of "gender enforcers" in young children's peer interactions. *Poster presented at SRCD*, Boston, MA.

Pahlke, E., Bigler, R. S., & Green, V. A. (2010). Effects of learning about historical gender discrimination on middle school-aged children's occupational judgments and aspirations. *Journal of Early Adolescence, 30*, 854–894.

Rideout, V. J., Foehr, U. G., & Roberts, D. F. (2010). *Generation M2: Media in the lives of 8- to 18-year-olds*. Menlo Park, CA: Henry J. Kaiser Family Foundation.

Russell, S. T., Kosciw, J., Horn, S., & Saewyc, E. (2010). Safe schools policy for LGBTQ students. *SRCD Social Policy Report, 24,* 1–17.
Rutland, A., Killen, M., & Abrams, D. (2010). A new social-cognitive developmental perspective on prejudice: The interplay between morality and group identity. *Perspectives on Psychological Science, 5,* 279–291.
Smetana, J. G. (2006). Social domain theory: Consistencies and variations in children's moral and social judgments. In M. Killen & J. G. Smetana (Eds.), *Handbook of moral development* (pp. 119–154). Mahwah, NJ: Erlbaum.
Smith, S. L., & Cook, C. A. (2008). *Gender stereotypes: An analysis of popular films and television.* Los Angeles, CA: Geena Davis Institute for Gender and Media.
Tofi, M. M., Farrington, D. P., & Baldry, A. C. (2008). *Effectiveness of programmes to reduce school bullying.* Swedish National Council for Crime Prevention.
Zosuls, K., Martin, C., Ruble, D., Miller, C., Gartner, B., England, D., & Hill, A. (2011). 'It's not that we hate you': Understanding children's gender attitudes and expectancies about peer relationships. *British Journal of Developmental Psychology, 29,* 288–304.

ERIN PAHLKE is an assistant professor of psychology at Whitman College. Her research interests include children's and adolescents' understanding of discrimination, social stereotyping, and gender and racial inequalities across contexts.

REBECCA S. BIGLER is a professor of psychology and gender and women's studies at the University of Texas at Austin. Her research interests include gender role development, social stereotyping and prejudice, and intervention to reduce gender and racial biases among children.

CAROL LYNN MARTIN is a professor of child development in the T. Denny Sanford School of Social and Family Dynamics at Arizona State University. She is also a director of the Lives of Girls and Boys Enterprise, which promotes innovative research and its application to the real life issues and challenges facing girls and boys. Her research interests include gender development and peer relationships.

Ethnic Classroom Composition and Peer Victimization: The Moderating Role of Classroom Attitudes

Jochem Thijs[*], Maykel Verkuyten, and Malin Grundel
ERCOMER, Utrecht University

This study examined the imbalance of power thesis by investigating the link between ethnic classroom composition and peer victimization in 94 Turkish–Dutch (minority) and 374 native Dutch (majority) preadolescents (ages 9–13) living in the Netherlands. These children came from the same multi-ethnic classrooms (N = 31) and were considered as mutual out-group members. Analyses showed that children with more out-group classmates reported more peer victimization but only when those classmates evaluated their own ethnic group more positively than the out-group. This interaction effect was similar for minority and majority children, and no longer significant once children's experiences with ethnic peer discrimination were partialled out. Results indicate that ethnicity is not inevitably used as a criterion to victimize out-group members who are less well represented in the classroom. The findings partly support the imbalance of power thesis.

Peer victimization is a considerable problem for a substantial number of children and refers to the experience of being the victim of aggressive or negative behaviors, including name-calling and social exclusion (Hawker & Boulton, 2000). Several studies have examined how peer victimization is related to the ethnic composition of children's school environment from the perspective of intergroup contact theory (Allport, 1954). Ethnically diverse classrooms are important contexts for intergroup contact as children (can) work together with other-ethnic classmates while supervised and supported by teachers. However, "mere" contact opportunity is not the same and not as effective for improving ethnic relations as actual, meaningful contact (Pettigrew & Tropp, 2006; Tropp & Prenovost, 2008; Wagner, Christ, Pettigrew, Stellmacher, & Wolf, 2006). Children may also have negative

---

[*]Correspondence concerning this article should be addressed to Jochem Thijs, ERCOMER, Utrecht University, Padualaan 14, 3584 CH Utrecht, the Netherlands [e-mail: j.t.thijs@uu.nl].

contact experiences with out-group classmates leading to less positive out-group attitudes (Vervoort, Scholte, & Scheepers, 2011). More specifically, the presence of out-group classmates is a precondition for the experience of peer victimization based on one's ethnicity. In a segregated, ethnically consonant environment children are relatively protected from ethnic peer prejudice and discrimination but with desegregation comes the possibility of ethnic peer victimization.

In this study, we examine the link between ethnic classroom composition and peer victimization in a sample of Turkish–Dutch (minority) and Dutch (majority) preadolescents (ages 9–13) from the same multi-ethnic classrooms. Taking the perspective of the individual child, we anticipate that a stronger presence of ethnic out-group classmates increases the risk of peer victimization. However, we also expect that this downside effect of ethnic diversity is not self-evident but dependent on the ethnic attitudes of out-group classmates.

Ethnic Composition and Peer Victimization

Some of the research on classroom and school ethnic composition has used complex measures of diversity like Simpson's (1949) index which involves the number of different ethnic groups in combination with their relative proportions (e.g., Juvonen, Nishina, & Graham, 2006). Other studies have used measures of the ethnic segregation by looking at the proportion of ethnic majority (e.g., Verkuyten & Thijs, 2002) or minority children (e.g., Vervoort, Scholte, & Overbeek 2010). Despite these differences in the operationalization of ethnic composition, several studies have yielded support for what is known as the imbalance of power thesis (Graham, 2006; Juvonen et al., 2006). According to this thesis, peer victimization would be the consequence of imbalanced power relations between different ethnic groups in the class or school context. In more diverse contexts, the balance of power is less likely to be tipped in favor of one particular ethnic group, and this should have positive consequences for peer relations. From the perspective of the individual child this means that ethnic peer victimization is less (vs. more) likely when the ethnic in-group is in a numerical majority position (vs. minority), regardless of its ethnic minority or majority status in society at large. There is research evidence for these assertions (e.g., Graham, 2006; Graham & Juvonen, 2002; Juvonen et al., 2006; Verkuyten & Thijs, 2002). Yet, there are some notable exceptions.

In a recent study in 68 Belgian primary schools, school segregation (proportion of ethnic minority students) predicted less peer victimization for ethnic minority children but it had no effect on the victimization experiences of ethnic majority children (Agirdag, Demanet, Van Houtte, & Van Avermaet, 2011). Moreover, similar to Vervoort et al. (2010) in the Netherlands, Durkin et al. (2011) found in the United Kingdom that both ethnic minority and majority children were more likely to report peer victimization when there were more ethnic minority students. They argued that a larger presence of ethnic minority students challenges the majority's dominant position, which increases group tensions and lead to intergroup hostility.

These findings raise two important points. First, classroom ethnic composition may have different meanings for different ethnic groups making it important to consider ethnic group differences. Diversity indexes like Simpson's (1949) ignore the specific ethnic groups included and from an intergroup perspective they "lack" precision. For instance, a low score on the Simpson index might mean that a particular student is predominantly surrounded by co-ethnics (ethnically consonant context) or by other-ethnics (ethnically dissonant context). However, these different situations may have different consequences for students' experiences with interethnic relations in the classroom. In this study, we consider Turkish–Dutch and native Dutch students as mutual out-groups, and we examine how their experiences with peer victimization are related to the relative out-group presence in the classroom.

A second implication is that a stronger presence of out-group students does not automatically increase the risk of peer victimization. It seems crucial to consider how the out-group is perceived and evaluated. Whether out-group members are targets of victimization is likely to depend on other factors than their presence in the classroom and the attitude towards the out-group might be particularly important. In this study, we examined whether the link between peer victimization and the presence of out-group classmates is moderated by the average ethnic bias of those classmates.

Ethnic Attitudes

The imbalance of power thesis assumes that ethnicity is used as a criterion to victimize out-group peers when the out-group is a numerical minority in the classroom and thus less powerful (see Graham, 2006; Juvonen et al., 2006). However, this negative use of ethnicity is not self-evident as many children find ethnic exclusion morally wrong and socially unacceptable (Killen & Rutland, 2011). In this study, we test the imbalance of power thesis by examining group-averaged ethnic in-group bias (the evaluation of the in-group minus the evaluation of the out-group) as a moderator of the link between ethnic classroom composition and peer victimization. Consistent with social identity theory (see Tajfel & Turner, 1979), many studies have shown that children tend to favor their ethnic in-group over ethnic out-groups (see Levy & Killen, 2008). However, whereas most children like their in-group, some, more than others, show out-group dislike (Cameron et al., 2001). Hence, there can be substantial variation in children's ethnic in-group bias.

Taking the perspective of the individual child we consider out-group classmates as potential perpetrators of ethnic victimization. More specifically, we examine the hypothesis that children are more likely to be victimized in classrooms with more out-group students but only if these students have relatively strong ethnic in-group bias. To our knowledge, previous research has not examined the actual ethnic attitudes of children's out-group classmates as a condition for experiences with peer victimization. However, there are two reasons for examining these attitudes. First, there is evidence for a link between prejudicial attitudes and discriminatory behavior (for a review, see Wagner, Christ, & Pettigrew, 2008). Thus, even if not all classmates are equally likely to victimize peers (Salmivalli, Lagerspetz, Björkqvist, Österman, & Kaukiainen, 1996), it is reasonable to expect that ethnic bias affects at least some of the interethnic interactions in the classroom. Second, the average ethnic bias within a group may act as a peer norm that influences interethnic relations and regulates discriminatory peer behavior. If there is a peer group norm of ethnic in-group bias, children may socially condone or even encourage ethnic peer victimization even if they do not victimize out-group peers themselves (see Salmivalli et al., 1996). Alternatively, children may be less likely to show discriminatory behavior if their in-group classmates have a strong antibias norm (see Rutland, Cameron, Milne, & McGeorge, 2005). Thus, it can be expected that children will be more likely to be victimized by out-group peers when these peers on average have a relatively strong ethnic in-group bias.

To properly evaluate the meaning of the anticipated interaction between out-group proportion and ethnic in-group bias it is important to examine children's experiences of ethnic peer victimization. According to the imbalance of power thesis, classroom ethnic composition has an effect on forms of peer victimization that are based on ethnicity, but most research has only focused on peer victimization "in general" (some exceptions are Durkin et al., 2011; Verkuyten & Thijs, 2002). Yet, children can be victimized for all kinds of reasons and some of those may be related to, or confounded with, their ethnic background. For instance, in many countries different ethnic groups have different socioeconomic status, and socioeconomic status appears to be related to peer victimization as well (Wolke, Woods, Stanford, & Schulz, 2001). If the effects of classroom ethnic composition on peer victimization can be attributed to perceived ethnic discrimination, this means that ethnicity is indeed implicated.

Our approach to studying classroom ethnic composition and interethnic attitudes differs from other perspectives and contact theory in particular. Consistent with this theory, we acknowledge that the opportunity for out-group contact can be related to less bias. However, contact theory addresses the consequences of actual intergroup contact, which is only probabilistically related to contact opportunity. Compared to actual contact, the effects of contact opportunity are small (Pettigrew & Tropp, 2006; Tropp & Prenovost, 2008). Moreover, children are no blank slates but come to their classrooms with preexisting ethnic attitudes which may be a barrier to positive contacts (see Finchilescu, 2010). Empirically and theoretically, out-group presence and ethnic attitudes are sufficiently independent to allow for combined effects on peer victimization.

This Research

The main hypothesis in this study is that the link between the proportion of out-group classmates and children's experiences of peer victimization depends on the ethnic in-group bias of those classmates. In addition, we test whether this expected interaction can be attributed to children's perceptions of ethnic discrimination (ethnic peer victimization). That is to say, we control for these perceptions by including a separate measure. We evaluate our hypotheses by examining children of Turkish or Dutch origin who shared the same classrooms. People of Turkish origin constitute the largest non-Western ethnic minority group in the Netherlands and they have low social status in Dutch society (Gijsberts & Dagevos, 2010) of which children tend to be aware. For instance, research has shown that native Dutch children are more negative about the Turkish out-group than vice versa (Thijs & Verkuyten, 2012). Likewise, Turkish–Dutch children have been found to report more ethnic peer victimization than Dutch children (Verkuyten & Thijs, 2002). In this study, we expect more ethnic in-group bias among the Dutch children, and therefore also a stronger effect of their presence for the victimization experiences of Turkish–Dutch children (cf., Agirdag et al., 2011). Yet, we expect that the interaction between out-group proportion and bias is similar for both groups.

We also control for three other classroom characteristics. Our focus is on Turkish–Dutch and Dutch children which means that we use a societal minority–majority distinction. Previous research in the Netherlands has shown that this distinction is particularly important for children's perceptions of discrimination (Verkuyten & Thijs, 2002). However, children of different minority groups can also victimize each other and Dutch classrooms contain different ethnicities. For this reason, we control for the presence of "other ethnic minority" students, that is, children who are not considered ethnically Dutch or Turkish. Next, we control for classroom size. Class size can be related to peer victimization (Wolke et al., 2001) and peer discrimination (Verkuyten & Thijs, 2002), and in Dutch schools classes with more minority children tend to be smaller in size (see Verkuyten & Thijs, 2002). Finally, we examine the influence of the anti-prejudice aspect of multiculturalism in the classroom (Banks, 2004). Dutch schools and teachers differ considerably in how they deal with ethnic diversity, and previous research has shown that both ethnic bias and the awareness and perceptions of ethnic discrimination are stronger in classrooms in which teachers deal with examples of ethnic exclusion and discuss the need for fairness toward all cultures (Verkuyten & Thijs, 2013). It is important to control for this form of multiculturalism as it might act as a third variable causing spurious shared variance between classmates' ethnic in-group bias and cross-ethnic peer victimization.

Method

Participants and Procedure

Grade 5–6 children from various schools in different parts of the Netherlands participated in the research. The children voluntarily and anonymously completed a questionnaire in their classroom under supervision. The questionnaire involved various topics including attitudes toward school, peer victimization, and ethnic attitudes. Based on children's reports of their own and their parents' ethnicity, 94 Turkish–Dutch children and 374 native Dutch children were selected for the present analysis (49.1% female). The gender distribution was similar in both groups, but the Turkish–Dutch children were somewhat older than the Dutch children, $M_{age} = 11.6$, $SD = 0.78$, versus $M_{age} = 11.18$, $SD = 0.79$, $p < .01$. The children were in 31 classrooms containing both Turkish–Dutch ($M_\% = 15.1$, $SD = 12.3$; range = 3.0 – 43.8) and Dutch students ($M_\% = 53$, $SD = 22.6$; range = 7.1–84).

Measures

Peer victimization. Children completed three items to rate the frequency of their personal experiences with name calling, teasing, and exclusion from play in the school context. These three types of experiences are important aspects of peer victimization and they have been successfully examined in previous research (e.g., Agirdag et al., 2011; Verkuyten & Thijs, 2006). The three items had a five-point scale ranging from 1 (no, never) to 5 (yes, very often), and they loaded on one principal component explaining 66.1% of the variance. Cronbach's alpha was 0.73 (0.71 for the Turkish children and 0.74 for the native Dutch children).

Perceived discrimination. Perceived ethnic discrimination was separately measured with a single item about children's perception of being discriminated on the basis of their ethnic background. Children were asked whether they ever were teased or called names because of their ethnicity (1 = *never* to 5 = *very often*). Previous research has shown that his type of question is a valid way to measure ethnic peer discrimination in preadolescent children (see Verkuyten & Thijs, 2006).

Proportion out-group classmates and "other ethnic" students. For each classroom we calculated the proportions of students who identified themselves and their parents as respectively Dutch and Turkish. These proportions were strongly and negatively related, $r = -.76$, $p < .01$ ($N = 31$). Next, we calculated the proportion of out-group classmates, which was the proportion of Turkish students for the Dutch children and the proportion of Dutch students for the Turkish–Dutch children. As this proportion measure was negatively skewed we performed a log transformation. In addition, we calculated the proportion of "other ethnic" students.

Classmates' ethnic in-group bias. In counterbalanced order and within a list of four target groups, students were asked to indicate how they felt about Dutch people and Turkish people using a response format consisting of seven faces, ranging from very happy (1; *big smile*) to very sad (7; *big frown*), and containing a neutral mid-point (3; *straight face*). This "seven faces' response format has been successfully used to examine group attitudes among early adolescents from different ethnic groups (e.g., Thijs & Verkuyten, 2012). Preliminary analysis showed that the order of the measures did not affect the responses. Hence, order was not included in the final analyses. For each group of respondents (respectively, Turkish–Dutch or Dutch) we calculated a measure of ethnic in-group bias by subtracting the (reverse scored) evaluation of the out-group (respectively, Dutch or Turks) from the (reverse scored) evaluation of the in-group (respectively, Turks or Dutch). For the Turkish–Dutch children ethnic in-group bias was significantly lower than for the Dutch children, respectively $M = 0.20$, $SD = 1.46$, and $M = 1.04$, $SD = 1.63$, $t(156.343) = 4.821$, $p < .01$, $\eta^2_{partial} = 0.42$. Moreover, only for the Dutch children ethnic bias was significantly larger than zero, $t(373) = 12.29$, $p < .01$. Next, we separately aggregated (i.e., averaged) the bias scores for the Turkish–Dutch and Dutch students in each classroom ($N = 31$), and we calculated a new variable labeled "bias out-group classmates." For the Dutch children it consisted of the average bias of their Turkish–Dutch classmates, and for the Turkish–Dutch children it was the average bias of their Dutch classmates.

Multiculturalism. The anti-prejudice aspect of multiculturalism in the classroom was assessed with four questions. Children were asked to imagine having a new classmate from another culture. First, they were asked whether this child would feel at home in the classroom. Subsequently, children were asked whether the teacher would say something about it should this classmate be harassed, whether they would tell their teacher about it, and whether other children would say something about it (see Verkuyten & Thijs, 2002). These questions (5-point scales) were asked to all children in the 31 classrooms (the 94 Turkish–Dutch children and the 374 Dutch children, and their "other ethnic" classmates) and answers were aggregated (averaged) in each classroom. At the classroom level ($N = 31$), the four aggregated items yielded a Cronbach's alpha of 0.72, and they loaded on one principal component explaining 54.7% of the variance.

Data Analytic Strategy

As students were sampled within classrooms, data were not independently collected. To correct for dependencies within each classroom we used multilevel analysis to evaluate our hypotheses (Snijders & Bosker, 1999). Two levels were specified: Level 1 pertaining to the individual children ($n = 468$), and Level 2 pertaining to the different classrooms ($n = 31$). Although classrooms were nested in schools, we did not include a third (school) level because 7 of the 19 schools were represented by only one classroom. All models were estimated using the Iterative Generalized Least Squares algorithm and relative model improvement was assessed by comparing the fit (deviance) of nested models (Snijders & Bosker, 1999). In the multilevel analyses, the continuous measures were standardized at Level 1 (z-scores) to enhance the interpretability of the findings. Finally, a contrast was specified to analyze the difference between the Turkish–Dutch children ("0.5") and the Dutch children ("–0.5").

Results

Preliminary Analyses

Prior to testing our hypotheses, we conducted two sets of preliminary analyses. First, we examined the means and intercorrelations of the classroom variables, separately for both ethnic groups (Table 1). Paired-samples t-tests at the classroom level ($N = 31$) showed that Dutch children were less likely to have out-group classmates than Turkish–Dutch children, $t(30) = -5.92, p < .01, \eta^2_{partial} = 0.54$, and also that the ethnic in-group bias of the Dutch out-group classmates (i.e., *their* preference of Dutch over Turkish people) was stronger than that of the Turkish–Dutch out-group classmates (i.e., *their* preference of Turkish over Dutch people) $t(30) = 2.64, p < .05, \eta^2_{partial} = 0.19$. Next, in both ethnic groups the correlation between the proportion of out-group classmates and their average ethnic bias was rather small and nonsignificant, which justifies the examination of their interaction. In addition, the relation between out-group proportion and the proportion of "other ethnic" classmates was positive for the Dutch children but negative for the Turkish–Dutch children, whereas the relation between out-group proportion and class size was negative for the former group but positive for the latter. This means that classrooms with more Dutch children (and less Turkish–Dutch children) contained less "other ethnic" children, and were larger in size. Note that the strong relation between out-group proportion and the proportion of other-ethnic students for the Turkish–Dutch children indicates a risk for multicollinearity. However, across both groups this relation was small, $r = .14, p < .01$ ($n = 468$). Finally, there was a significant correlation between multiculturalism in the classroom and the ethnic bias of the out-group classmates of the Turkish-Dutch children (i.e., the

Table 1. Intercorrelations, Means, and Standard Deviations for Class-Level Variables ($N = 31$)

	1	2	3	4	5	Dutch M (SD)	Turkish–Dutch M (SD)
1. Proportion out-group classmates[a]	–	−0.86**	0.21	0.18	0.40*	−2.21 (0.84)	−0.78 (0.64)
2. Proportion other ethnic children	0.32	–	−0.14	−0.12	−0.25	0.32 (0.16)	0.32 (0.16)
3. Bias out-group classmates[b]	0.02	−0.11	–	−0.59**	0.15	0.13 (1.21)	0.92 (1.11)
4. Multicultural-ism	0.01	−0.12	−0.10	–	0.10	3.90 (0.24)	3.90 (0.24)
5. Class-size	−0.56**	−0.25	0.18	0.10	–	21.87 (5.42)	21.87 (5.42)

Note. Correlation coefficients for the Dutch and the Turkish–Dutch children are given below and above the diagonal, respectively.
[a]This variable is log transformed. For Dutch children it equals the proportion of Turkish–Dutch students in the classroom, and for Turkish–Dutch children it equals the proportion of Dutch students in the classroom.
[b]This variable involves the classmates' relative preferences for *their* own group.
*$p < .05$, **$p < .01$.

Dutch peers; $r = -.59, p < .01$) but not for the out-group classmates of the Dutch children (i.e., the Turkish–Dutch peers; $r = -.10$, ns). This negative correlation shows that at the classroom level multiculturalism had a negative effect on the ethnic in-group bias of the Dutch children.

Second, to explore ethnic differences in peer victimization and ethnic discrimination uncorrected for the influence of the contextual measures, we specified a multilevel regression model for each of the variables with the ethnicity contrast, and age and gender (dummy variable) as predictors. There were no group differences for peer victimization, but the Turkish–Dutch children perceived more ethnic peer discrimination than the Dutch children, $b = 0.56, p < .01$. Age was unrelated to perceived discrimination but negatively and weakly to peer victimization, $b = -0.10, p < .05$. There were no gender differences for peer victimization and ethnic discrimination, and therefore gender was not included further in the analyses.

Out-Group Proportion and Peer Victimization

Out-group proportion. We specified two multilevel models to examine the effect of the proportion of out-group classmates on children's experiences with peer victimization. In addition to out-group proportion (which was a Level 1

Table 2. Effects of Out-Group Proportion and Ethnic In-group Bias on Peer Victimization

	Peer victimization	
	Model 1	Model 2
Level 1 predictors		
Children		
Ethnicity (Turkish vs. Native Dutch)	−0.33*	−0.44**
Age	−0.10*	−0.06
Out-group classmates		
Proportion[a]	0.15*	0.13
Bias[b]	–	0.06
Proportion × Bias	–	0.20**
Level 2 predictors (classroom)		
Multiculturalism	−0.12*	−0.08
Proportion other ethnic children	0.06	0.08
Class size	0.05	0.07
Variance		
Level 1	0.96	0.94
Level 2	0.00	0.00
Deviance	1310.40	1301.00

Note. [a]For Dutch children this variable equals the proportion of Turkish–Dutch students in the classroom. For Turkish–Dutch children it equals the proportion of Dutch students.
[b]This variable involves the classmates' relative preferences for *their* own group.
$*p < .05$, $**p < .01$.

variable as it was differently calculated for the two ethnic groups) and children's ethnicity, these models included four control variables: age (at Level 1), and multiculturalism, the proportion of "other ethnic" students, and class size (at Level 2). In the first step we only included the main effect of out-group proportion. The result is shown in the middle column of Table 2 (Model 1). Overall, out-group proportion had a small but positive effect implying that it increased the risk of peer victimization.

In a second step (Model 2) we added the ethnic in-group bias of students' out-group classmates and its interaction with out-group proportion. Comparison of the deviance statistics in Table 2 showed that this led to a significant improvement in model fit, $\chi^2(2) = 9.399$, $p < .01$. Out-group proportion no longer had a main effect but its interaction with bias was significant. To further examine this interaction, we conducted a set of simple slope analyses. We calculated the effect of out-group proportion for out-group classmates with high versus low ethnic bias, i.e., one standard deviation above the mean (unstandardized score of 1.63), and one standard deviation below the mean (unstandardized score of −0.97), respectively. These effects are shown in Figure 1. When bias was high, the effect of out-group

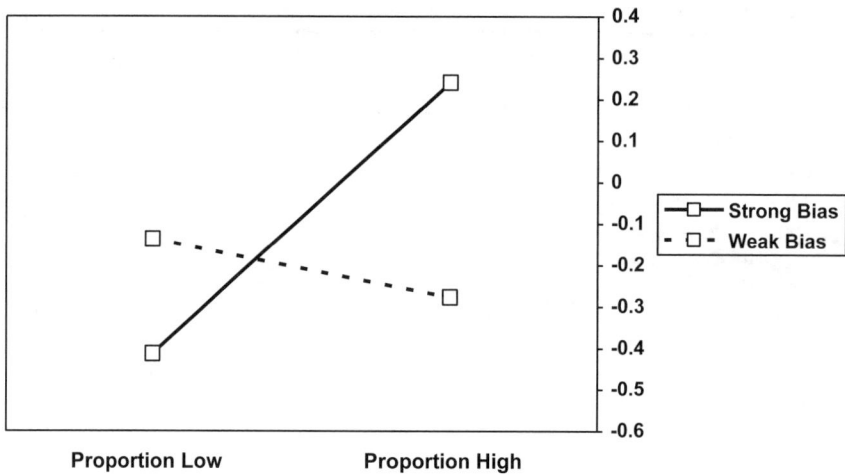

Fig. 1. The interaction effect of out-group proportion and ethnic in-group bias on peer victimization.

proportion on experiences with peer victimization was relatively strong, $b = 0.33$, $p < .01$, whereas for low bias out-group proportion had no significant effect on peer victimization, $b = -0.07$. Note that the nonsignificant main effect of proportion means that it was unrelated to peer victimization at the mean level of ethnic bias (unstandardized score of 0.33). Thus, only when out-group classmates had relatively strong ethnic in-group bias did their presence increase the risk of peer victimization.

Peer Discrimination

We examined whether the combined effects of out-group proportion and ethnic bias on peer victimization could be attributed to children's perceptions of ethnic peer discrimination. First, we re-ran the two models in Table 2 with the (standardized) single item for ethnic peer discrimination as the dependent variable. In the first model, the proportion of out-group classmates had a medium-sized positive effect on perceived discrimination, $b = 0.38$, $p < .01$. In the second model, the interaction between proportion and bias was positive and significant, $b = 0.22$, $p < .01$. Again, this implied a weaker effect of the proportion of out-group classmates when their ethnic in-group bias was low. Next, we re-ran the two models for peer victimization (originally in Table 2) with perceived discrimination as a separate additional predictor. With the impact of perceived discrimination partialled out, the main effect of proportion was no longer significant in Model 1, $b = 0.02$, and the interaction between out-group proportion and bias also was no longer significant in Model 2, $b = -0.12$. Thus, the classroom effects on peer victimization could be explained by their effects on ethnic peer discrimination. This indicates that ethnicity is the critical factor in the findings for peer victimization.

Ethnic Group

In a last set of analyses, we further examined the role of children's ethnicity. First, we tested whether the combined effects of out-group proportion and ethnic bias were similar for the Dutch and the Turkish–Dutch children. To do so, we extended the models in Table 2 by adding the two-way interaction of ethnicity with out-group proportion to Model 1, and its two- and three-way interactions with out-group proportion and ethnic bias to Model 2. Extending Model 2 did not lead to a significant improvement in model fit, and the three-way interaction between out-group proportion, ethnic bias, and ethnicity was not significant. This indicates that our main finding concerning the interaction between out-group proportion and ethnic bias was similar for Dutch and Turkish–Dutch children.

Model 1 did improve significantly after the extension, $\chi^2(2) = 8.73$, $p < .01$, and the effect of out-group proportion on peer victimization differed for the two groups, $p < .01$. For the Turkish–Dutch children it was strong and positive, $b = 0.61, p < .01$, but for the Dutch children it was not significant, $b = 0.03$. As the Turkish children had more out-group classmates than the Dutch children, we also explored whether this interaction with ethnicity could be attributed to a curvilinear effect of out-group proportion by adding its quadratic term. This term had no unique effect and the interaction with ethnicity remained significant. Thus, for the Turkish–Dutch children having more out-group classmates (i.e., native Dutch) was associated with more experience with peer victimization, whereas for the Dutch children the proportion of Turkish–Dutch classmates did not matter for their victimization experiences. This could not be attributed to the group difference in out-group proportion.

Finally, we explored whether the stronger (main) effect of out-group proportion for the Turkish–Dutch children could be attributed to their perceptions of ethnic peer discrimination. Hence, we added peer discrimination and its interaction with ethnicity to the version of Model 1 that included the other ethnic group interactions. Model improvement was significant, $\chi^2(3) = 64.538, p < .01$, and the effect of peer discrimination on peer victimization was significantly stronger ($p < .05$) for the Turkish–Dutch as compared to the Dutch children, respectively, $b = 0.51$ versus $b = 0.31$, both $p < .01$. However, the interaction between ethnicity and out-group proportion was no longer significant. Thus, for both groups of children, the classroom effects on victimization could be attributed to perceived ethnic peer discrimination.

Discussion

In this study, we evaluated the imbalance of power thesis in the classroom by examining the role of ethnic in-group bias of out-group peers for children's experiences with peer victimization. As predicted, we found that having more out-group classmates increased the risk of peer victimization but only when those classmates were relatively negative towards the victims' ethnic group. This means that out-group presence was unrelated to peer victimization for more than half of the children in our sample as their classmates' bias was below average. Hence, the link between ethnic classroom composition and peer victimization is not "mechanical" and the use of ethnicity to victimize out-group peers is not self-evident. Our analyses also showed that the combined effects of out-group presence and ethnic bias on peer victimization could be attributed to ethnic peer discrimination. Thus, the effects of ethnic classroom composition on peer victimization were due to victims' ethnicity, and not to confounding factors such as socioeconomic status (see Wolke et al., 2001).

The findings were quite similar for the ethnic majority (Dutch) and ethnic minority children (Turkish–Dutch). The expected interaction between out-group presence and bias was obtained for both groups and for both of them the effects of ethnic composition could be attributed to ethnic discrimination. However, as expected the main effect of higher out-group proportion on peer victimization was significantly weaker (and absent) for the majority compared to the minority children. Additional analysis showed that this could not be attributed to the fact that the minority children had substantially more out-group classmates than the majority children, as there was no curvilinear effect of out-group proportion. Instead, the differential effect of out-group proportion is probably due to group differences in ethnic in-group bias. Consistent with previous research (e.g., Thijs & Verkuyten, 2012) the ethnic in-group bias of the majority children was substantially higher than that of the minority children. Accordingly, for ethnic minority children, out-group presence entailed a stronger risk for peer victimization (cf., Agirdag et al., 2011). This has implications for research on ethnic differences in peer victimization. Given mixed research findings it has been concluded that the link between ethnicity and peer victimization is dependent on the local context (see e.g., Durkin et al., 2011), and that "individuals" ethnic representation within context may be more important than their specific ethnic group in predicting their experiences with peer harassment" (Bellmore, Witkow, Graham, & Juvonen, 2004, p. 1160). Our findings are partly in agreement with this conclusion but they also indicate that the ethnic groups and their status position in society do matter. Ethnic in-group bias was found to similarly increase the effect of out-group presence on peer victimization for minority and majority children, and this supports "a one model fits all" approach. However, the ingredients for this model differ for both groups as majority children were less often confronted with biased out-group classmates.

Ethnic peer victimization is not possible without the presence of ethnic out-group children but the same is true for positive interethnic contacts like friendships. According to contact theory (Allport, 1954) inter-ethnic contact improves ethnic attitudes, and this should have positive implications for interethnic relations. A meta-analysis of contact research has shown that contact can diminish bias also among children and even in the absence of optimal conditions (Pettigrew & Tropp, 2006; Tropp & Prenovost, 2008). This means that mere out-group presence can have some effect as well. In our study, the relative proportion and ethnic bias of out-group classmates were sufficiently independent to examine their combined effect on peer victimization. Yet, post hoc analyses at the individual level (not reported in the text) showed that the Dutch majority children were less biased when they had more Turkish classmates, which supports contact theory. Moreover, our approach is compatible with this theory because higher out-group presence for the potential targets of ethnic peer victimization often means less out-group presence for its potential perpetrators. For instance, Turkish–Dutch children with relatively few Dutch classmates were less likely to be victimized. In these classrooms, Dutch classmates had more opportunity for contact with Turkish–Dutch children, which diminished the ethnic bias of the former and thereby also reduced the likelihood of ethnic victimization for the latter. Likewise, the lower rates of ethnic victimization might also be due to more cross-ethnic friendships in those classrooms. Note that these additional findings are at odds with a threat interpretation of the effects of ethnic composition (see Durkin et al., 2011). Theoretically, a stronger out-group presence can increase threat but also lead to more (positive) intergroup contact, and there is empirical support for both mechanisms in schools (Stark, 2011). However, it has also been suggested that threat effects are relatively more likely when the relevant contextual units are large (e.g., national states) and that contact effects are dominant in the case of small contextual units (e.g., neighborhoods; Wagner et al., 2006). Our additional classroom findings are consistent with this notion.

The present findings have wider implications for scientific, societal and policy discussions about desegregated schooling. Over the last six decades various initiatives and policies have been proposed and implemented to promote ethnic diversity in schools. However, these measures are not undisputed, and the debates have revolved around various aspects of desegregation, including its effects on students' well-being, social relations and academic outcomes, but also its interference with parents' freedom to a select a school for their children (see Thijs & Verkuyten, 2013). These debates have shown that it is not easy to draw simple conclusions about the overall benefits of desegregation. Our study focused on students' experiences with peer victimization but even for this single domain the effect of ethnic classroom composition was not straightforward but dependent on the average attitudes of out-group classmates. This indicates that there is no single way in which students respond to the ethnic diversity surrounding them, and that it is important to go beyond simple main effects and examine desegregation in interaction or combination with other school or classroom characteristics. Moreover, educational interventions and policies should target these other contextual characteristics (e.g., the ethnic biases in the classroom) to minimize the potential downsides of ethnic diversity. Our findings for the anti-prejudice aspect of multicultural education are telling in this respect. This control variable was associated with less victimization (and perceived discrimination) but it was also negatively related to the ethnic in-group bias of the Dutch children (who were on average substantially more biased than the Turkish–Dutch children). These findings indicate that the possible effects of ethnic out-group presence on peer victimization may be diminished or compensated by anti-prejudice and multicultural educational practices.

To evaluate the present research, a number of limitations should be considered. First, our conclusions are based on cross-sectional analyses and the possibility of reciprocal influences should be acknowledged. In particular, ethnic peer victimization is in itself a negative form of contact, and theoretically children's ethnic in-group bias might be affected by their own peer experiences. However, additional analyses at the individual level showed that ethnic bias was not uniquely related to peer victimization or perceived discrimination. Future research should use longitudinal designs to draw firmer conclusions about the direction of effects. However, it makes more sense to examine peer victimization as an outcome of ethnic classroom composition rather than vice versa, and our analyses were consistent with other research and our theoretically based predictions. A second limitation of our study is that we only focused on Dutch and Turkish–Dutch children. But there are other ethnic groups in Dutch schools and all of them can play a role in peer victimization. Other minority group children (e.g., of Moroccan or Surinamese origin) were not sufficiently represented in our sample, and future studies could use selective sampling to include a diversity of minority groups. Yet we did control for the presence of "other ethnic" children in our sample, and by doing so we could more adequately test our expectations. Finally, our measure of perceived peer discrimination was limited because it consisted of only one item and focused on experiences with name calling and teasing but not on social exclusion. It is important to replicate our findings with multiple-item measures of ethnic peer discrimination.

This study shows that ethnic classroom composition can increase the risk for ethnic peer victimization depending on the ethnic attitudes of out-group classmates. Ethnic diversity implies opportunities for positive intergroup contact and learning about different cultures. However, diversity also implies the risk of being the target of ethnic peer victimization and this risk is stronger in school classes in which ethnic out-group peers make a relatively strong evaluative distinction in favor of their ethnic in-group. And because majority children tend to be most biased in their ethnic attitudes, peer victimization is most likely for ethnic minority children in "white" classrooms. For meaningful discussions and informed policy making, it is essential that researchers look beyond "simple" main effects of diversity and examine it together with students' attitudes and norms.

References

Agirdag, O., Demanet, J., Van Houtte, M., & Van Avermaet, P. (2011). Ethnic school composition and peer victimization: A focus on the interethnic school climate. *International Journal of Intercultural Relations, 35*, 465–473.
Allport, G. W. (1954). *The nature of prejudice*. Cambridge: Addison-Wesley.
Banks, J. A. (2004). Multicultural education: Historical development, dimensions, and practice. In J. A. Banks & C. A. M. Banks (Eds.), *Handbook of research on multicultural education* (2nd ed., pp. 3–29). San Francisco: Jossey-Bass.
Bellmore, A., Witkow, M. R., Graham, S., & Juvonen, J. (2004). Beyond the individual: The impact of ethnic context and classroom behavioral norms on victims' adjustment. *Developmental Psychology, 40*, 1159–1172.
Cameron, J. A., Alvarez, J. M., Ruble, D. N., & Fuligni, A. J. (2001). Children's lay theories about ingroups and outgroups: Reconceptualizing research on prejudice. *Personality and Social Psychology Review, 5*, 118–128.
Durkin, K., Hunter, S., Levin, K. A., Bergin, D., Heim, D., & Howe, C. (2011). Discriminatory peer aggression among children as a function of minority status andgroup proportion in school context. *European Journal of Social Psychology, 42*, 243–251.
Finchilescu, G. (2010). Intergroup anxiety in interracial interaction: The role of prejudice and metastereotypes. *Journal of Social Issues, 66*, 334–351. doi: 10.1111/j.1540-4560.2010.01648.x
Gijsberts, M., & Dagevos, J. (Eds.) (2010). *At home in the Netherlands? Trends in integration of non-Western migrants*. Annual Report on Integration 2009. The Hague: Social Cultural Planning Office.
Graham, S. (2006). Peer victimization in school: Exploring the ethnic context. *Current Directions in Psychological Science, 15*, 317–321.
Graham, S., & Juvonen, J. (2002). Ehnicity, peer harassment, and adjustment in middle school: An exploratory study. *Journal of Early Adolescence, 22*, 173–199.
Hawker, D. S. J., & Boulton, M. J. (2000). Twenty years' research on peer victimization and sychosocial maladjustment: A meta-analytic review of cross-sectional studies. *Journal of Child Psychology and Psychiatry and Allied Disciplines, 41*, 441–455.
Juvonen, J., Nishina, A., & Graham, S. (2006). Ethnic diversity and perceptions of safety in urban middle schools. *Psychological Science, 17*, 393–400.
Killen, M., & Rutland, A. (2011). *Children and social exclusion: Morality, prejudice, and group identity*. New York: Wiley-Blackwell.
Levy, S. R., & Killen, M. (Eds.) (2008). *Intergroup attitudes and relations in childhood through adulthood*. New York: Oxford University Press.
Pettigrew, T. F., & Tropp, L. (2006). A meta-analytic test of intergroup contact theory. *Journal of Personality and Social Psychology, 90*, 751–783.
Rutland, A., Cameron, L., Milne, A., & McGeorge, P. (2005). Social norms and self-presentation: Children's implicit and explicit intergroup attitudes. *Child Development, 76*, 451–466.
Salmivalli, C., Lagerspetz, K., Björkqvist, K., Österman, K., & Kaukiainen, A. (1996). Bullying as a group process: Participant roles and their relations to social status within the group. *Aggressive Behavior, 22*, 1–15.
Simpson, E. H. (1949). Measurement of diversity. *Nature, 163*, 688.
Snijders, T. A. B., & Bosker, R. J. (1999). *Multilevel analysis. An introduction to basic and advanced multilevel modeling*. London, United Kingdom: Sage.

Stark, T. H. (2011). *Integration in schools: A process perspective on students' interethnic attitudes and interpersonal relationships*. Groningen, the Netherlands: ICS.
Tajfel, H., & Turner, J. C. (1979). An integrative theory of intergroup conflict. In W. G. Austin & S. Worchel (Eds.), *The social psychology of intergroup relations* (pp. 33–47). Monterey, CA: Brooks/Cole.
Thijs, J., & Verkuyten, M. (2012). Ethnic attitudes of minority students and their contact with majority group members. *Journal of Applied Developmental Psychology, 33*, 260–268.
Thijs, J., & Verkuyten, M. (2013). School ethnic diversity and students' interethnic relations. *British Journal of Educational Psychology*. Advanced online publication. doi:10.1111/bjep.12032.
Tropp, L., & Prenovost, M. A. (2008). The role of intergroup contact in predicting children's interethnic attitudes: Evidence from meta-analytic and field studies. In S. Levy & M. Killen (Eds.), *Intergroup attitudes and relations in childhood through adulthood: An integrative developmental and social psychological perspective*. Oxford: Oxford University Press.
Verkuyten, M., & Thijs, J. (2002). Racist victimization among children in the Netherlands: The effect of ethnic group and school. *Ethnic and Racial Studies, 25*, 310–331.
Verkuyten, M., & Thijs, J. (2006). Ethnic discrimination and global self-worth in early adolescents: The mediating role of ethnic self-esteem. *International Journal of Behavioral Development, 30*, 107.
Verkuyten, M., & Thijs, J. (2013). Multicultural education and ethnic attitudes: An intergroup perspective. *European Psychologist, 18*, 179–190.
Vervoort, M. H. M., Scholte, R. H. J., & Overbeek, G. (2010). Bullying and victimization among adolescents: The role of ethnicity and ethnic composition of school class. *Journal of Youth and Adolescence, 39*, 1–11.
Vervoort, M. H. M., Scholte, R. H. J., & Scheepers, P. L. H. (2011). Ethnic composition of school classes, majority–minority friendships, and adolescents' intergroup attitudes in the Netherlands. *Journal of Adolescence, 34*, 257–267.
Wagner, U., Christ, O., & Pettigrew, T. F. (2008). Prejudice and group-related behavior in Germany. *Journal of Social Issues, 64*, 403–416.
Wagner, U., Christ, O., Pettigrew, T. F., Stellmacher, J., & Wolf, C. (2006). Prejudice and minority proportion: Contact instead of threat effects. *Social Psychological Quarterly, 69*, 380–390.
Wolke, D., Woods, S., Stanford, K., & Schulz, H. (2001). Bullying and victimization of primary school children in England and Germany: Prevalence and school factors. *British Journal of Psychology, 92*, 673–696.

JOCHEM THIJS is an assistant professor at the Faculty of Social and Behavioural Sciences, Utrecht University and researcher at the European Research Centre on Migration and Ethnic relations (ERCOMER) at Utrecht University. His research interests include (ethnic) relations in educational contexts, and educational adjustments of ethnic minority children.

MAYKEL VERKUYTEN is a professor at the Faculty of Social and Behavioural Sciences, Utrecht University and Academic Director of the European Research Centre on Migration and Ethnic relations (ERCOMER) at Utrecht University. He has research interests in racism, discrimination, and ethnic relations.

MALIN GRUNDEL finished the research master *Migration, Ethnic Relations and Multiculturalism* (MERM) at the Graduate School of Social and Behavioural Sciences of Utrecht University. She is currently a PhD researcher at Erasmus University Rotterdam, and interested in citizenship education, ethnic diversity, and social cohesion.

How Peer Norms of Inclusion and Exclusion Predict Children's Interest in Cross-Ethnic Friendships

Linda R. Tropp*, Thomas C. O'Brien, and Katya Migacheva
University of Massachusetts Amherst

The present research examines how perceived inclusive and exclusive peer norms for cross-ethnic relations contribute to predicting interest in cross-ethnic friendship among ethnic minority and majority children. Across two survey studies, European American and African American children (Study 1) and European American and Latino American children (Study 2) reported on the extent to which they perceived inclusive and exclusive peer norms for cross-ethnic relations, as well as their own interest in developing cross-ethnic friendships. Results from both studies showed that perceiving inclusive norms for cross-ethnic relations from in-group peers uniquely predicted children's interest in cross-group friendships, beyond what can be accounted for by perceiving exclusive norms from in-group peers and preexisting cross-group friendships. Similar effects were observed for ethnic minority and majority children, and even after controlling for children's prior cross-group friendships. Implications of these findings for future research and efforts to promote inclusion among ethnic minority and majority children are discussed.

Greater diversity in school environments can provide new opportunities for children from different racial and ethnic groups to come into contact and develop friendships with each other (Moody, 2001). Yet even when children from different groups have opportunities to interact, this positive potential may be undermined by prevailing norms that highlight differences between groups and promote exclusion based on those differences (see Abrams & Rutland, 2008; Killen, Mulvey, & Hitti, 2013). Adding to the growing literature on developmental intergroup processes (Abrams & Killen, 2014), the present research examines how peer norms for

---

*Correspondence concerning this article should be addressed to Linda R. Tropp, Department of Psychology, University of Massachusetts Amherst, Amherst, MA 01060 [e-mail: tropp@psych.umass.edu].

cross-ethnic relations may enhance or inhibit children's interest in developing cross-ethnic friendships.

Consistent with a long tradition of research on intergroup contact (Pettigrew & Tropp, 2011), many studies now indicate that contact—and particularly cross-ethnic friendships—can predict positive intergroup attitudes among children and adolescents (Binder et al., 2009; Feddes, Noack, & Rutland, 2009; Levin, Van Laar, & Sidanius, 2003; Tropp & Prenovost, 2008). Although cross-ethnic friendships are known to be especially powerful forces for improving intergroup attitudes (Davies, Tropp, Aron, Pettigrew, & Wright, 2011), we know relatively little about psychological factors that are likely to contribute to the development of children's cross-ethnic friendships.

A considerable amount of research suggests that perceived peer norms can affect children's attitudes toward other ethnic groups and their cross-ethnic friendships. As children approach adolescence, they become more likely to interact in new settings and with members of different groups, which are likely to enhance the salience of ethnic group identities (Hughes, Way, & Rivas-Drake, 2011). Peers become especially important sources of social information as children grow into adolescence and begin to form attitudes toward and relations with cross-ethnic peers (McGlothlin, Edmonds, & Killen, 2008; Nesdale, 2004).

Recent research shows that children are sensitive to peer norms of inclusion or exclusion (Abrams, Rutland, & Cameron, 2003), and that expectations of loyalty to the in-group can influence the extent to which children's intergroup attitudes are biased toward the in-group (Abrams, 2011). However, most studies in this literature focus generally on how peer inclusion or exclusion affects children's intergroup attitudes (e.g., Nesdale, Griffith, Durkin, & Maass, 2005), rather than focusing more specifically on perceived peer norms for cross-ethnic relations.

The few studies that do focus on perceived peer norms for cross-ethnic relations tend to show that perceiving more supportive norms for cross-ethnic relations predict more positive intergroup attitudes (Feddes, Noack, & Rutland, 2009) and greater preferences for cross-ethnic friendship (Jugert, Noack, & Rutland, 2011). Still, perceiving inclusive norms that support cross-ethnic relations, or exclusive norms that may undermine them, tend not to be examined as independent predictors. Prior work in social psychology (Brewer, 1999) and developmental psychology (Aboud, 2003; Nesdale, 2004) indicate that favorability toward the in-group and derogation of the out-group often function as distinct processes. Research has yet to test (i) how inclusive and exclusive norms from in-group peers may both contribute to predicting children's interest in developing cross-ethnic friendships, and (ii) whether inclusive norms for cross-ethnic relations predict interest in cross-ethnic friendships beyond the role of exclusive norms.

Furthermore, most of the research conducted to date has focused on the perspectives of children from ethnic majority groups, rather than considering simultaneously the perspectives of both ethnic majority and minority groups.

Greater emphasis on the role of ethnic differences in children's peer relations is needed (Graham, Taylor, & Ho, 2009), as processes involved in friendship formation are often shaped by ethnic dynamics in diverse social environments (Bigler & Liben, 2007; Killen, Crystal, & Ruck, 2007). Consideration of ethnic differences is also critical because ethnic minority and majority youth may have different perceptions of cross-ethnic relations (Ancis, Sedlacek, & Mohr, 2000; Molina & Wittig, 2006), as well as different responses to cross-ethnic contact (Gómez, Tropp, & Fernandez, 2011; Tropp & Prenovost, 2008). Ethnic minority youth may also encounter prejudice and ethnic victimization that can negatively impact social relations in ways that differ from the common experiences of ethnic majority children (Quintana & McKown, 2008; Verkuyten, 2006).

Thus, integrating social and developmental perspectives, the present research extends prior work by examining how perceived inclusive and exclusive peer norms for cross-ethnic inclusion may simultaneously contribute to predicting interest in cross-ethnic friendship among ethnic minority and majority children. Consistent with research suggesting the importance of supportive norms for cross-ethnic relations (e.g., Jugert et al., 2011), we expect that perceiving inclusive norms from in-group peers will predict children's greater interest in forming cross-group friendships. Further, we expect that inclusive peer norms for cross-ethnic relations will predict greater interest in cross-ethnic friendships beyond any effects of perceiving exclusive in-group peer norms or children's preexisting cross-group friendships. These issues were examined in two studies with middle school students who completed brief surveys individually in a classroom setting. In each study, children reported the extent to which they perceived peer norms indicating inclusion in cross-ethnic relations, and peer norms indicating exclusion in cross-ethnic relations, as well as their own interest in developing cross-ethnic friendships.

Study 1

Participants and Procedure

Participants were recruited from two largely racially homogeneous middle schools in New York City: European American children from a school in which only 7% of the student body was African American, and African American children from a school in which only 2% of the student body was European American. The racial backgrounds of participating children were determined through consultation with school staff and facilitators of a local program that brought children from the different schools and different racial backgrounds together. After obtaining parental consent, a total of 179 European Americans (85 boys and 93 girls), and 133 African Americans (59 boys and 50 girls, 24 did not report their sex) completed a brief survey in a classroom setting, as part of a larger study on children's intergroup attitudes and experiences. Participants' ages ranged from 9 to 12 among European American children ($M = 10.46$ years, $SD = 0.95$) and from 9 to 13 among African American children ($M = 10.43$ years, $SD = 1.09$).

In each school, and with a school staff member of the same racial background as the students, a European American researcher explained to the students that the purpose of the survey was to understand their experiences with different kinds of people. Students were informed that they should include no personally identifying information on the survey, that there were no right or wrong answers to any questions in the survey, and that their survey responses would be anonymous and confidential. The researcher also explained how to respond to the survey questions, with an unrelated sample question, to ensure that students understood how to complete the survey on their own. Upon completion, students placed their questionnaires into an envelope along with other completed surveys, to ensure the confidentiality and anonymity of their responses. Survey items were pilot tested with students from other middle schools in the northeastern United States, and a readability test (Flesch-Kincaid Reading Grade Level: 3.1) ensured that middle school students would readily understand the survey items.

Measures

Participants completed several single-item measures to represent the primary constructs of interest. Specifically, participants reported their perceptions of inclusive norms supporting cross-group relations from in-group peers by stating the extent to which friends from their racial group would accept children from the other racial group as friends (*How much would your friends in your racial group like to become friends with kids who are [White/Black]?*). Participants also reported their perceptions of exclusive norms about cross-ethnic relations from in-group peers by stating the extent to which friends from their racial group made jokes at the expense of children from the other racial group (*How much do your friends in your racial group tell jokes about kids who are [White/Black]?*). These items were scored on a scale ranging from 1 (*Not at All*) to 5 (*Very Much*). The association between the inclusive and exclusive in-group peer norm items was nonsignificant among both European American participants ($r = -.09$, $p > .05$) and African American participants ($r = .08$, $p > .05$); thus, these items were treated as separate, single-item measures in the subsequent data analyses.

Participants responded to a separate item concerning their own interest in forming cross-group friendships (*How much would you like to become friends with kids who are [White/Black]?*), scored on a scale ranging from 1 (Not at All) to 5 (Very Much). In addition, participants reported their prior cross-group friendship experiences (*How many of your close friends are kids who are [White/Black]?*), on a scale ranging from 1 (*None at All*) to 5 (*Very Many*). This latter item was included to statistically control for the effects of prior cross-group friendship experience

Table 1. Correlations among Variables for European American and African American Children (Study 1)

	1	2	3	4
1. Interest in cross-group friendship	–	0.33**	0.62**	0.03
2. Prior cross-group friendships	0.35**	–	0.42**	–0.02
3. Inclusive in-group peer norms	0.67**	0.38**	–	0.08
4. Exclusive in-group peer norms	–0.05	0.09	–0.09	–

Note. Correlations for European American children appear below the diagonal, and correlations for African American children appear above the diagonal. $*p < .05$; $**p < .01$; and $***p < .001$.

when examining relationships between perceived norms from in-group peers and reported interest in forming cross-group friendships.

Results

Preliminary analyses revealed that European American children reported greater interest in forming cross-group friendships ($M = 4.31$, $SD = 0.88$) than African American children ($M = 3.53$, $SD = 1.37$), $t(258) = 5.46$, $p < .001$. European American children also reported greater perceptions of inclusive in-group norms ($M = 4.09$, $SD = 0.95$) than African American children ($M = 3.20$, $SD = 1.40$), $t(260) = 6.08$, $p < .001$, as well as lower perceptions of exclusive in-group norms ($M = 1.87$, $SD = 1.26$) compared to African American children ($M = 2.22$, $SD = 1.43$), $t(301) = -2.26$, $p = .03$. At the same time, European American and African American children reported similar numbers of cross-group friends ($M = 2.76$, $SD = 1.14$ and $M = 2.67$, $SD = 1.47$, respectively), $t(260) = 0.552$, $p = .58$.

Correlations. Correlations among the variables were conducted independently for European American and African American children and are provided in Table 1. Both inclusive in-group norms and prior cross-group friendships correlated positively and significantly with interest in cross-group friendships among European American and African American children. However, exclusive in-group norms did not significantly relate to interest in cross-group friendships among European American or African American children.

Regression analysis. Using centered variables (Aiken & West, 1991), we conducted a hierarchical regression analysis to predict children's interest in forming cross-group friendships (Table 2). We entered participants' prior cross-group friendships, their ethnic group membership, and inclusive and exclusive in-group norms as predictors at Step 1. We included the two-way interaction terms between inclusive and exclusive in-group norms and ethnic group membership at

Table 2. Summary of Hierarchical Regression Analysis Predicting Interest in Cross-Group Friendship (Study 1)

	Step 1			Step 2		
Predictor variables	B	SE	β	B	SE	β
Prior cross-group friendships	0.08˙	0.04	0.09˙	0.07	0.05	−.08
Ethnic group	−0.18	0.12	−0.08	−0.26	0.39	−0.11
Inclusive in-group norms	0.58***	0.05	0.62***	0.55***	0.09	0.60***
Exclusive in-group norms	−0.01	0.04	−0.02	−0.10	0.12	−0.12
Ethnic group × inclusive in-group norms				−0.04	0.09	−0.05
Ethnic group × exclusive in-group norms				0.09	0.08	0.10
Inclusive × exclusive in-group norms				0.02	0.03	0.10
R^2		0.48***			0.48***	
R^2 change		0.48***			>0.01	
F change		57.37***			0.59	

Note. B = raw regression coefficient; SE = standard error; β = standardized regression coefficient. For the ethnic group variable, "European American" was coded as "0" and "African American" was coded as "1". ˙$p < .10$; *$p < .05$; **$p < .01$; and ***$p < .001$.

Step 2, to see whether interactions among these variables would predict interest in cross-group friendships beyond what could be predicted at the first step of the analysis.

At the first step of analysis, inclusive in-group norms emerged as a strong predictor of interest, $B = 0.59, SE = 0.05, β = 0.62, t(252) = 11.59, p < .001$, such that perceiving more inclusive in-group norms supporting cross-group relations predicted children's greater interest in forming cross-group friendships. This effect was obtained while controlling for children's prior cross-group friendships, which only marginally predicted children's interest. At the same time, exclusive in-group norms did not significantly predict children's interest in forming cross-group friendships, $B = -0.01, SE = 0.04, β = -0.02, t(252) = -0.37, p = .71$, beyond what could be predicted by their perceptions of inclusive in-group norms. At the second step of analysis, inclusive in-group norms remained a significant predict of children's interest in cross-group friendship, and none of the two-way interaction terms qualified this effect, βs ranging from −0.05 to 0.10, $p > .20$.

Discussion

As expected, results from this initial study suggest that perceived inclusive in-group norms supporting cross-group friendships are especially important for predicting children's own interest in forming cross-group friendships. Lending further support for our predictions, we observed similar patterns of effects among samples of European American and African American children, and we observed these effects even after controlling for children's prior cross-group friendships. As such, it appears that perceiving inclusive norms from in-group peers can meaningfully contribute to enhancing children's interest in cross-group friendships.

Nonetheless, a clear limitation of this initial study is that only single-item indicators were available in the data set to test the relationships of interest. A primary goal of our second study is, therefore, to determine whether these patterns of effects can be replicated using reliable, multi-item indicators of the relevant constructs. A second goal of our next study was to test whether we might observe similar patterns of effects among ethnic minority and majority youth in a different intergroup context. Patterns of friendship preferences may vary among children in ethnically homogenous and heterogeneous schools (see McGlothlin et al., 2008). Some work also suggests that while African American and Latino American adolescents may be affected by perceived discrimination in many similar ways (Benner & Graham, 2011), they may also be socialized to have different expectations for inclusion or exclusion in their social environments (Hughes et al., 2008). Thus, we conducted a second study with European American and Latino American children in more ethnically mixed school environments.

Study 2

Participants and Procedure

Participants were recruited from 63 6th and 7th grade classrooms in three public middle schools in Western Massachusetts. These schools were selected because the student populations included mostly European American and Latino American children (56% and 36%, 68% and 24%, 69% and 22% for each of the three schools, respectively), with relatively small numbers of children from other ethnic backgrounds (5–6%) or of mixed heritage (2–3%).

Upon arriving in each classroom, members of a multi-ethnic research team explained that the survey was about "why kids become friends with other kids." Using procedures similar to those in Study 1, a member of the research team explained how to respond to questions in the survey, and students were informed that there were no right or wrong answers to any questions in the survey, and that their responses would be confidential. To determine their racial and ethnic background, children were asked to respond to the following question: *"If you had to describe your race using the following words, would you say that you are..."* and they were welcome to check any combination of the following responses: White, Latino, Black, Asian, and/or Other (with additional space provided to write a more detailed response).

A total of 468 children who identified only as European American (208 boys and 260 girls) and 126 children who identified only as Latino American (60 boys and 66 girls) took part in the study. Some indicated a more specific ethnic heritage or country of family origin. European origins, such as "Italian" or "Poland", were classified as "European American", whereas Latin American origins, such as "Mexican" or "El Salvador", were classified as "Latino American." Students of mixed heritage were excluded from this analysis. Responses from 17 participants (12 European American, 5 Latino American) were omitted from analyses due to missing data on one of the predictor or outcome variables. After obtaining parental consent and indicating their own willingness to participate, the children completed brief surveys individually in a classroom setting, as part of a larger study on children's cross-group friendships. Participants' ages ranged from 9 to 13 among European American students ($M = 11.66$ years, $SD = 0.66$) and from 10 to 14 among Latino American students ($M = 11.68$ years, $SD = 0.76$).

Measures

Participants completed several multi-item measures to represent the primary constructs of interest. Responses were scored on a 5-point scale, from 1 (*Not at All*) to 5 (*Very Much*).

Inclusive and exclusive in-group norms. Four items assessed children's perceptions of inclusive norms from in-group peers supporting cross-group relations (Kids from my racial group want to be friends with kids from other racial groups, Kids from my racial group would be happy if I became friends with kids from other races, Kids from my racial group encourage me to make friends with kids from other races, Kids from my racial group like it when I "hang out" with kids from other races). Two items assessed children's perceptions of negative norms from in-group peers concerning cross-group relations (Kids from my racial group sometimes make jokes about kids from other races, Kids from my racial group sometimes tease kids from other races).

Principal components analyses with oblique rotation showed that only two components emerged with eigenvalues greater than 1. The four inclusive norm items all loaded onto a first component (loadings from 0.80 to 0.87 for European Americans, 0.88 to 0.93 for Latino Americans) and the two exclusive norm items loaded onto a second component (loadings from 0.92 to 0.93 for European Americans, 0.93 to 0.93 for Latino Americans). Alpha coefficients of reliability were sufficiently high for the four-item inclusive in-group norm measure ($\alpha = 0.87$ for European Americans, $\alpha = 0.92$ for Latino Americans) and for the two-item exclusive in-group norm measure ($\alpha = 0.83$ for European Americans, $\alpha = 0.84$ for Latino Americans).

Interest in cross-group friendship. Three items assessed participants' own interest in forming cross-group friendships, using the same item stem ("*In general, how much would you like to become friends with ..."*). European American children completed three versions of this item in relation to *"kids who are Latino/Black/Asian"* and responses to these items were averaged ($\alpha = 0.90$). Latino American children completed three versions of this item in relation to *"kids who are White/Black/Asian"* and responses to these items were averaged ($\alpha = 0.87$).

Prior cross-group friendship. In addition, participants reported on their preexisting cross-group friendships in response to two items asking about the number of children from different groups in their friendship circles "before coming to middle school" and those in their "circle of friends right now." European American children completed three versions of each item in relation to Latino, Black, and Asian children, and responses to these items were averaged ($\alpha = 0.75$). Similarly, Latino American children completed three versions of each item in relation to White, Black, and Asian children, and responses to these items were averaged ($\alpha = 0.75$).

Results

Initial analyses showed that European American and Latino American children reported similar levels of interest in intergroup contact ($M = 3.81$, $SD = 1.13$ and $M = 3.68$, $SD = 1.15$, respectively), $t(575) = 1.05$, $p = .29$, as well as similar perceptions of inclusive in-group norms ($M = 3.82$, $SD = 0.89$ and $M = 3.78$, $SD = 1.15$, respectively), $t(575) = 0.44$, $p = .66$. At the same time, Latino American children reported significantly greater numbers of cross-group friends ($M = 2.45$, $SD = 0.73$) than European American children ($M = 2.07$, $SD = 0.69$), $t(575) = -5.32$, $p < .001$. Latino American children also perceived significantly more exclusive in-group norms ($M = 2.40$, $SD = 1.35$) than European American children ($M = 2.12$, $SD = 1.19$), $t(575) = -2.26$, $p = .02$.

Correlations. Correlations among the variables were conducted independently for European American and Latino American children and are provided in Table 3. As in Study 1, both inclusive in-group norms and prior cross-group friendships correlated positively and significantly with interest in cross-group friendships among European American and Latino American children. However, exclusive in-group norms showed only a modest, negative correlation with interest in cross-group friendships among European American children, $r(454) = -.11$, $p = .02$, and exclusive in-group norms was not significantly related to interest in cross-group friendships among Latino American children $r(119) = -.10$, $p = .27$.

Regression analysis. As in Study 1, we conducted a hierarchical regression analysis to predict children's interest in forming cross-group friendships (see Table 4). We entered participants' prior cross-group friendships, their ethnic group

Table 3. Correlations among Variables for European American and Latino American Children (Study 2)

	1	2	3	4
1. Interest in cross-group friendship	–	0.41**	0.39***	–0.10
2. Prior cross-group friendships	0.34***	–	0.39***	–0.06
3. Inclusive in-group peer norms	0.37***	0.30***	–	–0.25**
4. Exclusive in-group peer norms	–0.11*	0.04	–0.25***	–

Note. Correlations for European American children appear below the diagonal, and correlations for Latino American children appear above the diagonal. $*p < .05$; $**p < .01$; and $***p < .001$.

Table 4. Summary of Hierarchical Regression Analysis Predicting Interest in Cross-Group Friendship (Study 2)

	Step 1			Step 2		
Predictor variables	B	SE	β	B	SE	β
Prior cross-group friendships	0.44***	0.07	0.27***	0.44***	0.07	0.27***
Ethnic group	–0.26*	0.11	–0.09*	–0.28*	0.48	–0.10*
Inclusive in-group norms	0.32***	0.05	0.27***	0.36***	0.10	0.30***
Exclusive in-group norms	–0.04	0.04	–0.05	–0.06	0.14	–0.06
Ethnic group × inclusive in-group norms				–0.06	0.10	–0.03
Ethnic group × exclusive in-group norms				0.04	0.08	0.02
Inclusive × exclusive in-group norms				–0.09**	0.04	–0.10**
R^2		0.20***			0.21***	
R^2 Change		0.20***			0.01*	
F Change		35.91***			2.64*	

Note. B = raw regression coefficient; SE = standard error; β = standardized regression coefficient. For the ethnic group variable, "European American" was coded as "0" and "Latino American" was coded as "1". $*p < .05$; $**p < .01$; and $***p < .001$.

membership, and inclusive and exclusive in-group norms as predictors at Step 1. We then included the two-way interaction terms between inclusive and exclusive in-group norms and ethnic group membership at Step 2, to see whether interactions among these variables would predict interest in cross-group friendships beyond what could be predicted at the first step of the analysis.

At the first step of analysis, inclusive in-group norms emerged as a significant predictor of interest, $B = 0.32$, $SE = 0.05$, $\beta = 0.27$, $t(572) = 6.59$, $p < .001$, such that perceiving more inclusive in-group norms supporting cross-group relations predicted children's greater interest in forming cross-group friendships. This effect was obtained while controlling for children's prior cross-group friendships and ethnic group membership, both of which also predicted children's interest, $B = 0.44$, $SE = 0.07$, $\beta = 0.27$, $t(572) = 6.72$, $p < .001$ and $B = -0.26$, $SE = 0.11$,

$\beta = -0.09$, $t(572) = -2.44$, $p = .02$. At the same time, exclusive in-group norms did not significantly predict children's interest in forming cross-group friendships, $B = -0.04$, $SE = 0.04$, $\beta = -0.05$, $t(572) = -1.15$, $p = .25$, beyond what could be predicted by their perceptions of inclusive in-group norms, prior cross-group friendships, and ethnic group membership. At the second step of analysis, inclusive in-group norms remained a significant predictor of children's interest in cross-group friendship. However, this effect was qualified by a significant interaction between inclusive in-group norms and exclusive in-group norms, $B = -0.09$, $SE = 0.04$, $\beta = -0.10$, $t(569) = -2.64$, $p = .01$, which contributed significantly to the overall proportion of variance accounted for in the analysis, $R^2_{change} = 0.01$, $F_{change} = 2.64$, $p = .05$. More inclusive in-group norms generally predict greater interest in cross-group friendship, yet this effect is somewhat stronger when exclusive in-group norms are low as compared to when exclusive in-group norms are high.

Discussion

Consistent with the findings of Study 1, results from Study 2 suggest that perceived inclusive in-group norms supporting cross-group friendships are particularly useful for predicting children's own interest in forming cross-group friendships. Perceiving inclusive in-group norms predicted interest in cross-group friendship, beyond what could be predicted by exclusive in-group norms and children's preexisting cross-group friendships. Similar patterns of effects were observed among both European American and Latino American children. Unlike in Study 1, Study 2 showed a significant interaction between inclusive and exclusive in-group norms, such that inclusive in-group norms were especially predictive of interest when exclusive in-group norms were relatively low. Taken together, these findings suggest that inclusive peer norms are especially important for predicting children's interest in cross-group friendship, yet we must still attend to both inclusive and exclusive norms that may be operating in the social environment.

General Discussion

The present studies examined the extent to which perceiving inclusive and exclusive norms for cross-group relations from in-group peers could predict interest in cross-group friendship among ethnic minority and majority children. Results from these studies suggest that perceiving inclusive norms for cross-group relations from in-group peers are especially important for encouraging children's interest in cross-group friendships. In both studies, perceiving inclusive in-group norms uniquely predicted children's interest in cross-group friendships, beyond what could be accounted for by perceived exclusive in-group norms and children's preexisting cross-group friendships. Moreover, similar effects were observed among both ethnic minority and majority children across the two studies, and ethnic minority and majority children also reported mean levels of interest in cross-group friendship well above the midpoint on the scale. Together, these findings suggest that both ethnic minority and majority children may generally be willing to develop cross-group friendships, and especially the more they perceive their in-group peers to be supportive of such cross-group relations.

We also note that these relationships between perceived in-group norms and interest in cross-group friendship were observed through both correlation and regression analyses. Even when examined independently, perceiving exclusive in-group norms showed only modest correlations with interest, while perceiving inclusive in-group norms correlated positively and significantly with children's interest in forming cross-group friendships. Thus, perceiving in-group peers to be supportive of cross-group friendships may be more closely tied to children's intentions to form such friendships than perceiving that in-group peers tease or make jokes about children from other groups. This suggests that interventions should not merely aim to curb children's expressions of intergroup rejection and exclusion but also work to establish norms of inclusion and nurture interest in cross-group relations (see Tropp & Mallett, 2011).

At the same time, it should be noted that the inclusive and exclusive norm measures used in the present research assessed somewhat different dimensions of peer responses to cross-group relations. The inclusive norm items assessed perceptions of in-group peer support for cross-group friendships, whereas the exclusive norm items assessed perceptions of the extent to which in-group peers engaged in exclusionary behavior toward other groups. As such, the inclusive norms measure may have been more explicitly tied to children's reported interest in cross-group friendships than the exclusive norms measure, which would correspond to a stronger correlation between inclusive norms and interest than the correlation between exclusive norms and interest. Future research should explore whether different patterns of effects might be observed when different dimensions of inclusive and exclusive norms are used to predict children's interest in cross-group friendships. Additionally, the present research did not test the extent to which inclusive and exclusive norms contribute not only to interest in cross-group friendship, but the development of such friendships. Thus, further work is needed to test how these norms, as well as reported interest, eventually predict the development of actual cross-group friendships.

We also observed some differences in effects among ethnic majority and minority children across the two studies. For example, in Study 1, European American and African American children reported similar numbers of cross-group friendships, whereas European American children reported fewer cross-group friendships than Latino American children in Study 2. It is possible that these patterns are due to differences in the contexts in which the data were collected. Children in Study 1 were recruited from racially homogenous schools, likely with similar opportunities to develop cross-group friendships inside and outside of school; by contrast, European American children constituted greater proportions of the student populations in the schools we studied, such that Latino American children would likely have greater opportunities to forge cross-group friendships with European American children.

European American children also reported significantly greater interest in cross-group friendships than African American children in Study 1, while European American and Latino American children did not differ significantly in their reports of interest in Study 2. It is conceivable that European American children may have inflated their reports of interest in cross-group friendship to some degree, to minimize the possibility that they might be perceived as prejudiced (Bonilla-Silva, 2006; Devine & Vasquez, 1998). It is also possible that prior exposure to ethnic prejudice and discrimination may help to explain why African American children reported less interest in intergroup contact in Study 1 relative to their European American peers (Devine & Vasquez, 1998; Migacheva & Tropp, 2013; Tropp, 2006). Additionally, differences in perceptions of discrimination and socialization experiences among African American and Latino American youth may further explain why African American children reported significantly less interest in intergroup contact than European American children in Study 1, yet no significant difference in interest was observed among European American and Latino American children in Study 2 (see Graham et al., 2009). Nonetheless, even with such differences, the overall patterns of effects were quite similar across the two studies, suggesting the importance of inclusive in-group norms to promote interest in cross-ethnic friendships among ethnic majority and minority children.

Conclusions

Taken together, and complementing other recent work from a developmental intergroup perspective (Abrams & Rutland, 2008; Killen et al., 2013), these studies emphasize the role of peer norms for children's cross-ethnic relations and illuminate how inclusive peer norms may be especially important for encouraging the development of cross-ethnic friendships. Although further research is still needed, findings from these studies suggest that a greater focus on inclusive peer norms could augment efforts to improve intergroup relations among youth. Indeed, when inclusive norms are absent, people are often inclined to believe that they cannot trust members of other groups (e.g., Kramer & Wei, 1999), or to assume that members of other groups lack interest in cross-ethnic relations (e.g., Shelton & Richeson, 2005). Nonetheless, people's own attitudes toward cross-ethnic relations are often more positive than what they perceive among members of their own groups or other groups (Tropp & Bianchi, 2006).

Additionally, extensive research has concentrated on the ways in which peer norms can have detrimental influences on youth (Prinstein & Dodge, 2008), yet peer norms can also exert many positive influences on youth attitudes and behavior (Allen & Antonishak, 2008). Recent studies show that when youth encounter ingroup norms that support cross-ethnic relations, they themselves report greater openness to cross-ethnic relations and interest in contact with other groups (e.g., Gómez et al., 2011). Future studies and interventions should therefore grant greater attention to the establishment of inclusive peer norms among youth, in order to facilitate positive cross-ethnic relations and the development of cross-ethnic friendships.

References

Aboud, F. E. (2003). The formation of in-group favoritism and out-group prejudice in young children: Are they distinct attitudes? *Developmental Psychology, 39*, 48–60.

Abrams, D. (2011). Wherein lies children's intergroup bias? Egocentrism, social understanding, and social projection. *Child Development, 82*, 1579–1593.

Abrams, D., & Killen, M. (2014). Social exclusion of children: Developmental origins of prejudice. *Journal of Social Issues, 70*(1), 1–11.

Abrams, D., & Rutland, A. (2008). The development of subjective group dynamics. In S. Levy & M. Killen (Eds.), *Intergroup attitudes and relations in childhood through adulthood* (pp. 47–65). Oxford: Oxford University Press.

Abrams, D., Rutland, A., & Cameron, L. (2003). The development of subjective group dynamics: Children's judgments of normative and deviant ingroup and outgroup individuals. *Child Development, 74*, 1840–1856.

Aiken, L. S., & West, S. G. (1991). *Multiple regression: Testing and interpreting interactions*. Newbury Park: Sage.

Allen, J. P., & Antonishak, J. (2008). Adolescent peer influences: Beyond the dark side. In M. J. Prinstein & K. A. Dodge (Eds.), *Understanding peer influence in children and adolescents* (pp. 141–160). New York: Guilford Press.

Ancis, J. R., Sedlacek, W. E., & Mohr, J. J. (2000). Student perceptions of campus cultural climate by race. *Journal of Counseling and Development, 78*, 180–185.

Benner, A., & Graham, S. (2011). Latino adolescents' experiences of discrimination across the first 2 years of high school: Correlates and influences on educational outcomes. *Child Development, 82*, 508–519.

Bigler, R. S., & Liben, L. S. (2007). Developmental intergroup theory: Explaining and reducing children's social stereotyping and prejudice. *Current Directions in Psychological Science, 16,* 162–166.

Binder, J., Zagefka, H., Brown, R., Funke, F., Kessler, T., Mummendey, A., Maquil, A., Demoulin, S., & Leyens, J.-P. (2009). Does contact reduce prejudice or does prejudice reduce contact? A longitudinal test of the contact hypothesis amongst majority and minority groups in three European countries. *Journal of Personality and Social Psychology, 96*, 843–856.

Bonilla-Silva, E. (2006). *Racism without racists: Color-blind racism and the persistence of racial inequality in America*. Lanham, MD: Rowman & Littlefield.

Brewer, M. B. (1999). The psychology of prejudice: Ingroup love or outgroup hate? *Journal of Social Issues, 55*, 429–444. doi: 10.1111/0022-4537.00126

Davies, K., Tropp, L. R., Aron, A., Pettigrew, T. F., & Wright, S. C. (2011). Cross-group friendships and intergroup attitudes: A meta-analytic review. *Personality and Social Psychology Review*, 332–351.

Devine, P. G., & Vasquez, K. A. (1998). The rocky road to positive intergroup relations. In J. L. Eberhardt & S. T. Fiske (Eds.), *Confronting racism: The problem and the response* (pp. 234–262). Thousand Oaks, CA: Sage.

Feddes, A. R., Noack, P., & Rutland, A. (2009). Direct and extended friendship effects on minority and majority children's interethnic attitudes: A longitudinal study. *Child Development, 80*, 377–390.

Gómez, A., Tropp, L. R., & Fernández, S. (2011). When extended contact opens the door to future contact. *Group Processes and Intergroup Relations, 14*, 161–173.

Graham, S., Taylor, A., & Ho, A. (2009). Race and ethnicity in peer relations research. In K. H. Rubin, W. M. Bukowski, & B. Laursen (Eds.), *Handbook of peer interactions, relationships, and groups* (pp. 394–413). New York: Guilford.

Hughes, D., Rivas, D., Foust, M., Hagelskamp, C., Gersick, S., & Way, N. (2008). How to catch a moonbeam: A mixed-methods approach to understanding ethnic socialization processes in ethnically diverse families. In S. M. Quintana & C. McKown (Eds.), *Handbook of race, racism, and the developing child* (pp. 226–277). Hoboken, NJ: Wiley.

Hughes, D., Way, N., & Rivas-Drake, D. (2011). Stability and change in private and public ethnic regard among African American, Puerto Rican, Dominican, and Chinese American early adolescents. *Journal of Research on Adolescence, 21*, 861–870.

Jugert, P., Noack, P., & Rutland, A. (2011). Friendship preferences among German and Turkish preadolescents. *Child Development, 82*, 812–829.

Killen, M., Crystal, D., & Ruck, M. (2007). The social developmental benefits of intergroup contact for children and adolescents. In E. Frankenberg & G. Orfield (Eds.), *Lessons in integration: Realizing the promise of racial diversity in American schools* (pp. 57–73). Charlottesville, VA: University of Virginia Press.

Killen, M., Mulvey, K. L., & Hitti, A. (2013). Social exclusion in childhood: A developmental intergroup perspective. *Child Development, 84*, 772–790.

Kramer, R. M., & Wei, J. (1999). Social uncertainty and the problem of trust in social groups: The social self in doubt. In T. R. Tyler, R. M. Kramer, & O. P. John (Eds.), *The psychology of the social self* (pp. 145–168). Mahwah, NJ: Erlbaum.

Levin, S., Van Laar, C., & Sidanius, J. (2003). The effects of ingroup and outgroup friendship on ethnic attitudes in college: A longitudinal study. *Group Processes and Intergroup Relations, 6*, 76–92.

McGlothlin, H., Edmonds, C., & Killen, M. (2008). Children's and adolescents' decision-making about intergroup peer relationships. In S. M. Quintana & C. McKown (Eds.), *Handbook of race, racism, and the developing child* (pp. 424–451). Hoboken, NJ: Wiley.

Migacheva, K., & Tropp, L. R. (2013). Learning orientation as a predictor of positive intergroup contact. *Group Processes and Intergroup Relations, 16*, 426–444.

Molina, L. E., & Wittig, M. A. (2006). Relative importance of contact conditions in explaining prejudice reduction in a classroom context. Separate and equal? *Journal of Social Issues, 62*, 489–509. doi: 10.1111/j.1540-4560.2006.00470.x

Moody, J. (2001). Race, school integration, and friendship segregation in America. *American Journal of Sociology, 107*, 679–716.

Nesdale, D. (2004). Social identity processes and children's ethnic prejudice. In M. Bennett & F. Sani (Eds.), *Development of the social self* (pp. 219–246). East Sussex: Psychology Press.

Nesdale, D., Griffiths, J., Durkin, K., & Maass, A. (2005). Empathy, group norms, and children's ethnic attitudes. *Journal of Applied Developmental Psychology, 26*, 623–637.

Pettigrew, T. F., & Tropp, L. R. (2011). *When groups meet: The dynamics of intergroup contact*. New York: Psychology Press.

Prinstein, M. J., & Dodge, K. A. (2008). Current issues in peer influence research. In M. J. Prinstein & K. A. Dodge (Eds.), *Understanding peer influence in children and adolescents* (pp. 3–13). New York: Guilford.

Quintana, S., & McKown, C. (2008). (Eds.). *Handbook of race, racism, and the developing child*. Hoboken, NJ: Wiley.

Shelton, J. N., & Richeson, J. A. (2005). Intergroup contact and pluralistic ignorance. *Journal of Personality and Social Psychology, 88*, 91–107.

Tropp, L. R. (2006). Stigma and intergroup contact among members of minority and majority status groups. In S. Levin & C. van Laar (Eds.), *Stigma and group inequality: Social psychological perspectives* (pp. 171–191). Mahwah, NJ: Erlbaum.

Tropp, L. R., & Bianchi, R. A. (2006). Valuing diversity and interest in intergroup contact. *Journal of Social Issues, 62*, 533–551. doi: 10.1111/j.1540-4560.2006.00572.x

Tropp, L. R., & Mallett, R. K. (2011). Charting new pathways to positive intergroup relations. In L. R. Tropp & R. K. Mallett (Eds.), *Moving beyond prejudice reduction: Pathways to positive intergroup relations* (pp. 3–17). Washington, DC: American Psychological Association.

Tropp, L. R., & Prenovost, M. (2008). The role of intergroup contact in predicting interethnic attitudes: Evidence from meta-analytic and field studies. In S. Levy and M. Killen (Eds.), *Intergroup attitudes and relations in childhood through adulthood* (pp. 236–248). Oxford: Oxford University Press.

Verkuyten, M. (2006). Ethnic peer victimization and psychological well-being among early adolescents. In X. Chen, D. C. French, & B. H. Schneider (Eds.), *Peer relationships in cultural context* (pp. 339–363). New York: Cambridge University Press.

LINDA R. TROPP is Professor of Psychology and Director of the Psychology of Peace and Violence Program at the University of Massachusetts Amherst. Her research concerns how members of different groups approach and experience contact with each other, and how group differences in status affect cross-group relations. She is co-author of *When Groups Meet: The Dynamics of Intergroup Contact* (2011, Psychology Press), editor of the *Oxford Handbook of Intergroup Conflict* (2012, Oxford University Press), and co-editor of *Moving Beyond Prejudice Reduction: Pathways to Positive Intergroup Relations* (2011, APA Books) and *Improving Intergroup Relations* (2008, Wiley-Blackwell).

THOMAS C. O'BRIEN is a graduate student in Social Psychology and in the Psychology of Peace and Violence Program at the University of Massachusetts Amherst. He graduated from Washington University in St. Louis with an A.B. in Psychology and Jewish, Islamic & Near Eastern Studies. Before, he interned for the International Center for Journalists in Washington, DC, and later edited articles and worked in web metrics for the Trans Regional Web Initiative. His research focuses on intergroup relations, including intergroup contact and motivations for public support of foreign policies.

KATYA MIGACHEVA is a James Marshall Public Policy Fellow with the Society for Psychological Study of Social Issues and currently serves as a lead fellow for the Tom Lantos Human Rights Commission in the U.S. House of Representatives. In this capacity, Katya works to bring human rights violations to the attention of the U.S. Congress, and seeks ways to incorporate social psychological knowledge to promote policy and advocacy efforts. She completed her PhD in Social Psychology through the Psychology of Peace and Violence Program at the University of Massachusetts Amherst. Her research focuses on the facilitation of positive intergroup contact, as well as the psychological understanding of the consequences of drastic societal transformations on intergroup relations.

What Makes a Young Assertive Bystander? The Effect of Intergroup Contact, Empathy, Cultural Openness, and In-Group Bias on Assertive Bystander Intervention Intentions

Nicola Abbott[*] and Lindsey Cameron
School of Psychology, University of Kent

The present research tests the indirect effects of intergroup contact on adolescents' bystander intervention intentions via four potential mediators: "empathy," "cultural openness," "in-group bias," and "intergroup anxiety." British adolescents (N = 855), aged 11–13 years, completed measures of intergroup (interethnic) contact and the identified indirect variables. Intended bystander behavior was measured by presenting participants with an intergroup (immigrant) name-calling scenario. Participants rated the extent to which they would behave assertively. The findings extend previous intergroup contact research by showing a significant indirect effect of intergroup contact on assertive bystander intentions via empathy, cultural openness and in-group bias (but not via intergroup anxiety). Theoretical implications and practical suggestions for future prejudice-reduction interventions are discussed.

In U.K. schools, intergroup bullying, and particularly interracial bullying (e.g., name-calling) has reached alarming levels: recent figures show that between 2007 and 2011, nearly 88,000 racist incidents were recorded in British schools (Ofsted, 2012). The impact of such bullying can be devastating, for example, past research has shown that victims of bullying often experience social exclusion from school peers (Olweus, 1993; Perry, Kusel, & Perry, 1988). In turn, the psychological consequences of social exclusion are well documented, including detrimental effects on young people's academic performance, self-esteem, and pro-social behavior (Leary, 1990; Nansel et al., 2001; Twenge & Baumeister,

---

[*]Correspondence regarding this article should be addressed to Nicola Abbott, School of Psychology, University of Kent, Canterbury, Kent, CT2 7NP, United Kingdom [e-mail: nja8@kent.ac.uk].

2005). Recently, social developmental psychologists have highlighted the potential role that assertive peer bystanders can play in efforts to tackle intergroup bullying (Aboud & Joong, 2008). However, assertive intervention by peer bystanders during incidents of bullying is rare (Hawkins, Pepler, & Craig, 2001), and little is known about the predictors of assertive intervention when young people witness name-calling among their peers. Contributing to the emerging literature on developmental *intergroup* processes (Abrams & Killen, 2014) the current research examines whether young people intend to respond assertively when witnessing intergroup bullying, and potential underlying predictors derived from intergroup literature.

Social exclusion amongst young people encapsulates a variety of social behaviors, including bullying (Killen, 2007). Recently offensive *name-calling* has gained prominence as the most common form of bullying in schools (e.g., Smith & Shu, 2000) and *intergroup* name-calling has also been identified as the most common form of intergroup bullying (Verkuyten & Thijs, 2002). Importantly, intergroup name-calling can lead to both personal and intergroup damage: it causes public humiliation to the victim, but also serves to maintain group status and reinforce norms supporting stereotypes and prejudice (Aboud & Joong, 2008). With this in mind, the current research will focus on intergroup name-calling.

One intergroup context that may be particularly harmful is name-calling directed toward immigrants. Recent research found high levels social isolation amongst adolescent immigrants, with 1 in 5 reporting feeling like an outsider (Oxman-Martinez et al., 2012). Furthermore, adolescent immigrants' may be particularly sensitive to the detrimental effects of social exclusion, including anxiety and depression (McKenney, Pepler, Craig, & Connolly, 2006; Strohmeier, Kärnä, & Salmivalli, 2011). Arguably, when bullying is directed toward an individual's race or ethnicity, the psychological impact on the victim is greater as the attribution of the event is internal, stable and uncontrollable (McKenney et al., 2006). In light of these findings, the current research focuses on young people's intention to intervene in intergroup bullying situations where the victim is an immigrant.

Recently, social developmental psychologists (Aboud & Joong, 2008) and educational practitioners have highlighted the potential role that *assertive* peer bystanders can play in efforts to tackle intergroup name-calling. Assertive bystanders are onlookers who challenge bullies and comfort victims (Salmivalli, Lagerspetz, Björkqvist, Öösterman, & Kaukiainen, 1996). Importantly, peer bystanders have been found to be present in as many as 85% of bullying incidents (Atlas & Pepler, 1998; Craig & Pepler, 1995). However, assertive intervention by peer bystanders during incidents of bullying is rare (Hawkins et al., 2001), and little is known about the predictors of assertive intervention when young people witness name-calling among their peers. Assertive bystander behavior may be particularly effective for tackling intergroup name-calling as assertive bystanders have the potential to establish new social norms and intergroup attitudes of tolerance and acceptance (Aboud & Joong, 2008). This study builds on this previous research by examining assertive bystander intervention in an *intergroup* name-calling context, and by testing potential predictors of intended assertive bystander behavior derived from research on *intergroup relations*: intergroup contact and potential underlying mechanisms (empathy, cultural openness, in-group bias and intergroup anxiety).

Predictors of Assertive Bystander Intentions

Intergroup contact. This is defined as a meaningful interaction between members of different social groups (Allport, 1954). Over the past 60 years there has been considerable support for the success of intergroup contact in reducing prejudice, among both adults and young people (Cameron, Rutland, & Brown, 2007; Crisp & Turner, 2009; Pettigrew, Tropp, Wagner, & Christ, 2011; Tropp, O'Brien, & Migacheva, 2014); particularly when Allport's (1954) proposed facilitating conditions are met (such as equal status contact). A number of underlying mechanisms through which intergroup contact reduces prejudice have been identified, including greater empathy (Batson et al., 1997), greater cultural openness (Nesdale & Todd, 2000), lower in-group bias (Bettencourt, Brewer, Rogers-Croak, & Miller, 1992), and lower anxiety (Miller, 2002) which each, in turn, can generalize to more positive attitudes of the group as a whole.

To our knowledge, there has been no research to date examining the impact of intergroup contact on assertive bystander intentions in an intergroup name-calling incident. However, intergroup contact has been linked to greater intentions to engage positively with the out-group (Turner, West, & Christie, 2013), therefore, we argue that intergroup contact could also increase children's willingness to assist an immigrant victim. We also aim to shed light on whether the underlying mechanisms of the contact-attitude relationship also underlie the relationship between intergroup contact and assertive bystander intentions.

Empathy. This can be defined as "the ability to experience the same feelings as those of another person in response to a particular situation' (Nesdale, Griffiths, Durkin, & Maass, 2005, p. 624). Pettigrew and Tropp (2008) identified empathy as a strong positive mediator of the relationship between intergroup contact and intergroup attitudes. Empathy has also been linked with pro-social or helping behaviors (Eisenberg & Fabes, 1990) and more recently, defending victims of bullying (Caravita, Di Blasio, & Salmivalli, 2009; Gini, Albiero, Benelli, & Altoè, 2008). Therefore, we predict that greater intergroup contact will be associated with higher empathy, which in turn will be associated with greater assertive bystander intentions.

Cultural openness. This can be defined as the extent to which an individual is open to, and interested in, the similarities and differences between their own and other groups (Nesdale & Todd, 2000). Intergroup contact is thought to reduce ethnocentrism, which enhances openness to other groups (cultural openness) and positive intergroup attitudes (Drapela, 1975; Nesdale & Todd, 2000). The current research predicts that intergroup contact will be associated with greater cultural openness, which in turn will be associated with greater assertive bystander intentions.

In-group bias. This is defined as a strong favoritism toward members of an individual's own group, as opposed to members of other groups (Hewstone, Rubin, & Wills, 2002). Past research has connected intergroup contact with lower in-group bias (Bettencourt et al., 1992; Hewstone & Swart, 2011). Furthermore, in-group bias has been linked with intergroup helping behaviors (Dovidio, Piliavin, Gaertner, Schroeder, & Clark, 1991). Thus, we predict that greater intergroup contact will be associated with lower in-group bias, which will in turn be associated with greater assertive bystander intentions.

Intergroup anxiety. Finally, a key underlying mechanism that has been found to account for the positive impact of intergroup contact on reducing prejudice is intergroup anxiety (Pettigrew & Tropp, 2008). Under the right conditions, intergroup contact alleviates the initial anxiety that often accompanies an intergroup interaction (Blascovich, Mendes, Hunter, Lickel, & Kowai-Bell, 2001). Therefore, we predict that intergroup contact will be associated with lower intergroup anxiety, which in turn, will be associated with greater assertive bystander intentions.

Considering the past research demonstrating the importance of empathy, cultural openness, in-group bias and intergroup anxiety for intergroup attitudes, we examine each simultaneously as potential underlying mechanisms of the effect of intergroup contact on assertive bystander intentions. A multiple mediation analysis was conducted to determine the role of each of the proposed underlying mechanisms. This analysis allowed us to determine which effect could best account for a significant increase in assertive bystander intentions, controlling for each of the other proposed mediators. Our multiple mediation model predicted two positive and two negative indirect effects. We argue that intergroup contact will be associated with greater levels of empathy and cultural openness, which in turn will both be uniquely associated with *higher* levels of assertive bystander intentions. Whereas, intergroup contact will be associated with *lower* levels of in-group bias and intergroup anxiety, which in turn will be uniquely associated with greater assertive bystander intentions.

Method

Participants

Participants ($N = 902$, 341 males and 553 females) were recruited from 8 secondary schools in the South East of England. The majority (94.79%) of participants identified as native to the United Kingdom, and 5.21% as immigrants to the United Kingdom. As the focal out-group in this study was immigrants, all participants who were born outside of the United Kingdom were excluded from the analysis ($N = 47$) leaving 855 participants (327 males, 520 females and 8 who did not disclose their gender). The mean age of the sample was 12.4 years ($SD = 0.505$, range: 11–13 years). The ethnic composition comprised of 88.5% White British, 1.2% White Irish, 2.1% White other, 3.5% Mixed, 0.4% Black African, 0.2% Black other, 0.4% Asian, 0.5% Chinese, 0.8% Other, and 2.4% did not disclose their ethnicity.

Materials

Participants completed a questionnaire including all measures which will be outlined in this section. First, the demographic information (gender, age, ethnicity, and country of birth) of the participant was requested.

Intergroup contact. This measure was modified from Nigbur et al. (2008). Participants were asked about contact with Black and Minority Ethnic individuals (herein referred to as BME, a common term used in the United Kingdom). Due to the extremely low levels of contact with immigrants, a measure of direct contact with immigrants was not appropriate. Adolescents were asked about the level of contact they have with BME individuals in five contexts: neighborhood, school, class, friends and sports teams or clubs. For example, "in your neighborhood where you live, would you say there are...", followed by five response options (mainly black people and ethnic minority people, mostly black and ethnic minority people with some white people, about half and half, mostly white with some black and ethnic minority people, and finally mainly white people). A pictorial 5-point scale was also used to illustrate different ethnic proportions. Responses were coded so that a low score indicated low contact and a high score illustrated high contact. An average score across the five contexts was calculated (Cronbach's α coefficient 0.63).

Empathy. Ten items were selected from Bryant's (1982) Index of Empathy for Children and Adolescents. Participants responded on a scale from 1 (*not at all like me*) to 4 (*a lot like me*). All four reversed items were removed from the analysis due to low reliability, leaving six items (Cronbach's $\alpha = 0.80$). An average empathy score was calculated.

Cultural openness. This measure was derived from Black (1990). The wording of the items was modified from asking about "other cultures" to focusing on immigrants. For example, "do people from other countries who now live in the UK interest you?". Participants responded to five items on a 4-point scale from 1 (*not at all*) to 4 (*very much*). Analyses showed high internal reliability (Cronbach's $\alpha = 0.82$), a mean score was then calculated.

In-group bias. This was modified from Cameron, Rutland, and Brown (2007) to refer to immigrants as opposed to refugees. The measure consisted of five positive and five negative attributes: honest, friendly, hardworking, clever and clean, lazy, unintelligent, dirty, unfriendly and dishonest. The items were presented twice, to measure attitudes toward the in-group (*people born in the United Kingdom*) and the out-group (*people born in another country who now live in the United Kingdom*) separately. Participants were asked to indicate, on a 4-point scale, "How many of [these people] you think are..." followed by each attribute. Response options were: 1 (*All*), 2 (*Some*), 3 (*Most*), and 4 (*None*). All items were reverse scored. Cronbach's α analysis showed high internal reliability for out-group positive and negative scale items (0.85 and 0.84, respectively), and good internal reliability for in-group positive and negative scale items (0.64 and 0.65, respectively). A total score was computed for in-group positive attributes, out-group positive attributes, in-group negative attributes, and out-group attributes. A cumulative difference score was computed by subtracting the total out-group negative attribute score from the total in-group positive score. This difference score was then added to the difference score for the total in-group negative score subtracting the total out-group positive score.

Intergroup anxiety. Intergroup anxiety was measured using 10 items adapted from Stephan and Stephan's (1985) intergroup anxiety scale. The instructions for the measure were modified to focus on immigrants as the focal out-group: "If you were to meet someone who was born in another country and has moved to the United Kingdom in the future, how do you think you would feel?". Of the 10 items presented 7 were negative affect items (awkward, suspicious, embarrassed, defensive, anxious, careful, self-conscious) and 3 were positive (happy, comfortable confident). All responses were measured on a 5-point scale, from 1 (*not at all*) to 5 (*very much*). First, the 3 positive items were reverse scored. Analyses showed high internal reliability for intergroup anxiety (Cronbach's $\alpha = 0.77$), a composite mean score for intergroup anxiety was then calculated.

Assertive bystander intervention. This was adapted from a bystander measure created by Palmer and Cameron (2010). In the version used in this study the participant is presented with the following vignette of an immigrant name-calling incident: "Imagine that it is the end of the school day, and as you are walking down the corridor you hear someone (Person A) shout a rude word to someone else (Person B) because they are from another country and now live in the United Kingdom. What would you do?". Following the vignette participants are presented with four possible responses that are each a form of assertive bystander behavior. The four items were: *"I would try and make Person B feel better," "I would tell Person B to ignore Person A," "I would tell Person A not to say nasty things,"* and *"I would tell a teacher or member of staff."* Ten bystander responses were originally presented, with additional possible responses including ignoring, watching and joining in. The current research focuses on assertive bystander intentions only, therefore, only those bystander responses concerning assertive bystander behavior were included. A confirmatory factor analysis with varimax rotation showed that the four assertive bystander items did indeed load on one distinct factor [0.82, 0.77, 0.75, and 0.62, respectively], this also corresponds with the findings of Palmer and Cameron (2010). For each behavior, participants indicate how likely they are to behave in that way on a 3-point scale (1 *"I would not do this"*, 2 *"I might do this,"* and 3 *"I definitely would do this"*). Analyses showed high internal reliability for these assertive bystander behavior items (Cronbach's $\alpha = 0.77$), a composite mean score was then calculated.

Design

A multiple mediation bootstrap analysis (Preacher & Hayes, 2008) was used to test the indirect effect of intergroup contact on assertive bystander intentions via empathy, cultural openness, in-group bias and intergroup anxiety.

Results

A summary of descriptive statistics and a correlation matrix for the study variables are provided in Table 1.

Multiple Mediation Analysis Procedures

The proposed multiple mediation model was then tested using the Preacher and Hayes (2008) bootstrapping method for indirect effects. Bootstrapping is a nonparametric approach to hypothesis testing and effect-size estimation that is increasingly recommended for many types of analyses, including mediation (Derek, Rucker, Preacher, Tormala, & Petty, 2011; Hayes, 2009). Rather than making assumptions of the distribution of the data, bootstrapping generates an

Table 1. Means, Standard Deviations and Correlations Among Main Study Variables

	Variable[a]	Mean (SD)	1	2	3	4	5	6
1.	Intergroup contact	1.96 (0.44)	–	0.097**	0.258**	−0.112**	−0.098**	0.157**
2.	Empathy	2.76 (0.51)		–	0.411**	−0.193**	−0.174**	0.480**
3.	Cultural openness	2.46 (0.67)			–	−0.392**	−0.380**	0.541**
4.	In-group bias	1.37 (4.16)				–	0.263**	−0.337**
5.	Intergroup anxiety	2.48 (0.64)					–	−0.252**
6.	Assertive bystander intentions	2.09 (0.53)						–

Notes. Standard deviation in parenthesis. *$p < .05$ and **$p < .001$.
[a]Contact scores have a minimum of 1 and a maximum of 5 with higher scores indicating greater intergroup contact. Empathy and cultural openness scores have a minimum of 1 and a maximum of 4 with higher scores indicating greater empathy and cultural openness respectively. In-group bias scores have a minimum of −30 and a maximum of 30 with higher (positive) scores indicating greater bias in favor of the in-group, lower (negative) scores indicating greater bias in favor of the out-group. Intergroup anxiety scores have a minimum of 1 and a maximum of 5 with higher scores indicating greater intergroup anxiety. Assertive bystander intervention scores have a minimum of 1 and a maximum of 3 with a higher score indicating greater assertive bystander intervention intentions.

empirical approximation of the sampling distribution of a statistic by repeated random resampling (with replacement) from the available data. Bootstrapping uses this distribution to calculate p-values and construct confidence intervals (CIs). Furthermore, this statistical procedure provides superior CIs that are corrected for bias and accelerated (Efron & Tibshirani, 1993; Preacher & Hayes, 2008, for details).

This analysis was based on 5,000 bootstrap samples to describe the CIs of indirect effects. Interpretation of the bootstrap data is achieved by observing whether a zero is contained between either the 90% or 95% CIs, thus indicating a lack of significance. As argued by Hayes (2009), an indirect effect is estimated as significant from the CIs not containing a zero, as opposed to the individual paths. This is due to the overall mediation model not being pertinent on whether the individual paths are either significant or nonsignificant.

Furthermore, in accordance with new recommendations for mediation we reject the emphasis on the significance of a total (c) and direct effect (c', e.g., Derek et al., 2011; Hayes, 2009). An independent variable may exert a stronger influence on a mediator (path a) than on the dependent measure (path c), which could lead to a stronger indirect effect than total effect. Thus, the a-b path can be significant, even when the c path is not. In line with Derek et al. (2011), if theoretically driven indirect effects exist, these effects can be explored regardless of the significance of the total or direct effect. Notably, for this research, indirect effects that are in opposing directions can obscure the total effects, as they are potentially competing with each other (for example, the effect of empathy opposes that of in-group bias).

Table 2. Indirect Effects of Intergroup Contact on Intended Assertive Bystander Intentions through Empathy, Cultural Openness, In-Group Bias and Intergroup Anxiety, and Contrasts Between Proposed Mediators

Mediator	Bootstrap estimate	SE	BCa 95% CI lower	BCa 95% CI upper
	Indirect effects			
Empathy	0.0432	0.0168	0.0113	0.0775
Cultural openness	0.1125	0.0235	0.0688	0.1597
In-group bias	0.0199	0.0086	0.0063	0.0406
Intergroup anxiety	0.0032	0.0045	−0.0033	0.0155
	Contrasts			
Empathy vs. cultural openness	−0.0693	0.0206	−0.1143	−0.0319
Empathy vs. in group bias	0.0233	0.0158	−0.0063	0.0558
Empathy vs. intergroup anxiety	0.0400	0.0167	0.0095	0.0737
Cultural openness vs. in-group bias	0.0926	0.0221	0.0528	0.1383
Cultural openness vs. intergroup anxiety	0.1093	0.0238	0.0665	0.1591
In-group bias vs. intergroup anxiety	0.0167	0.0095	0.0014	0.0401

Note. CI = confidence interval. Based on 5,000 bootstrap samples.

Table 2 displays the bootstrapped estimates for the total and specific indirect effects obtained from the main analysis. In line with our predictions, the indirect effects of empathy, cultural openness and in-group bias were significant, as demonstrated by CIs that did not contain zero. Specifically, greater intergroup contact was related to higher levels of empathy, which in turn, was associated with greater assertive bystander intentions. Greater intergroup contact was also related to higher levels of cultural openness, which in turn, was associated with greater assertive bystander intentions. Additionally, intergroup contact was associated with lower levels of in-group bias, which in turn, was related to greater assertive bystander intentions (see Figure 1). Contrary to our predictions, the total indirect effect of intergroup contact on intended bystander behavior through intergroup anxiety was not statistically significant, as the CIs contained a zero.

Importantly, this analysis enables examination of each predictor whilst controlling for each other predictor. That is, a significant indirect effect of one predictor means it is statistically significant above and beyond the effects of the other predictors in the model. For example, empathy was found to have a significant unique indirect effect on assertive bystander intentions, whilst statistically controlling for cultural openness and in-group bias. Contrasting the three significant indirect effects revealed that the indirect effect via cultural openness was significantly stronger than the indirect effect via empathy (point estimate of contrast −0.0693, with a 95% CI of −0.1143, −0.0319). The indirect effect of cultural openness was

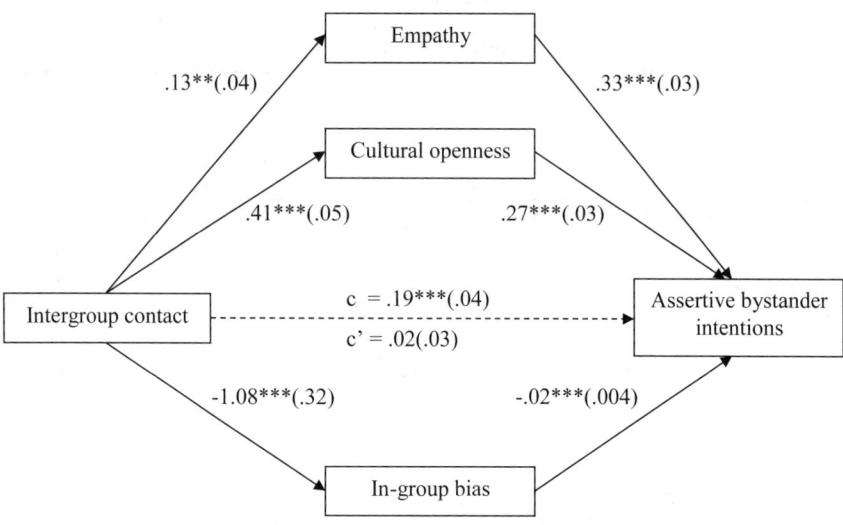

Fig. 1. A multiple mediation model of intergroup contact and assertive bystander intentions through empathy, cultural openness, and in-group bias. Unstandardized regression coefficients from a bootstrap procedure are provided along the paths. $*p < .05$; $**p < .01$; and $***p < .001$.

also significantly stronger than the indirect effect via in-group bias (point estimate of contrast 0.0926, with a 95% CI of 0.0528, 0.1383). The contrast between empathy and in-group bias revealed no significant difference (point estimate of contrast 0.0233, with a 95% CI of −0.0063, 0.0558).

In sum, regarding the strength of the predictors, the strongest indirect effect was found for cultural openness, which was stronger than both empathy and in-group bias. This was followed by the significant indirect effects of empathy and in-group bias (where no significantly stronger predictor was identified). Thus, both empathy and in-group bias each exert an indirect effect on assertive bystander intentions, over and above all other predictors, but neither was found to have a stronger indirect effect than the other.

Discussion

Past research has shown that victims of bullying are often excluded by their peers (Olweus, 1993) with immigrants identified as particularly vulnerable (McKenney et al., 2006). This study examined young people's assertive bystander intentions, and predictors of those intentions, in an intergroup (immigrant) name-calling situation.

By testing our model, we found that intergroup contact had an indirect effect on assertive bystander intentions via empathy, cultural openness and in-group bias. More specifically, greater intergroup contact was related to higher levels of empathy, higher levels of cultural openness and reduced intergroup bias, which in turn were associated with greater assertive bystander intentions. Contrary to our predictions, one potential mechanism, namely, intergroup anxiety was not a found to have a significant indirect effect. Interestingly, the effect of cultural openness was found to be significantly stronger than both empathy and in-group bias, thus we found it was the most important mechanism in fostering assertive bystander intentions.

The positive effect of cultural openness was in line with our predictions and previous research investigating the intergroup contact-prejudice relationship. Our findings suggest that intergroup contact influences assertive bystander intentions in the same way that it impacts attitudes: by reducing the individual's tendency toward ethnocentrism (Nesdale & Todd, 2000). Intergroup contact can promote a tendency to be open to other cultural groups, and to take an interest in the similarities and differences between the in-group and out-group, in turn, increasing assertive bystander intentions. Future research should examine more closely the particular aspects of cultural openness that predict assertive bystander intentions.

Past research illustrated a positive relationship between intergroup contact and empathy (Batson et al., 1997), and also between bystander empathy and defending behavior (Caravita et al., 2009; Gini et al., 2008). Consistent with these findings, we found that intergroup contact was linked to higher empathy, and in turn, greater assertive bystander intentions. Importantly, this study has combined the previously separate intergroup and bystander literature in relation to empathy, placing each into a model for assertive bystander intentions.

Finally, this study highlights the indirect effect of in-group bias, in that higher levels of intergroup contact were associated with lower levels of in-group bias, which in turn, was associated with higher intentions to intervene assertively. First, these findings are in line with intergroup contact theory which purports that in-group bias should decrease as a function of positive intergroup contact (Allport, 1954). Secondly, they concur with theory put forward by Dovidio et al. (1991), suggesting that lower in-group bias increases bystander arousal whilst simultaneously reducing the perceived costs of helping, resulting in greater helping behaviors, in this case assertive bystander intentions. Recently, Thijs, Verkuyten, and Grundel (2014) found ethnic in-group bias to moderate the effects of out-group contact on ethnic peer discrimination. Taken together with the current research, these findings suggest that both intergroup contact and in-group bias are crucial for promoting positive intergroup relations.

In general, cultural openness, empathy and in-group bias are all thought to impact helping behavior through valuing difference, or reducing perceived difference, in this case on an interpersonal level of contact. In addition to interpersonal contact, psychologists are beginning examine the effects of social categorization on promoting helping behavior by *altering the level of categorization that is most salient* (for review see Dovidio, Gaertner, Shnabel, Sagay, & Johnson, 2010). This is based on the idea of "we-ness' or a common in-group (a more inclusive in-group that consists of in-group and erstwhile out-group members), which is thought to be a potential avenue for reducing in-group bias and encouraging helping behavior (Gaertner & Dovidio, 2000). For example, if a school promotes a more inclusive common in-group, such as school membership, this could lead to greater pro-social and helping behavior across students. This is due to the common "school" in-group category becoming more salient than the other group categories, in this case categorization by ethnicity or country of origin. Thus, increasing the salience of a common in-group could also form the basis of future school-based interventions to promote assertive bystander intervention amongst students. Future research should examine how levels of categorization are linked with cultural openness, empathy and in-group bias, and how categorization could serve as a mechanism by which intergroup contact impacts on bystander behavior intentions.

Although the current research focuses on intergroup attitudes (such as in-group bias) as powerful forces in legitimizing intergroup social exclusion, there is also a moral component. Future research should examine moral reasoning, as the act to intervene assertively is relevant to moral development; in particular, the moral concepts of fairness and concern for another's welfare (Killen, 2007). We believe this to be fruitful area of future research, particularly as our research linked higher assertive bystander intention with higher levels of empathy. This finding could encompass a moral component, whereby greater assertive intentions resulted from a concern for another's welfare, comparable to the ability to experience the same feelings as another person (empathy). Furthermore, intergroup interactions can facilitate moral judgments by promoting perspective taking. Therefore, future research could further investigate our model of assertive bystander intervention, by examining moral reasoning alongside the indirect effect of empathy.

Contrary to our predictions, intergroup anxiety did not mediate the relationship between intergroup contact and assertive bystander intentions. This is surprising as the link between intergroup contact, anxiety and intergroup attitudes is well established in the literature (Pettigrew & Tropp, 2008; Stephan & Stephan, 1985). One possible explanation is that while anxiety toward interacting with an out-group member (intergroup anxiety) may be reduced by intergroup contact, it could be unimportant for intervening assertively in an intergroup name-calling situation. We argue that other forms of intergroup anxiety could instead be important in this context, for example, anxiety regarding whether the out-group victim would wish you to intervene, or anxiety about the reaction of fellow in-group members (Abrams, Rutland, Cameron, & Marques, 2003). Furthermore, research has shown that an *intrapersonal* form of anxiety, namely, self-efficacy in intervening, is an important predictor of bystander behavior (Gini et al., 2008). Future research should explore in greater detail the specific dimensions of self-efficacy and anxiety that could prohibit assertive bystander intervention in an intergroup name-calling context.

Limitations

This study examined adolescent's *intentions* to intervene assertively. However, whether adolescents would truly act assertively if they saw the intergroup name-calling scenario described is not known. Moreover, the lack of a measure of actual bystander intervention could also account for the lack of an association between intergroup anxiety and the purported assertive bystander behavior. We recognize the limitations of measuring behavioral intentions, however they are still of value. The theoretical framework of the Theory of Planned Behavior (ToPB: Ajzen, 1991) stresses the importance of behavioral intentions as it proposes that intentions are the most important predictor of whether an individual performs a particular action. Moreover, past ToPB research has found pro-social intentions to be a strong predictor of pro-social behaviors, such as charitable donations (Smith & McSweeney, 2007). However, empirical findings regarding the extent to which behavioral intentions predict actual behavior are varied and have been criticized (Armitage & Conner, 2001). We argue that measuring behavioral intentions is a first step in this new line of research, and future research should attempt to include measures of actual bystander behavior that meet ethical guidelines in this sensitive area of research. Future research could also investigate the same behavior toward a variety of different groups (e.g., compare in-group victim to out-group victim, or different out-group victims) to differentiate between bystander reactions to name-calling in general and name-calling specific to immigrants.

Implications

This study has theoretical and practical implications in both the intergroup contact and bystander intervention literature. The current findings build on the recent focus on the intergroup contact-behavior relationship (Hewstone & Swart, 2011; Turner et al., 2013), with a particular theoretical advancement in the under-researched area of the predictors of assertive bystander behavioral intentions. Importantly, this study also has important practical implications for future school-based interventions, highlighting the possibility of countering intergroup social exclusion with educational intergroup contact interventions and policies that also target interpersonal characteristics (e.g., empathy and cultural openness, and reduce in-group bias). In line with the work of Thijs et al. (2014), this current research further emphasizes the importance of moving beyond simple main effects of intergroup contact, to examine the effects of other school or classroom based characteristics (e.g., the ethnic in-group bias) to limit the negative effects and promote the positive effects of intergroup contact.

References

Aboud, F. E., & Joong, A. (2008). Intergroup name-calling and conditions for creating assertive bystanders. In S. R. Levy & M. Killen (Eds.), *Intergroup attitudes and relations in childhood through adulthood* (pp. 249–260). Oxford: Oxford University Press.

Abrams, D., & Killen, M. (2014). Social exclusion of children: Developmental origins of prejudice. *Journal of Social Issues, 70*(1), 1–11.

Abrams, D., Rutland, A., Cameron, L., & Marques, J. (2003). The development of subjective group dynamics: When in-group bias gets specific. *Developmental Psychology, 21*, 155–176.

Ajzen, I. (1991). The theory of planned behavior. *Organizational Behavior and Human Decision Processes, 50*(2), 179–211.

Allport, G. W. (1954). *The nature of prejudice*. New York: Doubleday Anchor.

Armitage, C. J., & Conner, M. (2001). Efficacy of the theory of planned behavior: A meta-analytic review. *British Journal of Social Psychology, 40*(4), 471–499.

Atlas, R., & Pepler, D. J. (1998). Observations of bullying in the classroom. *American Journal of Educational Research, 92*, 86–99.

Batson, C. D., Polycarpou, M. P., Harmon-Jones, E., Imhoff, H. J., Mitchener, E. C., Bednar, L. L., Klein, T. R., & Highberger, L. (1997). Empathy and attitudes: Can feeling for a member of a stigmatized group improve feelings toward the group? *Journal of Personality and Social Psychology, 72*, 105–118.

Bettencourt, B. A., Brewer, M. B., Rogers-Croak, M., & Miller, N. (1992). Co-operation and the reduction of intergroup bias: The role of reward structure and social orientation. *Journal of Experimental Social Psychology, 28*, 301–319.

Black, J. S. (1990). The relationship of personal characteristics to adjustment of Japanese expatriate managers. *Management International Review, 30*, 119–134.

Blascovich, J., Mendes, W. B., Hunter, S. B., Lickel, B., & Kowai-Bell, N. (2001). Perceiver threat in social interactions with stigmatized others. *Journal of Personality and Social Psychology, 80*, 253–267.

Cameron, L., Rutland, A., & Brown, R. (2007). Promoting children's positive intergroup attitudes towards stigmatized groups: Extended contact and multiple classification skills training. *International Journal of Behavioral Development, 31*(5), 454–466. doi:10.1177/0165025407081474

Bryant, B. (1982). An index of empathy children and adolescents. *Child Development, 53*, 413–425.

Caravita, C.S.C., Di Blasio, P., & Salmivalli, C. (2009). Unique and interactive effects of empathy and social status on involvement in bullying. *Social Development, 18*, 140–163.

Craig, W. M., & Pepler, D. J. (1995). Peer processes in bullying and victimisation: An observational study. *Exceptionality Education Canada, 5*, 81–95.

Crisp, R., & Turner, R. (2009). Can imagined interactions produce positive perceptions?: Reducing prejudice through simulated social contact. *American Psychologist, 64*, 231–240.

Derek, D., Rucker, D. D., Preacher, K. J., Tormala, Z. L., & Petty, R. E. (2011). Mediation analysis in social psychology: Current practices and new recommendations. *Social and Personality Psychology Compass, 5*(6), 359–371.

Dovidio, J. F., Gaertner, S. L., Shnabel, N., Sagay, T., & Johnson, J. (2010). Recategorisation and prosocial behavior: Common in-group identity and dual identity. In S. Stürmer & M. Snyder (Eds.). *The psychology of prosocial behavior*. Malden, MA: Wiley-Blackwell.

Dovidio, J. F., Piliavin, J. A., Gaertner, S. L., Schroeder, D. A., & Clark, R. D., III (1991). The arousal/cost-reward model and the process of intervention: A review of the evidence. In M. S. Clark (Ed.), *Prosocial behavior* (pp. 86–118). Newbury Park, CA: Sage.

Drapela, V. J. (1975). Comparative guidance through international study. *Personnel and Guidance Journal, 53*, 438–445.

Efron, B., & Tibshirani, R. (1993). *An introduction to the bootstrap*. Chapman and Hall: New York, London.
Eisenberg, N., & Fabes, R. A. (1990). Empathy: conceptionization, measurement, and relation to prosocial behavior. *Motivation and Emotion, 14*, 131–149.
Gaertner, S. L., & Dovidio, J. F. (2000). *Reducing intergroup bias: The common ingroup identity model*. Philadelphia, PA: Psychology Press.
Gini, G., Albiero, P., Benelli, B., & Altoè, G. (2008). Determinants of adolescents' active defending and passive bystanding behavior in bullying. *Journal of Adolescence, 31*, 93–105.
Hawkins, D. L., Pepler, D. J., & Craig, W. M. (2001). Naturalistic observations of peer interventions in bullying. *Social Development, 10*, 512–527.
Hayes, A. F. (2009). Beyond Baron and Kenny: Statistical mediation analysis in the new millennium. *Communication Monographs, 76*, 408–420.
Hewstone, M., Rubin, M., & Wills, H. (2002). Intergroup Bias. *Annual Review of Psychology, 53*, 575–604.
Hewstone, M., & Swart, H. (2011). Fifty-odd years of inter-group contact: From hypothesis to integrated theory. *British Journal of Social Psychology, 50*, 374–386.
Killen, M. (2007). Children's social and moral reasoning about exclusion. *Current Directions in Psychological Science, 16*, 32–36.
Leary, M. R. (1990). Responses to social exclusion: Social anxiety, jealousy, loneliness, depression, and low self-esteem. *Journal of Social and Clinical Psychology, 9*, 221–229.
McKenney, K. S., Pepler, D., Craig, W., & Connolly, J. (2006). Peer victimization and psychosocial adjustment: The experiences of Canadian immigrant youth. *Electronic Journal of Research in Educational Psychology, 9*, 239–264.
Miller, N. (2002). Personalization and the promise of contact theory. *Journal of Social Issues, 58*, 387–410. doi: 10.1111/j.1540-4560.00267
Nansel, T. R., Overpeck, M., Pilla, R. S., Ruan, W. J., Simons-Morton, B., & Scheidt, P. (2001). Bullying behaviors among US youth: Prevalence and association with psychosocial adjustment. *Journal of the American Medical Association, 285*(16), 2094–2100. doi:10.1001/jama.285.16.2094
Nesdale, D., Griffiths, J., Durkin, K., & Maass, A., (2005). Empathy, group norms and children's ethnic attitudes. *Applied Developmental Psychology, 26*, 623–637.
Nesdale, D., & Todd, P. (2000). Effect of contact on intercultural acceptance: a field study. *International Journal of Intercultural Relations, 24*, 341–360.
Nigbur, D., Brown, R., Cameron, L., Hossain, R., Landau, A. R., Le Touze, D. S., Rutland, A., & Watters, C. (2008). Acculturation, well-being and classroom behavior among white British and British Asian primary-school children in the south-east of England: Validating a child-friendly measure of acculturation attitudes. *International Journal of Intercultural Relations, 32*, 493–504.
Ofsted. (2012). *No place for bullying: How schools create a positive culture and prevent and tackle bullying* (Publication No.110179). Retrieved July 4, 2012, from http://www.schools-out.org.uk/policy/docs/No%20place%20for%20bullying.pdf.
Olweus, D. (1993). *Bullying at school: What we know and what we can do*. Oxford, UK: Blackwell.
Oxman-Martinez, J., Rummens, A. J., Moreau, J., Choi, Y. R., Beiser, M., Ogilvie, L., & Armstring, R. (2012). Perceived ethnic discrimination and social exclusion: Newcomer immigrant children in Canada. *American Journal of Orthopsychiatry, 82*, 376–388.
Palmer, S., & Cameron, L. (2010, July). Bystander intervention in subtle and explicit racist incidents. *Paper session presented at the meeting of Developmental Perspectives on Intergroup Prejudice: Advances in Theory, Measurement, and Intervention, EASP Small Group Meeting*, Lisbon, Portugal.
Perry, D. G., Kusel, S. J., & Perry, L. C. (1988). Victims of peer aggression. *Developmental Psychology, 24*, 807–814.
Pettigrew, T. F., & Tropp, L. R. (2008). How does intergroup contact reduce prejudice? Meta-analytic tests of three mediators. *European Journal of Social Psychology, 38*, 922–934.

Pettigrew, T. F., Tropp, L. R., Wagner, U., & Christ, O. (2011). Recent advances in intergroup contact theory. *International Journal of Intercultural Relations, 35*, 271–280.
Preacher, K. J., & Hayes, A. F. (2008). Asymptotic and resampling procedures for assessing and comparing indirect effects in multiple mediator models. *Behavior Research Methods, 40*, 879–891.
Salmivalli, C., Lagerspetz, K. M., Björkqvist, K., Öösterman, K., & Kaukiainen, A. (1996). Bullying as a group process: Participant roles and their relations to social status within the group. *Aggressive Behavior, 22*, 1–15.
Smith, J. R., & McSweeney, A. (2007). Charitable giving: The effectiveness of a revised theory of planned behavior model in predicting donating intentions and behavior. *Journal of Community & Applied Social Psychology, 17*(5), 363–386.
Smith, P. K., & Shu, S. (2000). What good schools can do about bullying: Findings from a survey in English schools after a decade of research and action. *Childhood, 7*, 193–212.
Stephan, W. G., & Stephan, C. W. (1985). Intergroup anxiety. *Journal of Social Issues, 41*, 157–176. doi: 10.1111/j.1540-4560.1985.tb01134.x
Strohmeier, D., Kärnä, A., & Salmivalli, C. (2011). Intrapersonal and interpersonal risk factors for peer victimization in immigrant youth in Finland. *Developmental Psychology, 47*, 248–258.
Thijs, J., Verkuyten, M., & Grundel, M. (2014). Ethnic classroom composition and peer victimization: The moderating role of classroom attitudes. *Journal of Social Issues, 70*(1), 134–150.
Tropp, L. R., O'Brien, T. C., & Migacheva, K. (2014). How peer norms of inclusion and exclusion predict children's interest in cross-ethnic friendships. *Journal of Social Issues, 70*(1), 151–166.
Turner, R. N., West, K., & Christie, Z. (2013). Out-group trust, intergroup anxiety, and out-group attitude as mediators of the effect of imagined intergroup contact on intergroup behavioral tendencies. *Journal of Applied Social Psychology, 43*, 196–205.
Twenge, J. M., & Baumeister, R. F. (2005). Social exclusion increases aggression and self-defeating behavior while reducing intelligent thought and prosocial behavior. In D. Abrams, M. Hogg & J. Marques (Eds.). *The social psychology of inclusion and exclusion* (pp. 27–47). Psychology Press: New York.
Verkuyten, M., & Thijs, J. (2002). Racist victimization among children in The Netherlands: The effect of ethnic group and school. *Ethnic and Racial Studies, 25*, 310–331.

NICOLA ABBOTT is currently a PhD researcher at the University of Kent, Canterbury, United Kingdom. She has research interests in intergroup contact, intergroup bullying, assertive bystander intervention, and school-based antibullying interventions.

LINDSEY CAMERON is a lecturer in Psychology at the University of Kent, Canterbury, United Kingdom. Her research is in social development, specifically children's understanding of social categories, awareness of stereotypes and intergroup attitudes, how these develop with age, and the sociocognitive and contextual variables that drive developmental changes in these constructs. Dr. Cameron's research aims toward developing theoretically based classroom interventions that address children's intergroup attitudes.

Intergroup Social Exclusion in Childhood: Forms, Norms, Context, and Social Identity

Mark Bennett[*]
University of Dundee

Humans are a profoundly social species, aligning with groups, forming group identification, and navigating the social world. One of the complex tasks of childhood is to understand when exclusion is necessary to make groups work well, and when it is wrong, creating unnecessary harm or unfairness. In this volume the authors grapple with many new aspects of exclusion not previously documented by taking a developmental and social psychological approach. The studies reveal original findings regarding how children both perpetuate and are recipients of exclusion, and the processes that accompany these experiences. In reflecting on the diverse range of work represented in this special issue, various themes emerge, such as the roles of context and norms in children's exclusionary behavior and judgment, the particular forms that exclusionary behavior can take, and the consequences that result as part of the developmental process. Most importantly, given that social identities frame a host of phenomena associated with group-based exclusionary phenomena, the field should reveal the central role that social identity plays in how exclusion and inclusion are understood.

As members of a profoundly social species, it should come as no surprise that human beings are highly sensitive to exclusion. Sensitivity to ruptures in relations with other people is evident even in the first weeks of life, as is clear in the "still face effect" (Tronick, Als, Adamson, Wise, & Brazelton, 1978). Moreover, toward the end of the first year of life infants are remarkably alert to joint attention phenomena, noticing in triadic contexts who is attending—and *not* attending—to whom (Beier & Spelke, 2012); thus, skills involved in the tracking of coalitions emerge very early in life. By 5 years, such is the sensitivity to signals of exclusion that even witnessing third-party ostracism heightens children's affiliative imitation (Over & Carpenter, 2009). Such findings clearly speak to the biological and evolutionary

---

[*]Correspondence regarding this article should be addressed to Mark Bennett, School of Psychology, University of Dundee, Dundee DD1 4HN, UK [e-mail: m.bennett@dundee.ac.uk].

The author like to thank Fabio Sani for comments on an earlier version of this article.

story that one day may be told about the very early origins and development of sensitivity to exclusionary behavior. For the present however, my task is to reflect on the papers comprising this special issue on group-based exclusion in childhood.

Given burgeoning interest in the development of identity, and especially group-based identity (e.g., Bennett & Sani, 2004; Levy & Killen, 2008), the focus of this special issue is timely and welcome, particularly since it complements and substantially alters the emphasis found in the extensive literature on *interpersonal* exclusion (e.g., Hymel, Vaillancourt, McDougall, & Renshaw, 2006). Social exclusion should clearly matter to psychologists because it is an intrinsically important topic that connects with issues that have long been of interest, such as social identity, morality, prejudice, and social norms. The 10 substantive papers in this volume reflect a robust body of research over the past decade that has investigated social exclusion from a developmental intergroup perspective (see Killen, Mulvey, & Hitti, 2013). The papers address a broad range of pertinent issues, such as the possible drivers of exclusion, whether exclusionary behavior can be mitigated, and the origins of social group affiliations. Moreover they do so across a broad range of social groupings, such as those based on ethnicity, gender, sexuality, and disability. Important implications emerging from many of the papers—implications that are consonant with the social identity tradition—are that social identities are consequential and moreover that contextual factors are immensely important in understanding group-based exclusion. The opening paper by Nesdale, Zimmer-Gembeck, and Roxburgh (2014) is an exemplary case in point.

Nesdale et al.'s (2014) study asked children to imagine experiences of acceptance or rejection by a group—in particular being chosen by peers, or not, to be on a team. The really important innovation in this study was that it went beyond the standard inclusion/exclusion contrast and included a third condition, which involved *ambiguous* rejection. In this condition it was indicated that the team preferred another child over the participant, but because the other child wanted to join a different team, the participant could, after all, join the team. Thus, the participant gained membership of the group, but by default rather than through the team's choice. As Nesdale et al. (2014) note, it is striking that even 6-year-old children were sensitive to their status as group members: over several measures, their responses differed depending on whether they had been accepted, rejected, or ambiguously rejected. Perhaps the most interesting findings were that children who had been "ambiguously rejected" identified with the group significantly more than did those who had been unambiguously rejected, and expressed more positive attitudes toward the group—although in contrast to "accepted" children, both indicated a desire to change groups! Thus, as group members, even if by default, children appear to make the best of it, while nonetheless harboring an interest in changing groups.

Ambiguous rejection is an experience with which many children will be familiar. Given this, future research would do well to explore the sort of "work" children may undertake to enhance their position as low status/peripheral/nonprototypical members of groups. In a survey of research on adults, Myers, Abell, Kolstad, and Sani (2010) identified four strategies that might be employed: increased conformity to in-group norms; derogation of nonprototypical in-group members; praise of prototypical in-group members; and derogation of out-group members. Investigating the use of such strategies seems particularly important when reflecting on the real groups to which children belong, especially since the available scope for movement to other groups is often very limited. Nesdale et al.'s (2014) notion of "social acumen" is likely to be important in this respect.

The papers of this special issue each operationalize exclusion in a particular way, including not choosing a child to be on a team (Nesdale et al., 2014), name-calling (Abbott & Cameron, 2014; Thijs, Verkuyten, & Grundel, 2014), preference for hypothetical peers (Huckstadt & Shutts, 2014), and liking/disliking of out-group members (Pahlke, Bigler, & Martin, 2014). Some papers however conceive of exclusion in more general, abstract terms; for example, Heinze and Horne (2014) asked participants to consider only the "exclusion" of a target person. To my eye, this variability raises various important issues, which are also raised by Abrams and Christian's (2007) framework for analyzing for analyzing social exclusion. First, at a methodological level the range of operationalizations shows that it would be useful if researchers more explicitly distinguished the general from the particular, ideally representing both in studies. They are likely to tap subtly different things. For example, although a participant might acknowledge a general inclination to exclude members of particular groups, they might not express a willingness to engage in typical forms of exclusionary behavior, except perhaps in extreme circumstances. Thus, it will aid our understanding to differentiate between the particular and the general. Second, it seems highly likely that the particular forms of exclusion will have different consequences; Nesdale et al.'s (2014) findings emerging from children's responses to ambiguous and unambiguous rejection make this point well. Finally, different forms of exclusion are likely to be age-related, with some (like name-calling) featuring prominently amongst young children, and others (like ostracism) being more typical in older children and adolescents. Thus, there is much to be gained from giving more detailed attention to the particular forms that exclusion can take, with a view ultimately to establishing a fuller taxonomy of exclusion. In this way an increasingly comprehensive and more nuanced picture of developmental change, and the consequences of exclusion, will be constructed.

Acknowledging that social exclusion can take different forms also raises a further set of issues concerning social perceptual skills on the part of the excluded. Clearly some forms of exclusion, like name-calling, are hard to miss, even by very young children. Others however require more sophisticated social perceptual skills.

In a review of the very limited research on this issue, Spears-Brown and Bigler (2005) indicated that "by age 10, children can recognize discriminatory actions that are both overt (e.g., name calling) and covert (e.g., being suspected of wrongdoing), understand that these actions may be caused by others' social stereotypes, and use contextual information to make decisions about whether discrimination is likely to have occurred. The underpinnings of this understanding appear to emerge as early as age 5 or 6" (p. 535). Despite these tentative proposals, much remains to be done and the model proposed by Spears-Brown and Bigler provides a valuable framework within which to pursue issues bearing upon children's perception of exclusion and discrimination.

Might there be differences in children's responses to interpersonal and intergroup exclusion (cf. Killen et al., 2013)? Abbott and Cameron (2014) speculate that in the case of exclusion "directed toward an individual's race, or ethnicity, the psychological impact on the victim is greater as the attribution of the event is internal, stable and uncontrollable." Whether group-based exclusion is indeed more painful or more enduring remains to be established and is an area ripe for further research. That said, it probably would not be possible to make a blanket statement on the matter, given individual differences in attachments to different personal and social identities. Differences may also be found between majority and minority group members. Moreover, there are likely to be developmental effects here too. For example, at the point in development at which children can begin to conceive of themselves predominantly in terms of their social group affiliations, their experience of group-based exclusion may shift. Seeing themselves as interchangeable with other category members, the adverse effects of group-based exclusion might be more readily rationalized and hence mitigated (e.g., "It's stupid for them to write me off just because I'm a member of this group"; "They don't know what sort of person I am"; etc.). Future studies that contrast the two types of exclusion will need to take into consideration relevant variables such as the importance of particular identities to the child, and whether s/he can conceive of the self mainly as a group member. Although none of the papers speak directly to this latter issue, one paper nonetheless suggests that it may not be until the age of six years that children begin to conceive of persons in sociocentric terms and therefore clearly differentiate the personal from the social in their own identity. Dunham and Emory's (2014) excellent contribution, the only one in the collection to consider the issue of developmental origins, looks at emergence of the tendency to prefer and positively evaluate the actions of social in-group members. Using a clever priming-based method, their studies suggest that mechanisms involved in human social group affiliations undergo "a striking increase in generality between ages 3 and 6, perhaps driven by a shift from an individual-level to a group-level or 'sociocentric' orientation."

What does a sociocentric orientation actually involve? In some of my own work with Fabio Sani, we have wrestled with the complex problem of how to conceptualize and measure "true" social identification in children, conceiving of it as the integration of in-groups within the self-system (e.g., Bennett & Sani, 2008; Sani & Bennett, 2009). Dunham and Emory's (2014) attempt to examine origins of social group affiliations is particularly illuminating and it will be important to their work on artificial groups to investigate sociocentrism involving real groups, since it is here that we are likely to see the earliest developments in social group affiliation. For example, work by Bar-Tal (1996) found that even before their third birthday, Israeli children judged photographs more negatively if they had been labeled as "Arab" than when the photograph had not been labeled. Such a finding may or may not reveal something about the very early emergence of self-identification as Israeli, but the sorts of methods devised by Dunham and Emory (2014) might help us to establish whether meaningful and affectively significant social group affiliations emerge very early in life.

So far, I have considered papers that address responses to, and perceptions of social exclusion, and also origins of genuine social group affiliations. I'd like now to turn my attention to papers that look at factors that lead to exclusion. Looking specifically at ethnic exclusion, Thijs et al. (2014) highlight the need to resist the temptation to look for simplistic causal stories. Their study examined the relationship between ethnic classroom composition and peer victimization in Turkish–Dutch (minority) and native Dutch (majority). What emerged was that children with more out-group classmates experienced higher levels of peer victimization, but crucially this was only so when classmates evaluated their ethnic in-group more positively than the out-group. As they note, the importance of these findings is that they indicate the need to "look beyond 'simple' main effects of diversity" and consider also attitudes and norms.

The role of in-group norms in social exclusion is abundantly clear in Heinze and Horne's (2014) paper. Their study looked at adolescents' judgments of the acceptability of exclusion based on sexuality and on nonconformity to in-group norms, such as appearance, an understudied area of research in the exclusion literature. Whilst all participants judged that it would be more acceptable to exclude their gay and lesbian peers compared to their straight counterparts, it is striking that amongst males, but not females, gender nonconformity in appearance (regardless of targets' sexual orientation) was also taken as a basis for exclusion. Clearly, if we are to understand the causes of exclusion it is crucial to look not only at generic processes, but also at the particular content of in-group identities. Group behavior is frequently guided by norms that are specific to particular social group identities—here, for example, norms governing appearance for males, but not females. Thus, an approach that foregrounds the concept of social identity is likely to be extremely valuable.

Speaking to the issue of how different levels of social relationship intersect and impinge on one another, Mulvey, Hitti, Rutland, Abrams, and Killen (2014) present the intriguing finding that, in the context of resource allocation, children like in-group members who challenge group norms, particularly a norm to distribute resources unequally between the in- and out-group. That is, in choosing between group loyalty and equal allocation, equality trumps loyalty. Thus, the paper highlights that wider social expectations and principles of equality can, in some cases, prevail over group-based conventions or expectations of bias. This is a surprising result, particularly in view of Platow, Hoar, Reid, Harley and Morrison's (1997) finding that adult group members are more likely to endorse a leader who gains them unfair advantage in intergroup contexts—but not in interpersonal contexts, where fairness is preferred. This raises the interesting question of whether and how people with within-group power and status can "challenge" general prosocial norms. This is an important line of inquiry for future research with children. Moreover, since Platow et al.'s work involved real, rather than hypothetical group members as in Mulvey et al.'s (2014) work, the possibility exists that the children's tendency to favor equality over group loyalty reflected particular concerns about appearing morally worthy in the eyes of the experimenter. Relatedly, Ruck and Tenenbaum (2014) find that adolescents draw on different types of justification and principle when arguing for endorsement than when arguing for rejection of asylum seekers' rights. The different types of reasoning that children deploy raises a key issue for future research, namely, who children have in mind as their audience when addressing matters related to exclusion, and whether (or when) they start to differentiate their private preference from their sense of what they think they are expected to do. Once again, the particular identities that are salient in a given context will play a central role in shaping children's responses.

Staying with the matter of norms, particularly in the context of cross-ethnic friendships, Tropp, O'Brien, and Migacheva (2014) argue for the need to consider the role of in-group norms of inclusivity. Clearly this is a very important topic if we take seriously the idea that, in providing guides to action, social identities are consequential. Two studies show that perceiving inclusive in-group norms for cross-ethnic relations is related to children's interest in cross-group friendships. Thus in Study 1, for example, a strong correlation was found between responses to the question "*How much would your friends in your racial group like to become friends with kids who are [White/Black]?*" and the question "*How much would you like to become friends with kids who are [White/Black]?*" This is an extremely interesting relationship to examine, and the issues for future research will be how, when and why the relationship strengthens or weakens. Nonetheless, in this particular study it seems possible that the two questions asked of children measure essentially the same construct: asking about behavioral intentions of "friends in your racial group" (i.e., one's in-group) is very nearly equivalent to asking about one's own behavioral intentions. Moreover, if questions about in-group norms came first [as is implied], then these would heighten the salience of the collective self (i.e., as in-group member), further increasing the probability that questions about behavioral intentions concerning cross-ethnic friendships would be responded to in terms of the collective self. The general point arising returns to the need for future research to give *explicit* consideration to contextual variations in the activation of social identities. From the position of self-categorization theory, it is now a truism to note that identities are fluid and contextually variable, but much more developmentally orientated research is needed to address contextual variation among identities, and the attendant variability in consequences for children's exclusion-related attitudes and behavior. Similarly social developmental research is only beginning to focus on variation along, and connections between, the interpersonal-intergroup continuum (Killen et al., 2013). Moreover, the papers in this issue highlight that research should not merely assume that the same sorts of phenomena that characterize adults will be found in children. For example, for the sorts of reasons implied by Dunham and Emory (2014), it may be that young children show a tendency to default to the interpersonal level of categorization. Thus, in order to address such issues, experimental designs should include within-child manipulations of context.

Given that social exclusion is typically a profoundly painful experience, the call for interventions in this field will be strong. The need to understand how best to change exclusionary attitudes and behavior is a pressing one. Although studies on adults have long demonstrated the difficulties associated with effecting desired change, one might suppose that children would be more corrigible to attempts to reduce their social exclusionary behavior. Two studies reported in this special issue show potential avenues for action whilst also illustrating the potential difficulty of achieving strong effects. Huckstadt and Shutts's (2014) study looked at preschoolers' preferences for able-bodied peers over disabled peers and importantly contrasted children from schools that did and did not have formal inclusion programs for the integration of children with disabilities. Over a variety of measures, no differences were found between children who had and had not direct personal experience of peers with disabilities. Conceivably, contact alone may be too blunt an instrument to effect change and greater gains could arise from further consideration of how adult and peer mediation of contact experiences might play a key role. In particular, structuring contexts in ways that enhance shared social identities may be important.

Pahlke et al.'s (2014) intervention, although lacking a control condition that would have aided interpretation of their data, nonetheless suggests that efforts need to be targeted very precisely—and moreover that we should be cautious in expecting too much from them. Their study contrasted two interventions: in one, the *pro-social condition*, children were taught to identify and respond to unfair social behaviors (such as teasing); in the other, the *pro-egalitarian condition,* they were taught the same but with additional attention specifically to gender bias (such as teasing about gender role nonconformity). Even after five lessons, there were no differences between the two groups in terms of gender egalitarian attitudes and intergroup liking. The sole difference was that those in the pro-egalitarian condition were better at identifying sexism in media and responding to peers sexist remarks. An important question is whether there would have been any generalization to, say, racism in the media or to peers' racist remarks.

The difficulties associated with effecting such change are now widely acknowledged. Ferguson, Miguel, Kilburn, and Sanchez (2007), for example, following their extensive meta-analysis of anti-bullying programs, noted that, at best, such programs "produce an effect that is positive and statistically significant but practically negligible." (p. 412). Given all such findings, future efforts need to find effective balances between ameliorative and preventative interventions. In thinking about ameliorative approaches, attempts to enhance "social acumen' and to teach skills of entry to social groups might have favorable consequences for those who are excluded or at risk of exclusion. More generally, it's worth noting that studies typically assume the invisibility of the individuals delivering the intervention, when in fact their social identity may well have a crucial bearing upon whether or not messages are perceived by participants as self-relevant. In Pahlke et al.'s (2014) study, for example, delivery by high status in-group members (in this case, cool teenagers perhaps?) ought to be the next obvious step for researchers. Once again, the central point here is that we need to be alert to the pivotal role of social identity in all aspects of work on group-based exclusion.

In a field such as this, given the multiple avenues of children's social exclusion, it is important to consider a wide range of options for promoting inclusion. For example, Mulvey et al.'s (2014) work suggests there are modes or realms of behavior in which a moral principle can trump children's biases toward group loyalty. A further, very encouraging finding comes from Abbott and Cameron (2014). Their paper indicates that day-to-day exposure to members of ethnic minorities may have benefits. In particular, their study revealed a significant indirect effect of intergroup contact on assertive bystander intervention intentions via cultural openness, empathy and (reduced) in-group bias. Although Abbott and Cameron (2014) refer to the important role of *personalized* intergroup contact, strictly speaking, their adapted measure tapped exposure based on perceived proportions of minority group members in the neighborhood, classroom, school, etc. It is encouraging that such incidental contact has positive effects. Nevertheless, further research is needed to disentangle effects of personal and incidental contact, since personalized contact may reflect preexisting attitudes toward out-groups.

Several of the papers show the now-familiar pattern of preferring in-group members whilst not actually rejecting out-group members. For example, Huckstadt and Shutts (2014) found typically developing children "do not hold extremely negative views of individuals with disabilities. . . . (E)ven though participants indicated that they would be more interested in befriending targets without disabilities in the Visible Preference task, the average preference ratings for targets in wheelchairs were not below the mid-point of the scale." Whilst ostensibly positive, it's crucial to note that even small preferences for in-group members can have major adverse effects for out-group members; de facto exclusion can arise merely from preferences for members of one group, not because of outright rejection of members of another group. And exclusion that arises from neglect is likely to be little different in its effects from that resulting from outright rejection. Indeed, brain-imaging studies have demonstrated that neglect by one's peers stimulates the same areas of the brain as does physical pain (Eisenberger, Lieberman, & Williams, 2003). In thinking about children with disabilities, it's all too easy to see how, even in the most benign of settings, children can become socially marginalized through being neglected rather than rejected. Thus, in interpreting specific judgments that children might make about members of particular groups, it's clearly important to see the wider systems in which those judgments are embedded.

Exclusion, then, can arise in subtle ways, not merely as a result of rejection. Even more insidious perhaps is that exclusion can come in forms that are barely noticed (at least by the excluding group). A case in point is the widespread exclusion of children from community and society. As I have noted elsewhere, "the position of children in contemporary Western societies is distinctly odd in socio-historical terms: seldom have children been quite as literally 'useless,' confined to relatively passive roles in the narrowly domestic arena, and largely excluded from participation in broader social and economic arenas" (Bennett, 2006, p. 342). Despite children's participation rights being enshrined in the United Nations' Convention on the Rights of the Child, their exclusion from participation in Western societies is extensive (Wyness, 2006).

An unaddressed but important theme for future research is that the "insularization' of children (Zeiher, 2001) is due in part to (largely misplaced) concerns about child safety—notably, "stranger danger," itself an alarming (if superficially legitimate) form of exclusion that identifies all individuals personally unknown to the self as a potential threat. Thus, notwithstanding the fact that insularization is well intentioned, its consequence is to greatly limit children's independent mobility and exposure to community life; moreover, I'd speculate that it is associated with psychological disorders such as heightened levels of anxiety. In recognition of the many costs both to children and society of this marginalization of children, some have proposed, radically, that the time has come to re-think citizenship to include children (Roche, 1999). Although we are far from being a society that routinely recognizes children's and adolescents' rights to societal participation (such as contributing to decision-making about urban planning, transport provision, leisure, healthcare, etc.), the case for children's citizenship, even if partial, has been made articulately and powerfully (Cockburn, 1998; De Winter, 1997). Other than highlighting this issue as an important case of exclusion that ought to be of interest to social and developmental psychologists, my wider point is that academics concerned with exclusion need to be alert to those cases that can slip under the radar of commonsense.

In providing new evidence and illustrations of how social and developmental perspectives can be effectively combined, this special issue represents a valuable contribution to the field. Nonetheless, diverse challenges remain. As I have noted at various points throughout this brief piece, the concept of social identity should play a central role in understanding children's group-based exclusion, particularly since the norms and values that are associated with particular identities will play a decisive role in framing and guiding social action. Moreover, the categorization of the self in terms of particular social categories gives rises to processes (such as the accentuation of in-group similarities and in-group–out-group differences), which also play a role in mobilizing particular identity-related judgments and actions. Explicitly placing the concept of social identity at the heart of research on group-based exclusion is, further, to acknowledge the wider context within which group-based phenomena occur and gain meaning. Thus, the concept of social identity may be viewed as providing a conceptual bridge from the individual to the wider context of social structure in which there typically exists a history of relations between groups in terms of status, power, etc. In short, there is likely to be considerable value in prioritizing the concept of social identity in this field. Clearly many important challenges flow from this, such as the need to specify the functional role of the self-concept in exclusion and inclusion processes. An even more basic challenge will be to develop measures that reflect the complex and dynamic nature of social identification.

Another implication of many of my remarks is that there is a need for *experimental* studies in this field, particularly those that manipulate aspects of the forms, norms, and contexts of exclusion. One significant challenge that arises from experimental work in this field is clearly that of constructing studies that are acceptable to ethical committees which may be anxious about measuring social exclusion for fear of creating it. The present studies (e.g., Nesdale et al., 2014) show that it is possible to do so, and a powerful argument is that it is an ethical responsibility to understand children's social exclusion in order to know how to tackle it. More generally, Dingwall (2008) has made an impassioned case for social scientists not be complicit with the relentless rise of ethical regulation, noting its "damage to wider interests in acquiring reliable and valid information about the social, political, economic and cultural life of our society" (p. 7). The time has come, I think, for researchers working in fields such as this to assert the ethical value of their work.

Exclusion is a familiar but painful experience with potentially profound consequences. The fact that exclusion is so powerful is unsurprising given that inclusion in social groups has been central to survival throughout our evolutionary past. Thus, MacDonald and Leary (2005) have suggested that human beings have evolved adaptations for responding to social exclusion and that "threats to social connections are processed at a basic level as a severe threat to one's safety" (p. 202). Reflection on the deeply-rooted nature of such processes prompts me to suggest that there will be many commonalities in the processes involved in the perception of, and response to, interpersonal and group-based exclusion in childhood and adolescence. This special issue has made a valuable journey into the largely uncharted territory of intergroup exclusion, demonstrating the viability of a variety of methods over numerous topics of inquiry. Future research will have more to say about the *relationship* between interpersonal and intergroup phenomena associated with exclusion. Indeed, the social psychological literature on intergroup exclusion, and the developmental literature on interpersonal exclusion have much to contribute to one another. As Abrams and Killen's (2014) introduction to this special issue suggests, exclusion happens at multiple levels, and because it is so often embedded in contexts in which the interpersonal and intergroup are intertwined, a fundamental challenge for the future is to develop integrative models that incorporate both the interpersonal and intergroup dimensions of exclusion.

References

Abbott, N., & Cameron, L. (2014). What makes a young assertive bystander? The effect of intergroup contact, empathy, cultural openness and in-group bias on assertive bystander intervention intentions. *Journal of Social Issues*, 70(1), 167–182.

Abrams, D., & Christian, J. N. (2007). A relational analysis of social exclusion. In D. Abrams, J. N. Christian, & D. Gordon (Eds.), *Multidisciplinary handbook of social exclusion research* (pp. 211–232). Chichester: Wiley-Blackwell.

Abrams, D., & Killen, M. (2014). Social exclusion of children: Developmental origins of prejudice. *Journal of Social Issues*, 70(1), 1–11.

Bar-Tal, D. (1996). Development of social categories and stereotyping in early childhood: The case of "the Arab" concept formation, stereotype and attitudes by Jewish children in Israel. *International Journal of Intercultural Relations*, 20, 341–370.

Beier, J. S., & Spelke, E. S. (2012). Infants' developing understanding of social gaze. *Child Development*, 83, 486–496.

Bennett, M. (2006). Societal cognition: Children's failures of understanding, the role of the wider society, and psychology's possible collusion. *Social Development*, 15, 339–343.

Bennett, M., & Sani, F. (Eds.) (2004). *The development of the social self*. New York: Psychology Press.

Bennett, M., & Sani, F. (2008). Children's subjective identification with social categories: A self-stereotyping approach. *Developmental Science*, 11, 69–75.

Cockburn, T. (1998). Children and citizenship in Britain. *Childhood*, 5, 99–117.

De Winter, M. (1997). *Children as fellow citizens: Participation and commitment*. Abingdon: Radcliffe Medical Press.

Dingwall, R. (2008). The ethical case against ethical regulation in humanities and social science research. *Twenty-First Century Society: Journal of the Academy of Social Sciences*, 3, 1–12.

Dunham, Y., & Emory, J. (2014). Of affect and ambiguity: The emergence of preference for arbitrary ingroups. *Journal of Social Issues*, 70(1), 81–98.

Eisenberger, N. I., Lieberman, M. D., & Williams, K. D. (2003). Does rejection hurt? An fMRI study of social exclusion. *Science*, 302, 290–292.

Ferguson, C. J., Miguel, C. S., Kilburn, J. C., & Sanchez, P. (2007). The effectiveness of school-based anti-bullying programs: A meta-analytic review. *Criminal Justice Review*, 32, 401–415.

Heinze, J. E., & Horne, S. S. (2014). Do adolescents' evaluations of exclusion differ based on gender expression and sexual orientation? *Journal of Social Issues*, 70(1), 63–80.

Huckstadt, L. K., & Shutts, K. (2014). How young children evaluate people with and without disabilities. *Journal of Social Issues, 70*(1), 99–114.
Hymel, S., Vaillancourt, T., McDougall, P., & Renshaw, P. D. (2006). Acceptance and rejection by the peer group. In P. K. Smith & C. H. Hart (Eds.), *Blackwell handbook of childhood social development* (pp. 265–284). Oxford: Blackwell.
Killen, M., Mulvey, K. L., & Hitti, A. (2013). Social exclusion in childhood: A developmental intergroup perspective. *Child Development, 84*, 772–790.
Levy, S. R., & Killen, M. (Eds.) (2008). *Intergroup attitudes and relations in childhood through adulthood.* Oxford: Oxford University Press.
MacDonald, G., & Leary, M. (2005). Why does social exclusion hurt? The relationship between social and physical pain. *Psychological Bulletin, 131*, 202–223.
Mulvey, K. L., Hitti, A., Rutland, A., Abrams, D., & Killen, M. (2014). When do children dislike ingroup members? Resource allocation from individual and group perspectives. *Journal of Social Issues, 70*(1), 29–46.
Myers, D., Abell, J., Kolstad, A., & Sani, F. (2010). *Social psychology.* London: McGraw Hill.
Nesdale, D., Zimmer-Gembeck, M. J., & Roxburgh, N. (2014). Peer group rejection in childhood: Effects of rejection ambiguity, rejection sensitivity, and social acumen. *Journal of Social Issues, 70*(1), 12–28.
Over, H., & Carpenter, M. (2009). Priming third-party ostracism increases affiliative imitation in children. *Developmental Science, 12*, F1–F8.
Pahlke, E., Bigler, R. S., & Martin, C. L. (2014). Can fostering children's ability to challenge sexism improve critical analysis, internalization, and enactment of inclusive, egalitarian peer relationships? *Journal of Social Issues, 70*(1), 115–133.
Platow, M. J., Hoar, S., Reid, S., Harley, K., & Morrison, D. (1997). Endorsement of distributively fair and unfair leaders in interpersonal and intergroup situations. *European Journal of Social Psychology, 27*, 465–494.
Roche, J. (1999). Children: Rights, participation and citizenship. *Childhood, 6*, 475–493.
Ruck, M. D., & Tenenbaum, H. R. (2014). Does moral and social conventional reasoning predict British young people's judgments about the rights of asylum-seeker youth? *Journal of Social Issues, 70*(1), 47–62.
Sani, F., & Bennett, M. (2009). Children's inclusion of the group in the self: Evidence from a self-ingroup confusion paradigm. *Developmental Psychology, 45*, 503–510.
Spears Brown, C., & Bigler, R. S. (2005). Children's perceptions of discrimination: A developmental model. *Child Development, 76*, 533–553.
Thijs, J., Verkuyten, M., & Grundel, M. (2014). Ethnic classroom composition and peer victimization: The moderating role of classroom attitudes. *Journal of Social Issues, 70*(1), 134–150.
Tronick, E., Als, H., Adamson, L., Wise, S., & Brazelton, T. B. (1978). Infants' response to entrapment between contradictory messages in face-to-face interaction. *Journal of the American Academy of Child and Adolescent Psychiatry, 17*, 1–13.
Tropp, L. R., O'Brien, T. C., & Migacheva, K. (2014). How peer norms of inclusion and exclusion predict children's interest in cross-ethnic friendships. *Journal of Social Issues, 70*(1), 151–166.
Wyness, M. (2006). *Childhood and society: An introduction to the sociology of childhood.* Basingstoke: Palgrave.
Zeiher, H. (2001). Children's islands in space and time: The impact of spatial differentiation on children's ways of shaping social life. In M. doBois-Reymond, H. Sunker, & H. H. Kruger (Eds.), *Childhood in Europe: Approaches, trends, findings* (pp. 139–159). New York: Peter Lang.

MARK BENNETT is Professor of Developmental Psychology at the University of Dundee, UK. From 2001 until 2010 he was editor of *Infant & Child Development* and he is currently Associate Editor for *British Journal of Developmental Psychology.* His primary research interests are developments in children's social identities and self-categorization, and their impact upon phenomena such as in-group favoritism, the perception of out-group homogeneity, and the acquisition of group-relevant information. In 2006 he was elected to the UK's Academy of Social Sciences.